Western Intervention and Informal Politics

This book examines the political and military dynamic between threatened local regimes and Western powers, and it argues that the power of informal politics forces local regimes to simulate statebuilding.

Reforms enabling local states to take care of their own terrorist and insurgency threats are a blueprint for most Western interventions to provide a way out of protracted internal conflicts. Yet, local regimes most often fail to implement reforms that would have strengthened their hand. This book examines why local regimes derail the reforms demanded by Western powers when they rely on their support to stay in power during existentially threatening violent crises. Based on the political settlement framework, the author analyses how web-like networks of militarized elites require local regimes to use informal politics to stay in power. Four case studies of Western intervention are presented: Iraq (2011–2018), Mali (2011–2020), Chad (2005–2010), and Algeria (1991–2000). These studies demonstrate that informal politics narrows strategic possibilities and forces regimes to rely on coup-proofing military strategies, to continue their alliances with militias and former insurgents, and to simulate statebuilding reforms to solve the dilemma of satisfying militarized elites and Western powers at the same time.

This book will be of much interest to students of statebuilding, international intervention, counter-insurgency, civil wars, and international relations.

Troels Burchall Henningsen is an Assistant Professor at the Institute for Strategy and War Studies at the Royal Danish Defence College.

Routledge Studies in Intervention and Statebuilding

The series publishes monographs and edited collections analysing a wide range of policy interventions associated with statebuilding. It asks broader questions about the dynamics, purposes and goals of this interventionist framework and assesses the impact of externally-guided policy-making.

Series Editors: Aidan Hehir, *University of Westminster, UK*, Pol Bargues, *CIDOB (Barcelona Centre for International Affairs), Spain*, and Vjosa Musliu, *Vrije Universiteit Brussel (VUB), Belgium*

Europeanization and Statebuilding as Everyday Practices
Performing Europe in the Western Balkans
Vjosa Musliu

Kosovo and Transitional Justice
The Pursuit of Justice after Large-scale Conflict
Edited by Aidan Hehir and Furtuna Sheremeti

Statebuilding Missions and Media Development
A Context-Sensitive Approach
Kerstin Tomiak

New Interventionist Just War Theory
A Critique
Jordy Rocheleau

De Facto States and Land-for-Peace Agreements
Territory and Recognition at Odds?
Eiki Berg and Shpend Kursani

Western Intervention and Informal Politics
Simulated Statebuilding and Failed Reforms
Troels Burchall Henningsen

For more information about this series, please visit: https://www.routledge.com/ Routledge-Studies-in-Intervention-and-Statebuilding/book-series/RSIS

Western Intervention and Informal Politics
Simulated Statebuilding and Failed Reforms

Troels Burchall Henningsen

LONDON AND NEW YORK

First published 2022
by Routledge
2 Park Square, Milton Park, Abingdon, Oxon OX14 4RN

and by Routledge
605 Third Avenue, New York, NY 10158

Routledge is an imprint of the Taylor & Francis Group, an informa business

© 2022 Troels Burchall Henningsen

The right of Troels Burchall Henningsen to be identified as author of this work has been asserted in accordance with sections 77 and 78 of the Copyright, Designs and Patents Act 1988.

All rights reserved. No part of this book may be reprinted or reproduced or utilised in any form or by any electronic, mechanical, or other means, now known or hereafter invented, including photocopying and recording, or in any information storage or retrieval system, without permission in writing from the publishers.

Trademark notice: Product or corporate names may be trademarks or registered trademarks, and are used only for identification and explanation without intent to infringe.

British Library Cataloguing-in-Publication Data
A catalogue record for this book is available from the British Library

Library of Congress Cataloguing-in-Publication Data
Names: Henningsen, Troels Burchall, 1978- author.
Title: Western intervention and informal politics : simulated statebuilding and failed reforms / Troels Burchall Henningsen.
Description: Abingdon, Oxon ; New York : Routledge, 2022. | Series: Routledge studies in intervention and statebuilding | Includes bibliographical references and index.
Identifiers: LCCN 2021037047 (print) | LCCN 2021037048 (ebook) | ISBN 9781032070070 (hardback) | ISBN 9781032070094 (paperback) | ISBN 9781003204978 (ebook)
Subjects: LCSH: Nation-building–Developing countries. | Intervention (International law) | Internal security–Developing countries. | Counterinsurgency–Developing countries. | Developing countries–Foreign relations–Western countries. | Western countries–Foreign relations–Developing countries. | Developing countries–Politics and government.
Classification: LCC D888.W47 H46 2022 (print) | LCC D888.W47 (ebook) | DDC 327.109724–dc23/eng/20211012
LC record available at https://lccn.loc.gov/2021037047
LC ebook record available at https://lccn.loc.gov/2021037048

ISBN: 978-1-032-07007-0 (hbk)
ISBN: 978-1-032-07009-4 (pbk)
ISBN: 978-1-003-20497-8 (ebk)

DOI: 10.4324/9781003204978

Typeset in Times New Roman
by MPS Limited, Dehradun

Contents

List of tables	vi
List of abbreviations	vii
Acknowledgements	ix

1	The puzzle of non-cooperative, but existentially threatened regimes	1
2	Informal politics and regime strategy	20
3	Chad: turning friends into enemies and enemies into friends	47
4	Mali: counterinsurgency by clients and patrons	72
5	Iraq: fighting the Islamic State with an unstable alliance	101
6	Algeria: security institutions fighting for their survival	129
7	Do politics, organizations, or persons derail reforms?	154
8	Betting on institutions or persons?	179
	Index	195

Tables

2.1	General questions guiding the case studies	38
7.1	Variance in importance of informal politics and the organization, training, and application of force	155
7.2	Variance in the importance of informal politics and the choices of alignment	160
7.3	Overview of Western demands for political and administrative reforms	166

Abbreviations

AAH	*Asa'ib Ahl al-Haq* (Shia militia and party in Iraq)
AIS	*Armée Islamique du Salut* (Islamist militia in Algeria)
ANT	*Armée Nationale Tchadienne*
AQIM	Al Qaeda in Maghreb
ATT	Malian President Amadou Toumani Touré
CDR	*Conseil Démocratique Révolutionnaire* (insurgent group in Chad)
CM-FPR	*La Coordination des mouvements et forces patriotiques de résistance* (alliance of pro-government militias in Mali)
CPDC	*Coordination des Partis Politiques pour la Défense de la Constitution* (alliance of civilian opposition parties in Chad)
CTS	Counter Terrorism Service
DGSSIE	*Direction générale des services de sécurité des institutions de l'État (Presidential guard in Chad)*
ECOWAS	Economic Community of West African States
ETIA	*Echelons Tactiques Inter-Armes* (ethnically mixed military units in Mali)
FIS	*Front islamique du salut* (Islamist party in Algeria who won the election in 1991)
FLN	*Front de Libération Nationale* (dominating party in Algeria since independence)
GATIA	*Groupe Autodéfense Touareg Imghad Et Allies* (Tuareg pro-government militia)
GIA	*Groupe Islamique Armé* (Islamist insurgent group in Algeria)
GSPC	*Groupe Salafiste pour la Prédication et le Combat* (Islamist insurgent group in Algeria, later AQIM)
IBK	Malian President Ibrahim Boubacar Keïta
IMF	International Monetary Fund
IS	Islamic State
JEM	Justice and Equality Movement (insurgent group in Darfur)

viii *Abbreviations*

KDP	Kurdistan Democratic Party
MAA-Bamako	*Mouvement Arabe de l'Azawad* (Arab pro-government militia in Mali)
MINUSMA	United Nations Multidimensional Integrated Stabilization Mission
MNLA	*Mouvement National pour la Libération de l'Azawad* (Tuareg insurgent group in Mali)
MPS	*Mouvement Patriotique du Salut* (dominant party in Chad)
MUJAO	*Mouvement pour l'Unicité et le Jihad en Afrique Occidentale* (Islamist insurgent group in Mali)
PMF	Popular Mobilization Forces
PSPSDN	*Programme spécial pour la paix, la sécurité et le développement au Nord-Mali* (development program in Mali)
PUK	Patriotic Union of Kurdistan
RND	*Rassemblement National Démocratique* (pro-regime party in Algeria)
SATG	Special Anti-Terrorist Group (US-supported anti-terror unit in Chad)
SLA	Sudan Liberation Army (insurgent group in Darfur)

Acknowledgements

My motivation throughout this research project was to understand and explain the actions of the regimes with whom the Danish and other Western Armed Forces have routinely cooperated since 2001. Frustrated by the common refutation of regime leaders as greedy, mentally unstable, or incapable, I came to understand most of them as shrewd political actors able to strategize in complex security environments with little power to actually control and mobilize elites. However, I needed the nudging and inspiration of others to move beyond simplistic explanations. At the graduate school at Roskilde University, my luck was to have the mentorship and friendship of Gorm Rye Olsen, who urged me to look deeper into the informal side of politics – politics made outside the airconditioned rooms. The manuscript was developed by the many constructive suggestions from the members of the Globalization and Europeanization Research Group. I would also like to thank Jon Kvist and Tobias Hagmann, who both contributed with important insights, and Lindsay Whitfield, who introduced me to the richness of the political settlement theory. My gratitude also goes out to fellow graduate students Anne Ingemann Johansen and Peter Horne Zartdahl.

At the Royal Danish Defence College, the Institute of Strategy and War Studies provided a constructive and supportive environment to finish the manuscript. I was so fortunate as to have the guidance of Peter Viggo Jakobsen who constantly nudged me forward through highly detailed and constructive feedback. Anja Dalgaard-Nielsen, Niels Bo Poulsen, and Annemarie Peen Rodt Poucher gave me the best possible conditions to dedicate my time to develop the manuscript. As a guest researcher at the Naval Postgraduate School, Monterey, I gained valuable insights from Ian Rice, Anna Simons, Kalev Sepp, and Leo Blanken among others. Moreover, the many officers who shared their experience of military assistance and stabilization gave me an insight into the details of such concepts as coup-proofing practices.

At Routledge, the series editors Aidan Hehir, Pol Bargués, and Vjosa Musliu urged me to elucidate the distinctiveness of each case, which shows

x *Acknowledgements*

the diverse ways that political settlements can unfold. My editor Andrew Humphrys and editorial assistant Bethany Lund-Yates also provided advice and encouragement throughout the process. Jytte Burchall gave me much appreciated guidance on improving the language of the manuscript. I would like to dedicate the book to my wife Anne Marie and my children Esther and Peter.

1 The puzzle of non-cooperative, but existentially threatened regimes

In June 2014, the office of the Iraqi Prime Minister Nour al-Maliki was buzzing with activity. The political survival of al-Maliki and his inner circle of trusted persons was at stake. Threats had surfaced from all directions, most spectacularly from the rise of the Islamic State. After two years of massive Sunni protests, the crisis escalated when the Islamic State returned to Iraq and quickly conquered land in the Sunni-dominated regions. The fall of Mosul, Iraq's second largest city, gripped Baghdad with fear because the Iraqi army had proven incompetent and unable to stop a determined foe. We know now that a month later a coalition of Iraqi political parties, Iran, and the United States forced al-Maliki out of office. At such a desperate time, one of Prime Minister al-Maliki's key decisions remains puzzling. Since withdrawing in 2011, the United States had repeatedly offered support to al-Maliki on the condition that he would make the Iraqi government and state open to Sunni Arabs (Lynch 2014). As late as June 2014, President Barack Obama said "The United States is not simply going [to] involve itself in a military action in the absence of a political plan by the Iraqis that gives us some assurance that they are prepared to work together" (cited in Brands and Feaver 2017, 38). Yet, al-Maliki resisted even when external assistance could have secured the survival of his regime. American ambitions for shaping Iraq through administrative and political reforms had declined since the invasion in 2003. There has been a shift from a wide-ranging agenda of democratization and all-encompassing statebuilding reforms to limited demands for the inclusion of the Sunni Arab population and a stop to repression of peaceful domestic opponents after the United States withdrew from Iraq in 2011. Why would al-Maliki resist such limited reforms that might have left him in power, in addition to receiving military and economic aid from the world's sole superpower?

A look at existentially threatened regimes adds a puzzle to the many debates on military interventions and statebuilding among peacebuilding and security studies, because these regimes apparently have strong incentives to cooperate with intervening powers. An existential threat to a regime is an urgent threat that is likely to cost the political life of the power holders within a short time frame. All regimes face threats against their political survival.

DOI: 10.4324/9781003204978-1

2 *Existentially threatened regimes*

In democratic states, the threat is institutionalized in elections. However, in many states, including democracies, threats to regimes primarily come from military coups, defections of client networks, insurgencies, foreign-imposed regime change, and from popular uprisings (Geddes et al. 2018, 179). In some states, threats from, e.g., irredentist insurgency movements take on a permanent character without being an existential threat to the regime in the capital. Coups and popular uprisings, on the other hand, may overwhelm the regime in a short period of time, often with little warning. For this reason, concerns for regime survival take primacy in states with a history of violent political change and contestation.

Threats to regimes are not necessarily threats against the population, the state, or the political institutions. Therefore, literature on regime survival considers the regime an independent, analytical level (Clapham 1996, Cooper 2019, Henningsen and Engbo Gissel 2020, de Waal 2015). The use of the concept of regime reflects that in many states the government and the state are made up of various factions with independent client networks and loyalty bonds inside and outside the state. In this book, the term *regime* refers to the de facto leader of the state and the inner circle of a few loyalist persons with a strong say in political decisions. Loyalists might be found within the government but might also take up executive positions in the state institutions, or they may even be private persons without whom strategic decisions cannot otherwise be made. The term *regime* is not used with normative connotations, nor is it reserved for autocratic political systems. However, the threat of losing power is most severe in states where the loss of power is likely to be permanent, or will result in severe consequences for the power holders and their client networks (Cooper 2019).

In some cases, as in Iraq in 2014, the existentially threatened regime calls for external intervention. External powers may already have considered intervening and may ask for an invitation. In other cases, an effort to attract external assistance may take on a form of sophisticated "image management" to mirror the security concerns of a potential intervener or a "taming" of international interveners by engaging in the international security discourse (Deoliveira and Verhoeven 2018, Fisher and Anderson 2017). Whether an external power chooses to intervene on behalf of the regime is an inherently political process. Western political leaders will often consider lost elections acceptable existential threats to regimes, and even a sign of a healthy political system. In other cases, some Western leaders may end up viewing lost elections as threats if they deem that the new regimes comprise security threats, as was the case in Algeria in 1991 and Egypt in 2013 (Kirkpatrick 2018). The political judgement of Western leaders may even lead them to accept coups and successful insurgencies against allied regimes, which is illustrated by the French inaction against the military coups in Mali in August 2020 and May 2021. Even in cases where Western powers or international organizations choose to intervene, their views on the conflict-dynamics will influence their strategy against the existential threat. If they

Existentially threatened regimes 3

find that the policies of the regime have contributed to the rise of the threat, interventions will most likely be followed by demands for reforms.

The view on conflict dynamics and the need for reforms has been influenced by changes in the international discourse on military interventions and statebuilding. Since the 1990s, the debate has shifted from issues concerning liberal peacebuilding to issues of stability, counter-terrorism, and local resilience (Karlsrud 2019). Liberal peacebuilding was a label for quite different intervention practices, from counterinsurgency to peacekeeping. The common denominator was a theory of success claiming that good-governance reforms of the state and democratization would create conditions for lasting peace. By addressing the grievances of the population, the state would gain legitimacy and support, which in turn would marginalize violent opposition (Sisk 2013). Interventions influenced by the thoughts of liberal peacebuilding differed in their emphasis. The large counterinsurgency operations in Afghanistan and Iraq mainly focused on security governance, whereas, e.g., the UN mission in Cambodia had a strong focus on democratization (Berdal 2019, Simangan 2018). Despite their differences, interventions based on the principles of liberal peacebuilding all diverged fundamentally from the perspective of regime security. Security was for the population, and only indirectly for the regime. More to the point, security was not only against violent non-state groups, but also against the regime's power abuse or inability to govern legitimately. For this reason, the interests of regime security were often at odds with the interests of the interveners (Jackson 2018, 3–4).

Today, the idea of state reforms as a strategy has given way to a multitude of pragmatic practices and concepts. The failures of militarized statebuilding in Afghanistan and Iraq undermined much of the legitimacy of liberal statebuilding. But the shift away from liberal peacebuilding was also caused by an intellectual move away from statebuilding approaches in interventions (Pospisil and Kühl 2016). Since the United States withdrew its combat troops from Iraq and Afghanistan in 2011 and 2014, respectively, Western military interventions have been small-scale and often indirect. To compensate, interventions are often assemblages of Western enablers, regional security providers, private military companies, and selected airstrikes (Demmers and Gould 2018). Moreover, interventions often have a narrow focus on security force assistance and stability at the expense of good-governance reforms or democratization. Intellectually, Western states, international donors, and academic researchers have changed their focus to concepts of resilience, complexity, and local peacebuilding (Moe and Müller 2017, Bargués-Pedreny 2020). Building resilience among local communities is based on a recognition that much power and legitimacy reside outside the state. Even though military intervention practices and the policy-discourse both have modest ambitions of statebuilding, they offer very different answers to the questions of security for whom and against what. Whereas the "local turn" in peacebuilding still considers the security of the population

4 *Existentially threatened regimes*

(or rather local communities among the population) against a number of complex challenges, many Western military interventions now focus almost exclusively on security threats from non-state, often Islamist, violent actors against local regimes and Western powers (Gelot and Sandor 2019). Many authoritarian regimes have eagerly embraced the focus on military threats and their solutions, and the decline in concerns for democratization and human security (Hagmann and Reynthens 2016).

Even though there has been a clear shift in the discourse and practice of military interventions in the late 2000s, exceptions show that the relationship between military interventions and peace- and statebuilding is also specific to a given military intervention. Even in the heyday of liberal peacebuilding, France intervened in Chad in 2006 and 2008 to protect the incumbent regime with few demands of reform. Today, the United Nations' multidimensional peacekeeping mission in Mali is true to many of the basic principles of the liberal peacebuilding (Mac Ginty 2019). Global shifts in military interventions or shifts in policy discourses do not entirely structure the political process of interpreting conflict-dynamics and establishing political priorities.

In instances of military interventions with few demands for statebuilding or concerns for the security of the local population, the lack of cooperation becomes even more puzzling. When an internal military threat becomes too grave for the regime to combat, or defeat becomes a possibility, the regime is in a very vulnerable position. Since 1991, Western powers have supported existentially threatened regimes in at least nine cases[1]. Only in a few of these cases did Western powers demand comprehensive statebuilding reforms or democratization, but in every case demands for reforms were made. Whether or not the regimes disagreed or feared reforms, their implementation would mean short-term survival against an overwhelming internal threat. The risk of losing power, and potentially their lives, by defying Western demands seems to go against their most fundamental interests. After Prime Minister al-Maliki was forced from power in Iraq, the reversal of fortunes on the battlefield illustrates the impact of Western military assistance. Still, as the example also demonstrates, regime leaders have chosen to reject Western demands for reforms even when on the brink of losing power. In the wake of the regime change in Iraq in 2014, President Barack Obama emphasized the difficulty of identifying dependable regimes with which to cooperate as the main problem for US interventions in Iraq and elsewhere (Goldberg 2015).

For some regimes the crisis continues after Western powers have intervened. Still, cooperation may be absent. In the summer of 2020 the Mali regime had still not implemented administrative reforms to the chagrin of France, the EU, the United Nations, as well as protestors and coup plotters. Since 2013, the successive Malian regimes have run the risk of not receiving, or losing, their lifeline of Western support when every other military or diplomatic strategy had failed. In 2005–2010, Chad received vital military assistance and still undermined reforms, thereby risking the withdrawal of

Existentially threatened regimes 5

any further military assistance. This undermining is all the more perplexing considering that the Chadian regime could not take continued Western assistance for granted even while the existential crisis persisted. Despite the fact that the local regimes might disagree with Western strategies, the prospect of having access to overwhelming military power and economic resources should, from a pragmatic point of view, convince them to begin implementing the desired administrative and political reforms. So why do regimes choose not to? This book seeks an answer to this puzzle by using the following research question as a guideline: *Why do existentially threatened regimes derail Western demands for administrative and political reforms when they depend on Western assistance for survival?*

The shift from liberal peacebuilding interventions to new forms of military interventions means that reforms encompass quite diverse activities. "Political reforms" refer specifically to reforms of formal political institutions, such as the introduction of democracy, and to systematic processes to foster peace, reconciliation, or autonomy to increase the legitimacy of the political system at the local or national level. "Administrative reforms" are reforms that aim to increase the capacity of state institutions to deliver service output, such as increased security or effective justice, as well as reforms to strengthen the legitimacy of institutions by increasing rule of law, respect for human rights, or inclusion of previously marginalized social groups in state institutions. When Western powers demand political and administrative reforms, regimes must question their own priorities and long-established strategies of regime survival. An examination of existentially threatened regimes is, therefore, likely to provide a window into the dynamics of regime survival. When the local regimes pretend to accept, resist, defuse, or undermine the Western-demanded reforms, they derail Western strategies. Their reaction to reforms is an important part of the dynamics of contemporary Western interventions.

An approach to examine domestic constraints and regime strategies

The character of the puzzle provides two points of departure for constructing an analytical framework to answer the research question. First, existentially threatened regimes appear to be unwilling or unable to change the domestic status quo, even when Western support is crucial and not guaranteed. Other explanations may be found in the specific relationship between the local regime and the intervener, such as shared historical ties. However, this study takes its departure in the observation that upholding the domestic status quo seems essential to regimes, and focuses on domestic explanations. Second, existentially threatened regimes face very different domestic and regional conditions in terms of, e.g., ethnic composition, socio-economic structure, and vulnerability to the influence of regional powers. Based on this attention to domestic conditions, the aim is to identify such domestic circumstances that

6   *Existentially threatened regimes*

make regimes likely to derail Western-imposed reforms. Therefore, the first working question this book will answer is: *what domestic factors prevent the regimes from meeting Western demands?* This part of the study builds on the existing literature on regime survival and Mushtaq Khan's formulation of the political settlement theory, which together provide the building blocks for explaining how domestic factors might constrain regimes during times of an existential threat to their survival.

The second step is to connect limiting domestic factors to the choice between derailing or implementing specific reforms. To this end, this study will identify the kind of strategic choices that are possible for regimes in the light of limiting domestic factors. An analysis of strategic action makes it possible to identify measurable indicators of the connection between limiting domestic factors and the regimes' reactions to Western demands. The second working question that the theoretical framework needs to answer is thus: *how do these internal factors shape the strategic choices of the regimes?* Identifying observable regime strategies mitigates the problem of obtaining reliable information on the decision-making process in regimes during an existential crisis. In that way, the analytical framework becomes applicable to cases outside this study, because it requires comparatively little data on the decision-making process within the regimes, but instead relies on observable outcomes.

The influence of informal politics on the derailment of Western reforms

This book argues that the reception of Western demands for reforms depends on the composition of the specific political settlement in the state subject to military intervention. As a rule, political settlements dominated by informal politics constrain regimes to choose strategies that derail reform attempts. Even if a regime wants to implement administrative and political reforms, the domestic elites benefiting from the informal institutions of the political settlement will have the power to undermine the regime's efforts during an existential crisis. Informal politics relates to different forms of negotiation of personal, non-codified rules, such as covert payments for support or tacit agreements on illegal enforcement of property claims. This kind of politics is not only in conflict with possible formal political institutions demanded by the West, it is also the linchpin that holds together a coalition of elites that would not benefit from administrative and political reforms. Although informal politics can have many expressions, a political settlement dominated by informal institutions limits the number of available regime strategies. The argument is that in those states Western military interventions may successfully protect the regime and suppress a common threat for a period, but the introduction of reforms will most likely trigger a backlash led by powerful domestic elites inside and outside the state. However, the four case studies of this book also demonstrate that variation

Existentially threatened regimes 7

exists within each political settlement as to what formal and informal arrangements elites depend on, and, therefore are willing to fight for.

The overarching answer to the first working question of what domestic factors prevent the regimes from meeting Western demands is that the regimes cannot change informal politics, because during a time of existential crisis they cannot break their ties with the ruling coalition of factions, which constitutes the foundation of the regime's claim to power. Based on Mushtaq Khan's understanding of political settlement as an institutional expression of power, this book argues that the dominance of informal politics and corruption reflects the underlying distribution of power among the ruling coalition that supports the regime. When a large part of the ruling coalition consists of factions that do not benefit from formal rule-of-law arrangements, informal rules, such as systematic rents, become necessary for the regime to keep the ruling coalition together. This book takes a specific interest in the militarized factions such as former insurgents or militias. They prosper economically and politically when informal political arrangements allow them to take up positions in the state institutions or set up illegal schemes that take advantage of their expertise in violence. During an insurgency crisis or a civil war, militarized factions become crucial to the survival of the regime. Their client networks may spread into the security forces, or they are able to mobilize their militias to fight the insurgents. It remains very difficult for the regime to break away from those factions and curtail their benefits from informal politics at a time when the regime is most vulnerable. The factions specialized in violence are sufficiently powerful to punish the regime and prevent a move away from the status quo.

The subsequent part of the argument answers the second working question, namely how do these internal factors shape the regimes' strategic choices. This book argues that only a limited number of strategies are available to the regime when strong factions of the ruling coalition depend on informal politics in various forms, and these factions are crucial to the regime's survival. Based on this condition, this book identifies three complementary strategies that all undermine potential administrative and political reforms, but adhere to the rules of informal politics and take into consideration the power of factions specialized in violence. First, factions within the ruling coalition control competing client networks within the security institutions, which makes the regime liable to pursue a strategy of *praetorian protection*. According to this strategy coup-proofing defines the choices made in relation to the security forces. Small elite forces personally loyal to the leader of the regime receive lavish funds, materiel, and personnel, but their main task is to protect the regime against coups, not insurgencies or other internal threats. By contrast the regime uses the security forces' regular units for suppression and combat, but keeps them disorganized and does not provide them with additional resources, even at a time of crisis. Improvement of the regular units might benefit other factions of the ruling coalition because the units are not necessarily loyal to the state

8 *Existentially threatened regimes*

or the regime. The result is a military strategy that relies on regular forces carrying out an ineffective punishment strategy meant to coerce insurgent groups and other militant actors to relent or lower their demands. Consequently, regimes in such circumstances may have authoritarian leanings, but the kind of repressive apparatus they can build is much less effective than that of an effective authoritarian state.

This book argues that regimes use additional strategies of *risk-averse alignment* when a punishment strategy fails to halt the internal threat. The interdependency of a regime and its ruling coalition means that the regime will most likely provide funds and materiel to militias loyal to factions within the ruling coalitions. Moreover, the relative insignificance of programmatic politics allows the regime to align with militias outside the ruling coalition or even groups within the insurgency alliance, who then turn their weapons against their former allies. Furthermore, the book argues that the importance of non-programmatic politics induces militias and even some insurgent groups to adopt a similarly pragmatic approach. In effect, the regimes (and militias) are willing to undermine the long-term authority of the state institutions in return for short-term regime security, which in turn reinforces the informal rules. Alignment with Western powers may be less predictable to regimes, because of the power asymmetry between the two parties. Therefore, regimes are likely to accept Western assistance only when domestic alignment strategies have failed, despite the advantages offered by Western military aid.

If Western powers become involved and demand reforms in return, the regime faces a seemingly impossible situation of being dependent on informal politics to keep the ruling coalition together and at the same time being dependent on a Western power pushing for reforms to curb informal politics. The regimes react by engaging in *simulated statebuilding*. Simulated statebuilding is understood as the regimes' nominal implementation of reforms, while actually continuing the practices of informal politics. The regimes take advantage of the lack of intelligence in times of crisis, as well as of Western reluctance to withdraw support to threatened states. The extent of the practice depends on the kind of foreign intervention. The practice may take an elaborate form in interventions with wide-ranging demands for reforms, whereas interventions aiming at short-term stabilization may see little simulated statebuilding. Moreover, when it is possible, local regimes use regional powers as hedges against Western reforms and potential withdrawal, even when the interests of regional and Western powers collide. Together, the survival strategies utilize informal politics and, consequently, strengthen the power of the factions specialized in violence.

The final argument put forward by this book is that Western powers are often aware of the practice of simulated statebuilding, but choose to ignore it at a time of crisis for the lack of a better alternative. Even when an intervener is committed to the principles of liberal peacebuilding, the short-term interests in regime survival and stability may work against a full-

Existentially threatened regimes 9

hearted commitment to reforms, if the regimes derail them. In other cases, interveners have few statebuilding ambitions, which may make simulated statebuilding inconsequential in the eye of the Western intervener. This book argues that Western powers silently accept simulated statebuilding, because they are incapable of changing the behaviour of the regime and attach the greatest importance to regime survival. Simulated statebuilding forces Western powers to settle for symbolic steps, such as the public announcement of reforms, or to accept inconsequential changes, such as the rotation of senior persons within the government or administration.

The diversity of the regime–intervener dynamics

These arguments jointly provide an answer to the puzzle of why existentially threatened regimes derail Western demands for administrative and political reforms when the regimes depend on Western assistance for survival. Empirically, the argument of the book builds on four case studies that demonstrate important aspects of the intricate strategic interaction between external interveners and local regimes, as well as between the local regimes and domestic elites. Of the nine cases noted earlier, the book builds it argument on four single-case studies of Algeria (1991–2000), Chad (2005–2010), Iraq (2011–2018), and Mali (2011–2020). They are all cases of existentially threatened regimes that received Western assistance in return for administrative and political reforms. Yet the cases also demonstrate the diversity in the ways that the political settlement manifests itself as to regime strategies, and in the ways that Western powers intervene. Many of the states in the Global South that are subject to Western interventions possess a mix of formal and informal elements in their political settlements (as do states in the Global North), which means that the exact choice of regime survival strategies is highly context-specific. Moreover, the four case studies show that the political dilemmas and pressures each regime faces vary according to the more specific distribution of formal and informal political arrangements, as well as the specific Western interests and demands for reforms.

The case study of Chad (2005–2010) illuminates the impact of almost pure informal politics on regime strategy and use of simulated statebuilding. Chadian politics was (and arguably is) dominated by a wide dispersion of power, by client networks that form the most important vertical power relations, and political parties that are loosely organized around non-programmatic politics. In contrast to the media portrait of Chad as a staunch and strong ally against terror in the Sahel region, the case study finds that the lack of a trustworthy security institutions forced President Idriss Déby to engage in a number of highly pragmatic alignments with former friends and foes among the militant elites of Chad. Insurgent groups received aid from Sudan, yet many of them chose to accept co-optation by the Chadian regime. The case also illustrates how regimes navigating informal politics react to a limited and reluctant Western military support by

10   *Existentially threatened regimes*

hedging its Western alignment with a diplomatic outreach to its foe, in this case Sudan. The two principal Western powers supporting Chad, the United States and France, were primarily concerned with a spill-over of the Darfur conflict into Chad. The two powers had very limited ambitions of administrative and political reforms, and offered little support to the World Bank and the EU in their work for wide-ranging reforms. The regime of President Déby made wide use of simulated statebuilding to avoid further democratization, rule of law reforms, and distribution of new oil income according to formal principals. The case of Chad casts light on the political dynamics of regimes skilled in operating in informal politics, but also limited by the fluid loyalties of domestic elites. Moreover, the war in Chad took place during the height of liberal peacebuilding, yet it is a case of limited military interventions, where external interveners disagreed on the statebuilding ambitions, which as a result became relatively low.

The second case is Mali (2011–2020), which is another case of regimes traversing the challenges of a political settlement dominated by informal politics. However, the external interventions and the statebuilding agenda pose stark contrasts to the interventions in Chad. In the wake of the Amadou Toumani Touré regime's failed hedging strategies against a military coup and the expanding territorial control of the insurgencies, France and later on the UN, the EU, and a number of other external powers intervened to stabilize Mali. The concert of interveners demanded a resumption of democracy after the military coup in 2012, as well as a number of reforms to increase the capacity and legitimacy of the Malian state that amount to a liberal statebuilding project. Yet, the military coup in August 2020 marks the end of the case study as well as a bleak story of unsuccessful external security sector reforms. The case study demonstrates how the regime of Ibrahim Boubacar Keita (2013–2020) continued the strategies suited for informal politics, despite the protection, money, and assistance from external interveners. The security institutions remained marred by dysfunction caused by co-optation and coup-proofing measures, and the military strategy primarily punished the signatories of the peace agreement. In parallel to aligning with external powers, the Keita regime continued and expanded alignments with militias in a way that contributed to the spread of violence to other ethnic groups. Moreover, the Keita regime simulated implementation of the peace process and key administrative reforms, which derailed the stability blueprint of military interveners and donors alike. The case study concludes that the (temporary) external protection of a regime is not enough to compensate for the weight of navigating a highly informal political settlement among a ruling coalition of opportunistic militant elites and widespread client networks.

However, in some cases, Western powers support regimes in states where power is less widely dispersed and formal politics satisfies most of the demands of the influential factions. In these cases, Western attempts to strengthen the administrative and political institutions may play into the

Existentially threatened regimes 11

hands of the regimes. Regimes in states dominated by formal politics are likely to gain a better grip on power by supporting and implementing reforms – at least those that fit in with the regimes' ideological outlook. Iraq (2011–2018) is a case of a mix of informal and formal institutions that made the regimes dependent on formal arrangements in certain areas. Informal arrangements were mirrored in formal political parties and organizations, which created a double pressure on the regimes. For example, parts of the militant elites had formal roles, such as the Peshmerga and later on the Popular Mobilization Front. However, tensions remained within the formal security institutions as to who executed authority. During the war against the Islamic State, the alignment strategy of Prime Minister Haider al-Abadi mainly consisted in holding together a highly unstable alliance that cut across informal and formal lines, and brought together Iran and the United States. The alignment was not a way to hedge against US abandonment, but a necessity due to Iran's close contact to several powerful Shia militias and parties. Although al-Abadi sided with the United States on the question of combating the corruption of the Iraqi state, the Prime Minister could not risk losing the support of the pro-Iranian parties and militias and Iran. Therefore, Iraq's case shows that political settlements with mixed forms of politics make some formal reforms possible, as long as the informal elements of the political settlement are not threatened. During the war against the Islamic State, the United States' primary interest was to work through the security assemblage held together by al-Abadi in order to avoid the commitment of more US combat troops on the ground, which meant that demands for reforms to ensure long-term stability had a lower priority than the short-term military confrontation. In the end, the balancing acts of al-Abadi unraveled due to the public outcry against the informal and formal accommodation of the entrenched elites, which resulted in a victory for the protest party Saairun in the parliamentary elections in 2018. The mixed character of the political context resulted in a political stasis of public demands for reforms, but informal undermining by militarized elites.

In the last case, Algeria (1991–2000), the regime navigated a political settlement where formal politics played an important role due to the concentration of power among the security institutions and the ruling coalition's adherence to the programmatic politics of secular republicanism. In the face of a widespread and well-organized Islamic insurgency in the wake of the cancelled 1991-elections, the Algerian security institutions pursued an effective elimination strategy that drew on both regular and elite forces. The regime made use of militias, but subjugated them to the authority of the security forces, and only co-opted insurgency groups after they had been mostly defeated on the battlefield. Externally, the regime aligned with France and international donors to receive economic benefits, but guarded the sovereignty of state in the process. Algeria adopted reforms that hurt the livelihood of the population in the short term, making it a rare case of acceptance of Western demands for reforms. Still, the many pockets of

12 *Existentially threatened regimes*

informality within the ruling coalition led to the simulation of reforms that would otherwise have hurt the interests of the ruling coalition, especially privatization of state-owned companies. However, the reintroduction of democracy was the most toxic reform both for Western supporters of the regime and internally in Algeria. The 1991 election gave the Islamists party FIS a landslide victory. Although Western powers, most notably France and the United States, officially promoted the reintroduction of democracy during the civil war, their fear of an Islamic take-over made the external powers more than willing to accept the outcomes of the less than free and fair elections in Algeria from 1995 and onwards. In general, Western powers accepted their indirect role of providing mainly economic support of the regime. The case of the civil war in Algeria illuminates the particular regime-intervener dynamics in states dominated by formal politics, which makes the implementation of externally demanded reforms that strengthen the authority of the state possible. On the other hand, the case is also an exception; a rare example of formal politics dominating in conflict-inflicted states. Even so, the case shows that even elites in a political settlement dominated by formal politics may require informal accommodation and simulated state-building, which intervening powers may be eager to accept.

Together the four case studies illustrate much of the diversity of the interactions between intervening powers and local regimes. They cast light on the variation in the combinations of formal and informal politics that frame the available strategies for the regime, as well as the diversity in Western intervention practices in terms of the military engagement and the significance of reform demands. On the other hand, the four cases also share commonalities. Most notably, three of the four countries are former French colonies, and three share a reliance on oil income to finance public expenses. Chapter 2 discusses the potential biases caused by the common traits in the history and economy of the political settlements, and Chapter 8 returns to the importance of French post-colonial politics as well as the potential for development in political settlements more generally.

How this study adds to the explanations of the politics of Western interventions

This book straddles the literatures on peacebuilding and security studies in the sense that theoretical developments within peacebuilding studies inform the study, while the main contribution of the book is to the debate on the political dimensions of military interventions within security studies. The critique of liberal peacebuilding has led to a search for alternative theoretical ways to understand the local political context that liberal statebuilding attempts sought to change. One avenue is to investigate the formal and informal political arrangements rather than the root causes of a conflict. States which share characteristics associated with the outbreak of civil wars often follow very different trajectories in terms of political stability, which have

Existentially threatened regimes 13

led to an interest in how political and economic institutions accommodate grievances among representatives of societal groups (see e.g. Ingiriis 2018, Jackman 2019, Lewis and Sagnayeva 2020, Phillips 2016).

However, the concept of political settlement remains contested. One strand of literature considers political settlement a negotiated agreement among elites, most likely at the end of a violent conflict. The agreement structures future political and economic possibilities and impossibilities, although the agreement might see ongoing changes (Di John and Putzel 2009, Kelsall 2018, Kelsall and Hau 2020). This approach is strongly associated with policy descriptions of inclusive political settlements that aim to include hitherto excluded groups. The other strand of literature, conceptualizes political settlements as an expression of dynamic social conflicts. From this perspective, a settlement is not a negotiated agreement, but a combination of power and institutions that changes when the underlying balance of power among societal groups shifts (Khan 2010, 2018, Behuria et al. 2017). External attempts to create an inclusive political settlement are, therefore, unlikely to be viable. The latter approach informs the theoretical outlook of this study, which also makes three minor additions to the analytical and empirical understanding of political settlement-as-conflict. First, by analysing political settlements threatened by different levels of militant opposition, this study demonstrates that political settlements may continue to function during civil wars. Second, this study associates highly informal political settlements with a specific set of regime survival strategies, although the case studies show the variation in their implementation across different political settlements. Third, it adds new case studies to the study of political settlements in relation to international interventions, namely the civil war in Algeria in the 1990s, Chad in the 2000s, as well the two contemporary cases of Iraq and Mali, as briefly presented in the previous section.

This book contributes mainly to the nascent debate within security studies on the political dimension of the interplay between intervening powers and local regimes. Until now, contributions to this debate have relied on the general theories of principal-agent theory and alliance theory. The introduction of a theoretical approach from the peacebuilding literature, which explains dynamics and conflicts at the domestic political level, provides a different perspective and answers to the reactions of local regimes. The principal-agent theory offers a parsimonious explanation and points to the need for Western strategies to manipulate the local regimes' cost-benefit calculation (See e.g. Byman 2006, Ladwig III 2016, 2017, Biddle et al. 2018, Hazelton 2018, Berman and Lake 2019, Boutton 2021). By assuming that local regimes act rationally to pursue regime survival, potentially at the expense of the population or the state, it is possible to explain why local regimes lack the political will to comply with Western demands (see e.g. Ladwig III 2017, 32–34). From this perspective, the regime will try to get as much economic and military assistance as possible without implementing reforms that might undermine their hold on power. This assumption is

14 *Existentially threatened regimes*

supported by so-called adverse selection, which means that the regimes most prone to this kind of behaviour are precisely those most likely to face insurgencies and consequently to become allies of Western powers. However, the underlying assumption is that the regime lacks the will, not the ability, to cooperate. That is, the theory has less explanatory power in cases of regimes with a strong incentive to cooperate because they share a threat perception with an external power. This study diverges from principal-agent theory in that it explains why local regimes are unable to implement reforms, even when they have a strong incentive to do so. The implication is that attempts to manipulate the cost-benefit calculus of existentially threatened local regimes are unlikely to affect the regimes' strategies, and, thus, that shortcomings in Western strategies cannot fully explain the lack of cooperation.

The second dominating approach utilizes a rational choice and realist-rooted alliance theory, which assumes that client states might attempt to free-ride unless they perceive a sufficient threat, and that they are uncertain of the commitment of the intervener or have to implement vital reforms themselves (See e.g. Elias 2017, 2018, 2020, Quirk 2017, Tankel 2018). Even though the alliance is between states with very different material capacities, this approach rejects the assumption that the asymmetrical power relation translates into political leverage for the stronger state. In one of the most recent contributions Barbara Elias criticizes the principal-agent model for downplaying the negotiating power of the local regime (2020). If the intervening power is more reliant on the local regime than vice versa, the local regime gains a bargaining chip that may allow it to free-ride, despite its lack of military and economic power. Elias argues that as long as an external power can unilaterally implement a reform, the local regime is likely to free-ride to avoid the economic and internal political costs of cooperation. Conversely, when their interests align and the Western power is reliant on local regimes for implementation, Elias finds that regimes often cooperate to gain the benefits of the reform. This finding is mainly based on case studies of large-scale external engagements, such as the Soviet Union in Afghanistan and the United States in Vietnam. However, the four case studies in this book reveal contradicting evidence that decisions on cooperation and reforms are much more closely tied to the limitations of elite politics. Indeed, three of the case studies show that the regimes had very little room for manoeuvre. Moreover, it explores how local regimes and intervening powers shroud non-cooperation in a mutual pretence of cooperation, held up by the regimes' practice of simulated statebuilding and the intervening powers' calculation that regime survival matters more than administrative and political reforms.

The method and structure of the study

An examination of four diverse case studies serves the purpose of exploring the width of the potential interplays between external interveners and existentially threatened local regimes across different combinations of formal

Existentially threatened regimes 15

and informal politics in the political settlement, and across different forms of external interventions. The choice of four cases is meant to be a fruitful trade-off between in-depth knowledge and generalizability. Increasing the number of cases by drawing on quantitative databases has downsides, as this type of data on states dominated by informal politics proves error-prone, and does not contain information on the behaviour of the regimes as to the three proposed regime strategies. On the other hand, the ambition to compare cases of informal and formal politics, including historical cases, excludes a detailed single-case study based on extensive fieldwork.

The theoretical framework of the state-in-society approach and political settlement theory points to informal politics as a key factor that limits the regimes' choice of strategy. Therefore, the book's principal method for designing the case studies is co-variation between the importance of informal politics and the regimes' choice of strategy. Each case study gauges the importance of informal politics in the political settlement and examines the choice of regime strategies. To ensure variance in the level of informal politics, the selection includes two cases of states with political settlements dominated by informal politics and two cases of political settlements dominated by formal or mixed forms of politics, as detailed previously. The empirical part unfolds in two steps. First, each of the four cases is examined as a single-case study using the method of a structured, focused analysis that asks a fixed set of questions related to the importance of informal politics and the strategic behaviour of the regimes. Whenever the available sources allow, the single-case studies make empirical observations of the influence that elites with expertise in violence exercise on the choices made by the regime. The second step is a discussion based on a cross-case comparison of the results that sets up the book's theoretical framework against a political-psychological and organizational explanation of the regimes' behaviour.

Roadmap

Chapter 2 constructs a domestically grounded theoretical and analytical framework of why regimes derail Western-imposed administrative and political reforms. The chapter places the book within the theoretical perspectives of the state-in-society approach and political settlement theory. After developing the core argument that elites within the ruling coalition depend on the continuation of corruption and other informal practices, and are crucial to the survival of the regime, the chapter formulates three propositions as to what strategies informal politics allows the regime to pursue. Finally, the chapter shortly discusses the case selection and the logic behind the ensuing comparative case study.

Chapters 3 and 4 apply the theoretical framework to two cases of states dominated by informal politics, namely the previously introduced cases of Chad (2005–2010) and Mali (2011–2020). The purpose of examining two

16 *Existentially threatened regimes*

cases of existentially threatened regimes that operate in a context of informal politics is to highlight the different character of two Western interventions in an informal political setting, although the outcomes of Western demands for reforms were similar. Moreover, the case of Chad exemplifies the potential impact of regional powers involved through proxies, whereas the Malian case saw less regional involvement.

Chapters 5 and 6 examine the two cases where the logic of informal politics is less important, namely Algeria (1991–2000) and Iraq (2011–2018). Thereby, the chapters contrast the case studies of Chad and Mali by examining the impact of formal politics on regime strategies and interaction with external interveners. However, the two cases also demonstrate how informal politics may exist side by side with informal practices, which contributes with a more nuanced understanding of informal practices and the political limitation that local regimes navigate. The case of Algeria is the only case without Western military involvement, whereas Iraq highlights the politics of intervention through a security assemblage of state and non-state actors.

Chapter 7 makes a cross-comparison of the four cases to examine the impact of variation in mainly informal politics, but also discusses the impact of different military and civilian elements of Western interventions and the role of regional powers. In addition, the chapter broadens the analyses of the four case studies by evaluating the domestic politics explanation of the book against two alternative explanations. Organizational dysfunctions in intelligence agencies or the armed forces could lead the regime to underestimate the insurgent threat or the risk of Western withdrawal. In parallel, the crises facing the regimes might come as a result of aberrant psychological traits of the regime leaders. The chapter discusses whether the high proportion of inexpedient organizational and psychological biases is due to the particular hostile, chaotic, and clandestine character of informal politics.

Chapter 8 draws the conclusion and discusses the implications of the importance of informal politics to Western intervention. Especially, the chapter focuses on the shift towards low footprint interventions. To tease out the particularities of this approach, the chapter compares the French and the US approaches to utilizing local elites, and discusses the benefits and drawbacks of basing a Western strategy on personal relations, which might not only increase the influence of Western powers, but also entail moral and political ramifications of cooperating with corrupt and unpopular regimes.

Note

1 Since 1991, Western powers have supported existentially threatened local regimes in the following cases: Afghanistan (2002–), Algeria (1991–2000), Chad (2005–2010), El Salvador (pre-1990–1991), Guatemala (pre-1990–1996), Iraq (2011–2017), Mali (2011–2021), Sierra Leone (1991–2002), and Somalia (2006–2021).

References

Bargués-Pedreny, Pol. 2020. "Resilience Is 'always More' Than Our Practices: Limits, Critiques, and Skepticism About International Intervention." *Contemporary Security Policy* 41 (2): 263–286. 10.1080/13523260.2019.1678856

Behuria, Pritish, Lars Buur, and Hazel Gray. 2017. "Studying Political Settlements in Africa." *African Affairs* 116 (464): 508–525. 10.1093/afraf/adx019

Berdal, Mats. 2019. "NATO's Landscape of the Mind: Stabilisation and Statebuilding in Afghanistan." *Ethnopolitics* 18 (5): 526–543. 10.1080/17449057.2019.1640508

Berman, Eli and David. E. Lake (eds). 2019. *Proxy Wars: Suppressing Violence Through Local Agents*. Ithaca & London: Cornell University Press. 10.7591/97815 01733093

Biddle, Stephen, Julia Macdonald, and Ryan Baker. 2018. "Small Footprint, Small Payoff: The Military Effectiveness of Security Force Assistance." *Journal of Strategic Studies* 41 (1–2): 89–142. 10.1080/01402390.2017.1307745

Boutton, Andrew. 2021. "Military Aid, Regime Vulnerability and the Escalation of Political violence." *British Journal of Political Science* 51 (2): 507–525. 10.1017/ S000712341900022X

Brands, Hal, and Peter Feaver. 2017. "Was the Rise of ISIS Inevitable?" *Survival* 59 (3): 7–54. 10.1080/00396338.2017.1325595

Byman, Daniel. 2006. "Friends Like These: Counterinsurgency and the War on Terrorism." *International Security* 31 (2): 79–115. 10.1162/isec.2006.31.2.79

Clapham, Christopher. 1996. *Africa and the International System: The Politics of State Survival*. Cambridge: Cambridge University Press. 10.1017/CBO9780511549823

Cooper, Frederick. 2019. "Gatekeeping Practices, Gatekeeper States and Beyond," *Third World Thematics: A TWQ Journal* 3(3): 455–468. 10.1080/23802014.201 8.1557959

Demmers, Jolle, and Lauren Gould. 2018. "An Assemblage Approach to Liquid Warfare: AFRICOM and the 'Hunt' for Joseph Kony." *Security Dialogue* 49 (5): 364–381. 10.1177/0967010618777890

Deoliveira, Ricardo Soares, and Harry Verhoeven. 2018. "Taming Intervention: Sovereignty, Statehood and Political Order in Africa." *Survival* 60 (2): 7–32. 10.1 080/00396338.2018.1448558

Di John, Jonathan and James Putzel. 2009. *Political Settlements*. Issues Paper. Birmingham: Governance and Social Development Resource Centre.

Elias, Barbara. 2017. "The Likelihood of Local Allies Free-Riding: Testing Economic Theories of Alliances in US Counterinsurgency Interventions." *Cooperation and Conflict* 52 (3): 309–331. 10.1177/0010836717701966

Elias, Barbara. 2018. "The Big Problem of Small Allies: New Data and Theory on Defiant Local Counterinsurgency Partners in Afghanistan and Iraq." *Security Studies* 27 (2): 233–262. 10.1080/09636412.2017.1386935

Elias, Barbara. 2020. *"Why Allies Rebel: Defiant Local Partners in Counterinsurgency Wars."* Cambridge: Cambridge University Press. 10.1017/9781108784979

Fisher, Jonathan, and David M Anderson. 2017. *Africa's New Authoritarians: Aid, Securitisation and State-Building*. London: Hurst Publishers.

Geddes, Barbara, Joseph Wright, and Erica Frantz. 2018. *How Dictatorships Work: Power, Personalization, and Collapse*. Cambridge: Cambridge University Press. 10.1017/9781316336182

18 Existentially threatened regimes

Gelot, Linnéa, and Adam Sandor. 2019. "African Security and Global Militarism." *Conflict, Security and Development* 19 (6): 521–542. 10.1080/14678802.2019.1688959

Goldberg, Jeffrey. 2015. "'Look... It's My Name on This': Obama Defends the Iran Nuclear Deal." *The Atlantic*, May 2015.

Hagmann, Tobias, and Filip Reynthens. 2016. *Aid and Authoritarianism in Africa: Development without Democracy*. London: Zed Books.

Hazelton, Jacqueline L. 2018. "The Client Gets a Vote: Counterinsurgency Warfare and the U.S. Military Advisory Mission in South". *Journal of Strategic Studies*. Advance Online Publication, 1–28. 10.1080/01402390.2018.1428566

Henningsen, Troels B., and Line Engbo Gissel. 2020. "Non-Cooperation with the International Criminal Court in Gatekeeper States: Regime Security in Deby's Chad." Cambridge Review of International Affairs, online version. 10.1080/0955 7571.2020.1828281

Ingiriis, Mohamed Haji. 2018. "Building Peace from the Margins in Somalia: The Case for Political Settlement with Al-Shabaab," *Contemporary Security Policy* 39 (4): 512–536. 10.1080/13523260.2018.1429751

Jackman, David. 2019. "Violent Intermediaries and Political Order in Bangladesh." *The European Journal of Development Research*, 31 (4): 705–723. 10.1057/s41287-018-0178-8

Jackson, Paul. 2018. "Introduction: Second-Generation Security Sector Reform." *Journal of Intervention and Statebuilding* 12 (1): 1–10. 10.1080/17502977.2018.142 6384

Karlsrud, John. 2019. "From Liberal Peacebuilding to Stabilization and Counterterrorism." *International Peacekeeping*, 26 (1): 1–21. 10.1080/13533312.2018.1502040

Kelsall, Tim. 2018. "Towards a Universal Political Settlement Concept: A Response to Mushtaq Khan," *African Affairs*, 117 (469): 656–669. 10.1093/afraf/ady018

Kelsall, Tim, and Hau Matthiasvom. 2020. *Beyond Institutions: Political Settlements Analysis and Development*. Institut Barcelona d'Estudis Internacionals working paper 2020/56.

Khan, Mushtaq. 2010. *Political Settlements and the Governance of Growth-Enhancing Institutions. Governance for Growth*. London: London School of Economics.

Khan, Mushtaq. 2018. "Political Settlements and the Analysis of Institutions: An Introduction," *African Affairs* 117 (469): 636–655. 10.1093/afraf/adx044

Kirkpatrick, David. 2018. *Into the Hands of Soldiers: Freedom and Chaos in Egypt and the Middle East*. New York: Viking.

Ladwig III, Walter C. 2016. "Influencing Clients in Counterinsurgency: U.S. Involvement in El Salvador's Civil War, 1979–92." *International Security* 41 (1): 99–146. 10.1162/ISEC_a_00251

Ladwig III, Walter C. 2017. *The Forgotten Front: Patron-Client Relationships in Counter Insurgency*. Cambridge: Cambridge University Press. https://doi.org/10.1 017/9781316756805

Lewis, David G., and Saniya Sagnayeva 2020. "Corruption, Patronage and Illiberal Peace: Forging Political Settlement in Post-conflict Kyrgyzstan", *Third World Quarterly* 41 (1): 77–95. 10.1080/01436597.2019.1642102

Lynch, Marc. 2014. "How Can the U.S. Help Maliki When Maliki's the Problem?" *The Washington Post*, June 12, 2014.

Existentially threatened regimes 19

Mac Ginty, Roger. 2019. "Assessing Dynamics of Change in Peacekeeping," *International Peacekeeping* 26 (5): 549–551. 10.1080/13533312.2019.1677289

Moe, Louise Wiuff, and Markus-Michael Müller. 2017. "Introduction: Complexity, Resilience and the 'Local Turn' in Counterinsurgency." In *Reconfiguring Intervention: Complexity, Resilience and the "Local Turn" in Counterinsurgent Warfare*, edited by Louise Wiuff Moe and Markus-Michael Müller, 1–27. London: Palgrave Macmillan UK. 10.1057/978-1-137-58877-7_1

Quirk, Patrick W. 2017. *Great Powers, Weak States, and Insurgency*. Cham: Springer International Publishing. 10.1007/978-3-319-47419-9

Phillips, Sarah. 2016. "When Less Was More: External Assistance and the Political Settlement in Somaliland." *International Affairs* 92 (3): 629–645. 10.1111/1468-234 6.12601

Pospisil, Jan, and Florian Kühl. 2016. "The Resilient State: New Regulatory Modes in International Approaches to State Building?" Third World Quarterly 37 (1): 1–16. 10.1080/01436597.2015.1086637

Simangan, Dahlia. 2018. "When Hybridity Breeds Contempt: Negative Hybrid Peace in Cambodia." *Third World Quarterly* 39 (8): 1525–1542. 10.1080/014365 97.2018.1438184

Sisk, Timothy. 2013. *Statebuilding*. Hoboken: John Wiley & Sons.

Tankel, Stephen. 2018. *With Us and Against Us: How America's Partners Help and Hinder the War on Terror*. New York: Colombia University Press. 10.7312/tank1 6810

Waal, Alex de. 2015. *The Real Politics of the Horn of Africa: Money, War and the Business of Power*. London: Polity.

2 Informal politics and regime strategy

Each military intervention creates a unique constellation of interests, strategies, and power, which reflects historical trajectories and the upheaval caused by the intervention. On the other hand, some political settlements have common traits that generate certain political possibilities, and the strategies of Western interventions have similarities, because they tap into dominating international discourses on military interventions (Tenenbaum 2017). Therefore, the aim here is to construct a theoretical framework that is sensitive to the specifics of the political interplay among domestic elites and between the local regime and Western interveners, while at the same time it can register common dynamics related to regime survival strategies during existential crises. More specifically, the theoretical framework will build on existing theories on developmental states and the civil wars literature. The purpose is to lay out how certain political settlement configurations require the regime to turn to a limited set of survival strategies that undermine Western-imposed reforms. To allow the theoretical framework to be empirically applied and examined, the chapter aims to develop a comparative case study design and to select four cases that vary as to the importance of informal politics and Western forms of intervention.

The chapter maintains that regimes have a restricted set of strategic choices, when they have to conduct politics in a political settlement dominated by elites with expertise in the use of violence, or other elites who depend on informal institutions. During an existential crisis the relative power of the domestic elites are sufficient to prevent the regimes from strengthening formal administrative and political institutions. In turn, informal institutions limit the regimes' room for action and force them to rely on three strategies that are detrimental to political and administrative reforms, namely praetorian protection, risk-averse alignment, and simulated statebuilding. Furthermore, the chapter chooses a comparative case study design consisting of four cases that vary as regards the importance of informal politics and vary as to Western intervention practices. By using a co-variational design, the ensuing empirical study sidesteps the problem of accessing veiled regime decision-making and negotiations.

DOI: 10.4324/9781003204978-2

Informal politics and regime strategy 21

Four main sections make up the chapter. The first section positions the framework within the state-in-society approach and political settlement theory. The second section deals with the reasons why the relative power of the domestic elites supporting informal politics increases during an armed conflict, and why this prevents regimes from implementing Western-initiated reforms. The third section tackles the question of how domestic elites and informal politics shape the strategies available to the regime. The final section develops the comparative case study design and selects the cases, which guide the remaining part of the book.

Strong societies, weak states, and the need for informal politics

The first generation of theories on regime survival mainly apply a Weberian conceptualization of legitimacy. The theories seek to explain how legitimacy allows regimes to survive and rule despite limited institutional state capacity. The debate has been mostly concerned with whether the regimes instrumentalize traditional legitimacy (Chabal and Daloz 1999, Jackson and Rosberg 1984) or a mix of traditional and rational-legal legitimacy (Clapham 1996, Erdmann and Engel 2007, Lemarchand 1972, Van de Walle 2012, Pitcher et al. 2009). However, many of these studies observe the empirical phenomenon that strong domestic elites who mobilize and exercise social control also seek to expand their authority and legitimacy into parts of the state. This dynamic of contestation and conflict over authority is arguably difficult to encompass through the static concepts of patrimonial or neopatrimonial legitimacy.

Joel Migdal offers an interpretation of weak states that differs from a state-centric, legitimacy-oriented approach, namely that state institutions are penetrated by domestic elites and that individuals or even organizations within the state are loyal to domestic elites outside the state (1988, 210, 2001, 53–54). Instead of considering how a regime or state tries to appeal for popular consent and impose its authority on diverse domestic elites, I follow Migdal' s approach and consider both state and society as arenas for societal elites struggling for social control. State organizations are arenas for domestic elites, such as tribes, religious societies, or militias to occupy and exploit from. Because the state has little autonomy, the regime and the societal elites become the most important level of analysis (Migdal 1988, 206ff). The regime must deal with elites in and outside the state and even in some of the closest decision-making forums, elites with independent control of elements of the state institutions.

Yet, Migdal, too, may be criticized for neglecting the considerable variation and changes among states that he characterizes as weak in the Global South. In some states, domestic elites work through formal political institutions to a high degree, whereas in other states domestic elites interact directly with the regime through informal channels. In some states, interactions between the elites are relatively peaceful and allow the regime a long planning horizon, whereas other states are dominated by conflicts among

22 *Informal politics and regime strategy*

the different elites, and the question of regime survival becomes so acute that regimes are able to deal with only the most pressing, short-term related issues. To account for this variation and how it affects the regimes' strategies and implementation of Western-imposed reforms, this framework turns to the theory of political settlements.

Mushtaq Khan applies the following definition "a political settlement is a combination of power and institutions that is mutually compatible and also sustainable in terms of economic and political viability" (2010, 4). The definition conceives institutions in the same vein as Douglas North, namely as humanly devised constraints that structure political, economic, and social interactions (1991, 97). However, the political settlement theory differs from the new institutional economics approach of North, because it emphasizes the underlying power distribution that enables some actors to enforce the institution actively[1]. Institutions might be formal and effective if enforced by powerful and autonomous formal state organizations, or they might be informal, such as patron-client relations, and be enforced by elites with no formal authority, but with adequate power.

A political settlement concerns the fundamental character of any polity. The concept of political settlement accounts for variation among states, because the distribution of power and the exact composition of institutions have broad similarities across states while still retaining unique local expressions. The idea of political settlement gets to the heart of the matter concerning internal armed conflicts. A society has (at least temporarily) achieved a degree of political stability when its institutions satisfy the demands of a sufficiently strong part of the domestic elites, who in turn support the political settlement and become the ruling coalition (Phillips 2016, 623). Nevertheless, the definition differs from the widely used understanding of political settlement-as-an-agreement within the peacebuilding literature, as discussed in the introduction. Most often in the peacebuilding literature, the concept refers to specific political arrangements that are typically the outcome of peace agreements (Behuria et al. 2017, p. 508). Unlike a peace settlement, a viable combination of power and institutions does not have to be explicit, and the formal and informal institutional configuration can change over time to accommodate a shift in the underlying power distribution.

The social struggle among elites to make power and institutions mutually compatible will eventually lead to the conception of institutions that are beneficial to the ruling coalition (Khan 2010, 8). In many developmental states, large parts of the ruling coalition are non-productive factions, such as former insurgents, religious networks, or ethnic groups that rule themselves and are unlikely to benefit from formal institutions (ibid, 5).[2] To bring the political settlement in line with the distribution of power, the regime needs to allow for informal institutions. Informal institutions are rules that are systematic enough to be identified, yet are not formally written down and enforced by formal (state) organizations (ibid, 10). The informal institutions that require enforcement from non-state actors are of special interest.

Informal politics and regime strategy 23

A non-productive faction, such as a militia whose only "commodity" is violence, is well-situated to enforce informal rules of protection or regulation. Those factions would lose power in a case where the state is able to enforce the rule of law and deliver safety to its citizens. However, the regime cannot codify the influence of certain militias or other armed groups into formal rules without causing a conflict with other factions within, or elites outside, the ruling coalition. Informal institutions solve that problem.

Money is integral to most informal institutions, even though the institutions can also specify non-monetary privileges. Corruption, money laundering, and fraud are not deviant ways of behaviour, but are money flows that keep a ruling coalition together. In a narrow sense, corruption is payment to people in privileged positions in order to gain an unwarranted advantage. Though corruption is a global phenomenon, the most critical money flows that uphold a political settlement typically go in the other direction. The regime needs money to keep its ruling coalition together, and members of the ruling coalition need money to reward their client network. To this end, off-budget funds are necessary to avoid redistributing state funds for personal payments in public. Alex de Waal points to the way in which regimes accumulate informal political budgets, separate from the budget of the state, in order to finance informal political agreements (2015, 22–25). The core of this practice is to make money unaccounted for by manipulating payments. For example, regimes can agree to unfavourable acquisition contracts in return for unaccounted money, or set up firms that deliver goods and services to the state at above market price (Gillies 2020). Cash strapped regimes have other possibilities. A political settlement can be economically viable by allowing factions to enforce informal rules, such as criminal schemes, or regulate markets. Thereby, they gain an economic inducement to support the political settlement without requiring the redistribution of limited state funds.

In this book, informal politics is understood as the regime's and the ruling coalition's negotiation and enforcement of informal institutions, whereas formal politics refers to the negotiation and enforcement of formal rules within formal political and administrative organizations. The emphasis is on politics rather than institutions, because it highlights the regime's negotiations with non-productive elites as part of its survival strategies. One example is the negotiations that lead to a de facto recognition of the power held by excluded elites, and that could turn into an institution over time. As Paul Staniland argues, informal arrangements might include tacit acknowledgement of the spheres of influence controlled by insurgent groups, or collusion with insurgents in criminal activities (2012, 247–248). To be able to capture how such new institutions might be established, the focus needs to be on informal politics, rather than merely on the existing informal institutions.

24 *Informal politics and regime strategy*

Measuring the importance of informal politics

Any political settlement can be placed on a spectrum from purely formal politics, with no need for informal politics to keep the ruling coalition together, to purely informal politics with no formal expression. No states are placed on either end of the spectrum. Instead, formal politics is, to a varying degree, intertwined with informal politics that undermines, distorts, or replaces the workings of formal state organizations and political decisions. To determine the importance of informal politics, each political settlement must be analyzed prior to the period in which the regime is existentially threatened in order to understand the exact interactions between formal and informal politics. In the ensuing case studies, the political settlements are analyzed on three dimensions, namely the history of the underlying power distribution, the extent of clientelism, and the impact of programmatic politics.

First, the underlying power distribution is determined by a historical summarization of the power of the factions that make up the ruling coalition, and the development in the distribution of power between excluded elites and the ruling coalition. The greater the number of important militarized elites – such as factions within the security forces, militias, or insurgents – involved in the establishment of the current political settlement, the more likely informal politics is to be a dominant feature. Moreover, if excluded elites are almost as powerful as the ruling coalition, the expectation is that elites specialized in violence within the ruling coalition will remain militarized and, thus, non-productive (Tadros and Allouche 2017, 196–197). Consequently, a turbulent history caused by strong excluded elites would be an indication that informal politics is a dominant feature of the political settlement.

The second dimension is clientelism, which is by far the most important informal instrument to accommodate non-productive factions, because it allows a patron to hand privileges to clients in return for loyalty without having to formalize the rule[3]. Widespread clientelism distorts the way formal state institutions function and undermines the implementation of formal rules. Therefore, if non-productive elites dominate the ruling coalition, the indication would be a high number of patron-client relations and the distribution of large funds outside the budget. The exact scale of clientelism and off-budget funding can never be fully determined, due to the hidden and personal character of such practices (Behuria et al. 2017, 520). Also, client networks permute into multi-layered networks that spread among societal groups with few visible traits. In the light of these hidden features, the extent of clientelism must be assessed based on existing qualitative analyses of the availability of off-budget funds and the practices for distributing funds.

The last dimension, the importance of programmatic politics, is also an outcome of political settlements. In contrast to the non-programmatic and personal character of clientelism, formal politics concerns the parties' ability to mobilize segments of society based on programmatic ideas, that is ideologically cohesive policy proposals, some of which benefit voters collectively, and which the parties try to implement once in power (Kuo 2018, 28). Only when there is little need for catering to the demands of non-productive elites through informal institutions, do political settlements allow for programmatic politics to be carried out. Observing the behaviour of political parties provides an indication of the importance of programmatic politics. If political parties pursue coherent policies that are in line with their declared programmatic ideas, the expectation is that politics takes place within mostly formal institutions. This is based on existing studies of party politics. Finally, programmatic politics is considered in relation to examining the extent of clientelism, to gauge the degree to which programmatic ideas also determine the distribution of privileges.

Empirically, all states contain elements of informal politics, which might be more dominant in certain state organizations or certain policy areas. To avoid overly cumbersome terminology, the expression states as dominated by formal politics is used when non-productive elites are marginal in the ruling coalition, when the clientelistic distribution of privileges and funds is less important than public and programmatic principles, and when parties mostly adhere to programmatic principles. The expression states dominated by informal politics is used when non-productive elites dominate the ruling coalition, clientelism is the most commonplace practice, and programmatic politics is of marginal importance to political parties. Political settlements with a mixture of these three traits are referred to as states with mixed politics, which is admittedly an awkward term as informal and formal politics always interact. The next section shifts attention to the specific dynamics of violent crises in political settlement dominated by informal politics in order to tease out the room for manoeuvre of the incumbent regime.

Why informal politics shapes the choices

An existential threat from an insurgency or rebellious factions within the ruling coalition questions the viability of the political settlement. Even within the political settlement-as-conflict literature widespread violence directed against the regime is associated with the breakdown of the political settlement (Khan 2018a). An existential threat forces the regime to rely on the means at hand to counter the threat, but if the ruling coalition does not possess the necessary power, fundamental changes in the political settlement may take place. However, the following section argues that in most cases of armed resistance, political settlements function (at a certain level) until a potential regime defeat. In cases of widespread violence, the regime is likely to honour informal institutions, because it becomes even more dependent on the factions specialized in violence within the ruling coalition. The specialists in violence represent the regimes' best, if not only, chance of remaining in power. The outcome is that the regime reinforces informal politics to reward

26 *Informal politics and regime strategy*

the factions within the ruling coalition. Finally, the section argues that Western involvement does not change the regime's dependence on the elites within the ruling coalition.

On paper, the regime can make use of the formal security forces to withstand the insurgency. However, just as the political settlement generally determines the workings of the state organizations, so do the security forces reflect the political settlement. In a political settlement dominated by informal politics, one of the ways for the regime to accommodate the demands of non-productive factions specialized in violence is to include them in the security forces and allow them to operate according to informal rules (Malejacq 2016, Allen 2020). Powerful militias can take control of large elements of the security forces. Lower-level clients of factions can take up local offices, such as chief of police or regional military commander, and use their positions to, e.g., extort resources from the population (Barebee 2020). In cases where the political settlement has faced several crises or generally has a high level of violence, factions specialized in violence are likely to mobilize their military potential as part of a general lack of trust and cohesion in society (Malejacq 2019, Marten 2015). Militarized factions can easily translate their expertise in violence into a comparative advantage in the security forces, or they might benefit from informal rules allowing them to operate outside the security institutions as militias or criminal networks.

From this perspective, it would be fruitful to consider the ruling coalition as an alliance of militarized factions with overlapping and sometimes conflicting interests, not a coherent set of security institutions. Moreover, the factions that have large client networks might find it difficult to control them if the clients are powerful. A client might be a regional leader of the federal police, but also a power broker in the person's own right, with a separate set of clients in a local community (Reno 2019, 452–453). During a crisis, such an intermediate power broker might disagree with the patron, because a proposed course of action would hurt the client network. A view of the web-like networks of patrons and clients in its totality would very likely uncover a multitude of locally rooted interests. The regime cannot simply command the formal security institutions but must convince militarized factions within the ruling coalition to align their client networks against the insurgents, if the factions are able to do so (Quirk 2017). The result is that, in order to stay in power, the regime relies on militarized factions and clients from the ruling coalition, who command parts of the security forces and possibly militias outside the state.

If the offensive suddenly threatened the survival of the regime without a prior shift in the balance of power, the regime would strive to maintain the formal and informal political arrangements of the political settlement. Challenging the very foundation of the regime's grip on power hardly makes sense when little other than the ruling coalition keeps it in power, and the crisis forces it to adopt a short-term horizon. A long-term project to reform formal institutions gradually might improve the regime's hold on power over the years. However, at a time of crisis, the regime would lose its ruling

Informal politics and regime strategy　27

coalition, since the power of the militarized factions lies in the continuity of informal institutions. After all, they have their own clients to satisfy, clients who might also shift loyalty if the regime cuts off patronage or other privileges. In a time of crisis the regime is in an unfavourable negotiating position.

Western interveners may be uncommitted to the regime and offer little protection from dissatisfied factions within the ruling coalition. The introduction discusses instances in which Western powers consider the regime a political liability. More to the point of this study, Western interventions may indirectly threaten the survival of the regime even when the Western powers align with the regime but demand reforms. Accommodating those demands to strengthen the formal institutions would create a split within the ruling coalition. Dissatisfied militarized factions are ideally positioned to launch a coup or revolt during the chaotic period of an insurgency offensive, as they possess a relatively strong military capacity. The coups in Mali in 2012 and 2020 both demonstrate this danger. In an historical overview of Western sponsorship of client regimes between 1946 and 2010, Adam Casey finds that Western patronage did not improve client regime survival, because unlike the Soviet Union Western powers did not provide coup prevention aid (2020). Moreover, regime change may accompany interventions, as Western powers are inclined to want visible signs of change, such as changing the head of state or the resignation of ministers. Even when pragmatic concerns for stability drive Western powers, a regime associated with the dominance of informal politics is unlikely to gain Western protection, if it cannot deliver at least some level of stability among the ruling coalition. During a crisis, the regime's dependence on militarized factions within the ruling coalition and the factions' dependence on informal politics prevent the regime from meeting Western demands for strengthening formal institutions.

In essence, these dynamics limit the agency of the regime during an existential crisis. The next step of the framework is to consider the kinds of military and political strategies that are available to the regime in order to counter the internal threat, given the domestic need to maintain the dominance of informal politics.

How informal politics shapes the regimes' strategy

When a political settlement contains a large element of informal institutions, the regime must devise strategies that submit to the fact that many parts of the formal state organizations function according to informal logics. By and large, this means that the security institutions in particular become less effective, but also that pockets of loyal political clients within the security institutions are willing to fight for regime survival. The unreliability of most parts of the security institutions limits the regime's strategic freedom of choice in two ways in particular. First, factionalism and the risk of coups make the regime suspicious of the security institutions, which may lead it to rely on balancing the existential threat by aligning with other factions and previously

28 *Informal politics and regime strategy*

excluded elites or external powers. Second, a dilemma arises in cases when the regime aligns with external powers that demand a strengthening of formal rules that go against the interests of other members of the ruling coalition. The section begins by clarifying the use of the concept of strategy and subsequently proposes three major kinds of strategies that constitute the repertoire of regimes in informal political settings. The result is strategies that are at odds with possible Western attempts to reform.

Analysis of strategies

Strategies matter, but regimes in informal settings do not have unlimited freedom to craft them. The need to cater to the ruling coalition's need for informal accommodation limits the goals that the regime can pursue and the means available. The defining aspect of strategy is the underlying idea, or theory, of how civilian or military means can be organized and used to achieve a policy goal (Hoffmann 2020). The strategy process may involve the systematic work of an organization testing different ideas, but in many cases strategy is based on the intuition of a few persons. In an informal setting, the deliberations of a regime are unlikely to have a formalized strategic process. On the other hand, regime leaders are seasoned in the particularities of informal politics, which involves a deep understanding of threats to regime survival and the dynamic nature of informal politics (de Waal 2015). Years of constant interactions with included and excluded elites shape regime leaders' ideas about how to survive an existential crisis. Therefore, I would expect regular patterns of behaviour to coalesce out of the maelstrom of day-to-day informal politics.

According to Lawrence Freedman, strategy "is about getting more out of a situation than the starting balance of power would suggest. It is the art of creating power" (2013, xii). The creative aspects of particular strategies cannot be encapsulated a priori, but will reflect the particularities of a specific context or even the idiosyncrasies of specific leaders. What can be included in a theoretical framework is the limitations to the creative process, the outline of the kinds of strategies that are possible and likely given the restraints of the political settlement. In addition, strategies often involve trading known cost for uncertain risk or vice versa. Choices of low risks and costs are obvious, and choices of high risks and costs are likely to be self-defeating. The assumption is that regimes favour strategies that have a low risk of turning factions or their clients within the ruling coalition into enemies, even though this might increase economic and political cost (understood as rearrangement of rules). After all, the redistribution of wealth and privileges to elites within the ruling coalition is part of daily politics.

The strategy of praetorian protection

In all states, security forces are a double-edged sword as they provide regimes with a means to repress internal and external threats, but also pose a

Informal politics and regime strategy 29

potential threat to the regimes due to their coercive power (Feaver 1996, 149). However, the question of political control and loyalty becomes all-encompassing in a political settlement that includes several informal institutions of patron-client relations that personalize loyalty and establish links between factions, clients, and elements of the security forces (Roessler 2016). How can a regime trust the loyalty of senior commanders if they are also part of client networks associated with ethnic communities, or a warlord's client network, that demand their personal loyalty? The problem of trust and loyalty goes in two directions. First, the militarized factions of the ruling coalition are likely to place clients in the security forces, e.g., through the use of 'ethnic stacking' (Morency-Laflamme and McLauchlin 2020), albeit ethnicity is most likely a too crude descriptor of the discriminatory practices behind selection of clients. The factions cannot completely trust each other, as access to training and materiel keeps them militarized and potentially ready to turn on one another. Second, the factions at the top of the patron-client relationship might mistrust lower-level clients in the security forces. Nathaniel Allen suggests that the practice of ethnic stacking or other discriminating practices might take different forms at different points in the hierarchy of the security institutions, but the purpose is always to increase loyalty (2020). Although the lower-level clients may have prior relations to the patron at the senior level, their relative power has a potential to increase due to their position in the security forces, for-example as generals, making them demand more benefits, or negotiate a more favourable patronage for loyalty to a different faction (Knowles and Matisek 2019, 15ff). The result is possible mistrust not only among the factions but also within each client network.

The lack of trust in the security forces is not a minor concern to many regimes, but one that affects their choices in relation to warfare. The threat of a coup is still a pressing issue in many states in Africa, the Middle East, and Central Asia[4]. To engage in coup-proofing is to degrade the military component of the counter-insurgency and counter-terrorism. In fact, coup-proofing has such far-reaching consequences that there is a strong correlation between states with high degrees of coup-proofing and a lacklustre military performance against internal and external threats (Powell 2019, Roessler 2016, Talmadge 2015). Consequently, this study argues that the regime adopts a strategy of committing resources primarily to coup-proofing and, thereby, settling on a less than efficient military campaign against the insurgents.

The degrading of the military component requires the regime to settle on a simple and limited strategy that punishes excluded elites or rebellious parts of the ruling coalition. This means that the security forces engage in direct combat with the insurgents, whilst ignoring the interests of the population (Berlingozzi and Stoddard 2020, Day and Reno 2014, 112, Hazelton 2017). However, such an enemy-centric strategy is unlikely to lead to an unconditional defeat or marginalization of the insurgents, due to the use of coup-proofing measures.

30 *Informal politics and regime strategy*

A lack of intelligence, coordination between units, or motivated and well-equipped forces allow elusive insurgents to dodge a military blow (Byman 2006). Instead, by inflicting costs on the insurgents, the regime may alter their strategic calculus. Indiscriminate but inefficient application of force for political signalling is attainable, as the strategy has few requirements as to the level of competency within the security forces (Käihkö 2012, 196, Watermann 2021, 123). A successful praetorian protection strategy prevents coups. However, success against insurgents depends on the decisions of the rebellious elites. Ideally, they may decide to abandon their violent struggle, but the insurgents may also lower their demands of regime change or regional autonomy. However, even if the punishment strategy fails to influence the political calculus of the insurgents, keeping the insurgents at bay would suffice to keep the political settlement in place.

Measuring strategies of praetorian protection

Analytically, the main task is to separate a strategy of praetorian protection from an overall low level of competencies within the security forces. Therefore, the first step is to look for ways that the regime discriminates between trusted and untrusted units in terms of deployment, function, funding, materiel, and training before and during the crisis. If pockets of regime-loyal forces are to engage in coup-proofing they must be stationed close to the president, or officially tasked as the presidential guard, to receive lavish funding, to train efficiently with Western military units, and to have the relatively newest and most efficient equipment (Powell 2019). I expect regular units, on the other hand, to be disadvantaged through rotations of personnel, insufficient equipment, or inadequate funding, which are common coup-proofing measures (Talmadge 2015, De Bruin 2018). Even when regular forces receive training from Western forces, they are likely to suffer the same kind of disadvantages as before the training. In supplement to scholarly work on local military arrangements, the case studies rely on interviews with and reports from Western military officers involved in capacity building.

Identifying a strategy of punishment requires us to look at the observable, tactical engagements of the security forces. A punishment strategy uses tactical engagements to sow fear and show resolve to alter the calculus of the insurgents, rather than attack the key military weaknesses of the insurgency. In this scenario, the expectation is that indiscriminate attacks would occur with many civilian casualties. In addition, the tactical engagements are not expected to attack the insurgents' crucial infrastructure or well-defended positions, due to the incapacity of the regular forces. To measure such behaviour is often difficult, due to lack of reporting or suppression of information by the warring parties. By utilizing geo-localized databases on instances of violence, NGO reports, as well as institutes dedicated to trace the development of conflicts, such as the Institute for the Study of Wars, it becomes possible to triangulate the observations. However, the adequacy of

Informal politics and regime strategy 31

the data on tactical behaviour varies across conflicts and each case study will discuss the issue in more details.

In states dominated by formal politics, security institutions are likely to be dedicated fully to counter the threat. The threat of coups still exists, but requires senior commanders to claim the loyalty of some military units, whether regular or elite forces. As Risa Brooks notes, providing the security institutions with sufficient resources to gain senior commanders' loyalty becomes a way of coup-proofing regimes in authoritarian states that depend on the security institutions to stay in power (1998, 24–32). Therefore, regular units are expected to receive almost comparable amounts of funding, materiel and training as elite units. Security forces operating according to more formal rules would not settle on a strategy of punishment but seek to marginalize or destroy them. This is not necessarily a Western-inspired population-centric strategy to isolate the insurgents from the population, but more likely an enemy-centric strategy. An enemy-centric strategy would increase the size of the regular forces, dedicate elite units and the intelligence apparatus to the sole purpose of attacking the insurgents and their support network, with the aim of annihilating the insurgents or marginalizing them (Byman 2016).

Overall, the low risk associated with this strategy and the possibility of staying in power by compromising between coup-proofing and counter-insurgency, arguably make praetorian protection an attractive strategy to regimes navigating informal politics. Regimes may develop creative ways to combine punishment with political negotiations that diminish the insurgency threat. However, should the half-hearted use of punishment prove insufficient, the regime would need to rely on a second set of strategies.

Risk-averse alignment

In a situation where the strategy of praetorian protection has failed to alter the calculus of its internal enemies, the regime would need additional resources to handle the internal threat. In an informal political setting of widely distributed power, the regimes have little alternative but to rely on other actors to provide extra manpower, materiel, or finance. However, aligning with other actors can have unintended consequences and even be dangerous. Arming militias loyal to one faction of the ruling coalition or co-opting insurgent groups might change the underlying distribution of power within the political settlement or create conflict among the factions. Aligning with regional or Western powers might disturb domestic politics even more, because external powers wield more power and might have a different political agenda.

The development of alignment-based strategies leaves the regime with ample room for creative combinations of alignments, political accommodation, and coordination of the military effort. The proposition is merely that political settlements dominated by informal politics induce regimes to favour domestic over external alignments, because the repertoire of off-budget funds,

32   *Informal politics and regime strategy*

cross-cutting client networks, and informal institutions already exists and facilitates co-optation of domestic militant actors. Moreover, the regime only needs to shift the military balance of power to avoid losing power. Unlike the truism within Western counterinsurgency thinking that the insurgents are winning by not losing, this proposition expects that it is easier for the local regime to accept a long-term internal conflict than to risk undermining the ruling coalition.

In the same vein, the expectation is that the regime's main concern is to take on as few risks as possible, when evaluating options for domestic alignments. Arming, training, and supporting factions, or the factions' clients within the ruling coalition, to establish or strengthen pro-government militias is the safest bet, even though their military prowess might be low (Ash 2016, 709ff). Aligning with previously excluded elites would entail more risks, because the factions of the ruling coalition are likely to fear a loss of power. Co-opted or tolerated militias are not vetted based on a meritocratic evaluation, and their loyalty, in most cases, remains attached to the societal groups from which they are recruited, or they retain an anti-government rhetoric after the co-optation (Ahram 2016,Aliyev 2020). Depending on the outlook of the excluded elites, the alliance may build on the basis of a mutual hostility against a common threat, collusion to share economic benefits, or access to patronage. The regime may even try the riskier option to co-opt groups within the insurgent alliance. However, to accommodate the co-opted groups, the regime would have to take away funds or privileges from the ruling coalition and, thereby, run the risk of a conflict within this coalition. The benefit is primarily to weaken the insurgent alliance, as the co-opted insurgent units serve little military function, because their loyalty is extremely questionable (Seymour 2014).

Only when domestic alignments fail to remedy the regime's existential crisis is the expectation that the regime to chooses an external alignment. Alignment especially with Western powers provides the regime with a more effective, but riskier, choice. The vulnerability of the regime is often enough to attract Western support. Nevertheless, the active strategies of "image management" and "taming" of interventions, as discussed in the introduction, attract Western security interventions by framing internal problems in the context of global issues, such as migration and terrorism. The regime bears little direct cost associated with foreign assistance, and might even profit from an influx of finance to shore up the regime (Fisher and Anderson 2017, de Oliveira and Verhoeven 2018). External alignment is risky for two reasons. First, as discussed earlier, the external powers offer little protection against threats from the ruling coalition, and demands for formal reforms are likely to create hostility among the ruling coalition. Second, external powers have the freedom to abandon the regime with little immediate harm to their own security (Elias and Weisiger 2020). A sudden loss of military backing represents a substantial risk to the regime, as evident in Afghanistan after the US withdrawal in 2021. Domestically, the only insurance for the regime would be to keep domestic alignments in place, which

Informal politics and regime strategy 33

might be enough to handle the insurgency threat after being abandoned by an external power.

Overall, strategies of alignment are expected to take a specific risk-averse and pragmatic form in informal settings. The insignificance of programmatic politics and the broad distribution of power make it possible and necessary for the regime to align across societal divides, even if the regime prefers aligning with militias within the ruling coalition. However, a pragmatic alignment strategy will undermine the long-term authority of the state institutions, but will provide short-term regime security, which in turn reinforces the informal rules. In the short term, pro-regime militias carry few risks for the regime, on the other hand however, in the long run they will reduce the regime's ability to control other factions and their clients further.

Measuring risk-averse alignment

To track the internal and external alignments and their timing it is necessary to consider ways in which they can be observed. Empirically, internal alignments are the most difficult to trace, but some elements of publicity are to be expected, because the militias and insurgency groups need attention to mobilize clients and supporters, and later to be identifiable, in order to gain access to co-optation, negotiations of cease-fires or peace agreements, which might yield economic and political benefits (Seymour 2014, 125ff). Therefore, tracking the formation, splits, fusions, and co-optation of militias is in many cases feasible, although it might not be possible to detect smaller factions, if they act very locally or make no attempts to attract attention to their activities. Detailed political, economic, or anthropological studies of particular ethnic groups or militias contain fine-grained information, as do many day-to-day think tank reports on particular militias.

Following the overall argument of the book, domestic alignments are expected to vary widely between political settlements dominated by formal politics and those dominated by informal politics. In political settlements dominated by informal politics, the proposition foresees an upshot in the number of pro-government militias receiving weapons from the security forces. In addition, if mobilized militias from the ruling coalition are not able to change the military balance, the proposition of risk-averse alignment would expect co-opted insurgent groups to be formally enrolled in the security forces, but in practice to be left out of the security forces' operations without being disarmed. Co-opted elites are in a position to demand benefits, such as lucrative positions within the state, or to be allowed to use their military power for economic gains.

When regimes make external alignments, the proposition expects to observe major differences in the importance attached to the principle of sovereignty. In political settlements dominated by informal politics, the regimes are expected to be unconcerned about issues of sovereignty, but highly focused on the alignment's impact on regime survival. Therefore,

34 *Informal politics and regime strategy*

these regimes are expected to accept foreign combat troops, as long as regime survival is not endangered by the external alignment. If the regime is able to choose between two opportunities for external alignment, the proposition would expect them to choose the one which poses the least amount of risk to regime survival, even if the external power provides a lower degree of military capacity. The reason for this is, again, that a low-simmering conflict is less of a concern than aligning with an external power that threatens the stability of the ruling coalition.

In a more formal setting, the proposition expects the regime to care more about the authority of the state institutions and the sovereignty of the state. If circumstances force the regime to work with militias, the regime's care for the authority of the state will presumably lead the regime to subdue militias legally and practically into formalized auxiliary forces, and task them with the protection of local communities, albeit under the surveillance of the armed forces. If parts of the insurgency alliance seek negotiations with the regime, they will be disarmed rather than utilized in the war. When making external alignments, regimes will resist military interventions altogether out of care for sovereignty, but translate economic and materiel support into more efficient security forces. The alignment patterns of regimes in informal settings result in the last expected regime strategy, namely simulated statebuilding that seeks to handle both informal domestic demands and formal external demands.

Simulated statebuilding

A regime has every reason to worry about the prospect of Western-imposed political or administrative reforms, because it relies on the continuation of informal politics to keep the ruling coalition together. Earlier, the chapter argued that Western demands for reforms are likely to threaten the interests of powerful elites within the ruling coalition. In such instances, the regime might quickly become isolated and endangered, and Western powers would not protect an isolated regime. The proposition of simulated statebuilding argues that to mitigate this cross-pressure, the most sensible kind of strategy for the regime is to simulate reforms of formal political and administrative institutions. Pretending to carry out reforms might be enough for the regime to secure continued Western assistance, at the same time as it reassures the ruling coalition of the continuation of informal politics. Rigging elections, organizing political parties as cloaks for client networks, or inserting clients into reformed security forces are all ways of simulating institutional reforms without changing the politics and institutions of the political settlement.

Publicly, the regime is likely to accept demands for formalization of administrative and political reforms while privately continuing former practices. Writing about democratic reforms in Senegal in the 1990s, Jean-François Bayart labels this interaction "a game of make-belief" (2000, 226). During the 1990s, many regimes became used to Western rhetoric of democratization or

Informal politics and regime strategy 35

good governance. After 9/11 2001 they adopted narratives of counter-terrorism, counter-extremism, and the curbing of migration in order to turn them into instruments to secure diplomatic connections to Western powers (Fisher & Anderson 2017, Hagmann and Reynthens 2016, de Oliveira and Verhoeven 2018). Because formal declarations, or new legislation, hold little power in an informal setting, the regimes are formally free to cater to the demands of Western powers. The regime can manufacture tangible evidence of cooperation, as basic information asymmetry is likely to persist, even in cases where the Western powers dedicate most resources to control the use of aid. Furthermore, the increased use of Islamist symbols and narratives among insurgency groups in Africa and the Middle East has made it easier for regimes to portray existing initiatives against internal threats as measures in the war against terrorism.

A successful strategy of simulated statebuilding gives access to materiel, aid, or even Western troops at a low cost. As discussed earlier, Western disengagement or a temporary cut-off of aid is a dangerous risk associated with this strategy. To reduce such a risk, the regime might simultaneously align with regional powers to hedge against a potential Western withdrawal. Internal conflicts in informal settings often become cross-border security problems that attract the attention of regional powers (Silve and Thierry 2018). In many cases, Western and regional powers do not have a mutual understanding of the need for statebuilding. This requires that the regime handles an even greater number of interests in order to stay in power, but with the potential benefit of mitigating the risk of alignment. Simulated statebuilding during an existential crisis is an example of the more widespread practice of avoiding reforms. Since the launch of conditionality in the structural adjustment programmes in the 1980s, several studies have identified how aid recipients developed strategies to circumvent conditionality (Tangri 1999, Van de Walle 2001, Andrews 2013, Whitfield 2009). What sets the strategy apart during an existential crisis is the potentially fatal effects of a Western cut-off of aid. However, the contradicting pressures from domestic elites and Western powers make such a high-wire strategy the only possibility in cases where strategies of domestic alignment have failed.

In principle, a steadfast use of conditionality even at the height of a crisis might force the regime to accept a conflict with the ruling coalition rather than losing Western aid. Ladwig finds that demands for reforms are more successful when Western powers combine demands with threats and inducement (2017, 292ff). However, simulated statebuilding makes a steadfast conditionality strategy much more difficult. If Western powers figure out that reforms are being informally undermined, they face a dilemma. Cutting off aid, despite reforms being formally implemented, requires detailed evidence and a public display of the regime's shortcomings. Moreover, pressing concerns for stability are likely to lead Western powers to accept the practice of simulated statebuilding. Therefore, this proposition expects Western

36 *Informal politics and regime strategy*

powers to settle for formal reforms and turn a blind eye to most cases of informal undermining.

Measuring simulated statebuilding

In most weak states, many bi- and multilateral foreign aid programmes continue to be implemented even in the midst of internal armed conflicts. Because of the considerable overlap between the agenda of foreign aid programmes and the administrative and political reforms that are part of Western military interventions, there is a need to distinguish between general foreign aid and aid related to the military intervention. Therefore, the attention is on the context of the demands for reforms, and only include reforms designed to improve the position of the state vis-à-vis the insurgency or those that address what the Western powers or international organizations perceive as being root causes of the conflict. Obviously, regimes that are part of political settlements with large elements of informal politics are more likely to face multiple demands for reforms to formalize the state. However, even those in political settlements dominated by formal politics will often be urged to implement reforms. Authoritarian regimes come up against pressure for democratization or respect for human rights, and even democracies might face demands for, e.g., inclusion of minorities.

The proposition of simulated statebuilding would expect local regimes to publicly express support and acceptance, and Western powers or international donors to publicly register the regime's willingness to cooperate. It poses a methodological challenge for the external observer to detect informal ways of undermining reforms. This study relies on the work of independent researchers who focus on specific reform initiatives and supplements their findings with donor agencies' evaluation of their own initiatives, whilst remaining aware of the potential bias in self-evaluations. The alternative would entail in-depth studies of bureaucratic behaviour that would not be possible in relation to four separate cases spread over three decades (Bierschenk and Olivier de Sardan 2014, 2019). Logically, the bias of the sources should be towards under-reporting the degree of informal undermining, because of the lack of knowledge and institutional interests in reporting successes. A bias towards underreporting works against the proposition of simulated statebuilding, and is a less problematic bias from a methodological standpoint.

By contrast, the proposition would expect the response of regimes navigating formal politics to fall into one of two categories. One would be a public and de facto acceptance of reforms, if they strengthen administrative and political institutions useful to suppressing an internal threat. Since they rely on the power of the state institutions, the regimes have strong incentives to improve them. The alternative response would be a public rejection, if the reforms go against the programmatic policies of the regime. In a political settlement in which the ruling coalition relies on certain formal principles, the regime would have few options but to adhere to those principles.

Informal politics and regime strategy 37

However, at an empirical level it is necessary to allow for more intricate regime reactions, given that informal practices might dominate in some state organizations. The Western powers are likely to wield secret diplomatic pressure for reforms and punishment for non-compliance. The case studies disregard such hidden activity and instead focus on public pressure and cuts in aid. Besides the unobservable character of secret pressure it is also inconsequential, unless the regime faces a cutback in aid. Western powers would need to justify the termination of aid or the withdrawal of support to a regime in times of crisis, when the support originally depended on public or parliamentary backing. In a case where a regional power interferes in a conflict, NGOs such as Small Arms Survey are likely to have documented the flow of weapons, military units, or instructors.

A comparative case study approach

To study informal practices and the interplay between local regimes and Western powers presents a difficult methodological challenge. At what point can an analysis claim to have fully unearthed secret, unofficial, and verbal negotiations? The purpose of this last section is to lay out a method that limits the demand for access to the informal negotiations of state and non-state decision-makers during a crisis, while still providing a detailed mapping of the regime's behaviour. Moreover, the section explains the logic behind the choice of the four cases.

Four single-case studies and a cross-case comparison constitute the main analytical contents of the book. The theoretical framework deduced the expected kind of regime strategies based on the logic of informal politics during an existential crisis. Therefore, the case studies rely on the logic of covariation between the importance of informal politics and regime strategies. That choice reflects the difficulty of tracking informal negotiations and decision-making. However, when empirical observations allow, the case studies document the influence of the ruling coalition on the strategy of the regimes. In order to structure the case studies in a way that allows comparison, a set of generalized, standard questions structures each case (George and Bennett 2005, pp. 86–88). These questions are taken directly from the considerations of measurement in the previous sections of this chapter, and of course from the research and working questions presented in the introduction. The first series looks at the importance of informal politics in the specific political settlement, since this prescribes the theoretical expectations of the regime's strategies. The remaining three series deal with the three expected strategies of praetorian protection, risk-averse alignment, and simulated statebuilding. Table 2.1 gives an overview of the 14 questions applied and the division of the case studies into four series.

The general questions reflect a compromise between the importance of contextual detail and the need to allow a structured comparison of the four diverse cases. Each case study might not do full justice to the complexities

38 *Informal politics and regime strategy*

Table 2.1 General questions guiding the case studies

Series	General questions
Importance of informal politics	1 To what extent is informal politics a key characteristic of the political settlement?
	2 What role have non-productive elites played in the making of the current political settlement?
	3 To what extent are funds and privileges distributed according to personal, non-programmatic criteria with the use of off-budget money?
	4 To what extent do political parties pursue coherent policies that are in line with their declared programmatic ideas?
Praetorian protection	5 Does the regime allocate sufficient resources in terms of manpower, financing, and weapons only to units loyal to the regime, even when an insurgency existentially threatens the regime?
	6 Do the regimes' efforts to coup-proof undermine Western support to increase the efficiency of the security forces?
	7 Does the military strategy of the regime consist of indiscriminate and inefficient violence to raise the cost of insurgency, rather than an elimination strategy with the aim of annihilating the insurgents?
Risk-averse alignment	8 Does the regime favour alignments with domestic elites, even after making external alignments?
	9 Is the regime willing to co-opt rivals or insurgent groups and provide them with extended privileges?
	10 Does the regime favour aligning with the external power that poses the least risk to regime survival, even though the external power has a weaker military capacity?
Simulated statebuilding	11 Does the regime openly resist or refuse to carry out political or administrative reforms, which Western powers demand as a condition for providing aid?
	12 Does the regime informally undermine all reforms by continuing or renewing the practices of informal politics in the affected institution?
	13 Are Western powers satisfied by symbolic reforms, and if not, do they punish the regime?
	14 Does the regime use regional powers as a hedge against Western withdrawal, even when the interests of the Western powers and the regional powers collide?

of each conflict, but they deal substantially with regime strategies and can be read as individual studies of Western supported regime survival. Nevertheless, the four case studies also serve as the elements of a cross-case comparison of the diverse interplay between informal politics, regime strategy, and Western interventions.

Cross-case comparison and case selection

The aim of choosing four cases is to illustrate the diversity of the political dynamics in the meeting between local regimes and Western interveners during Western interventions. Thus, the selection criteria become highly important to ensure diversity, but also to identify commonalities among the cases in order to discuss possible biases in the findings caused by the case selection. By including two cases where formal politics played a sizeable part and cases that vary as to Western intervention practices, the cross-case comparison in chapter seven can examine the impact of informal politics, as well as the intricate interplay between various forms of Western intervention practices and regime strategies. Moreover, the diverse set of cases provides a varied empirical groundwork for comparing the explanatory power of the political settlement approach with the two competing explanations of organizational dysfunction and foreign policy blindness.

In the first steps of delimiting the universe of cases, Armed Conflicts Dataset, version 20.1, 1989–2019 from the Uppsala Conflict Data Programme provides valuable information, before a qualitative assessment can identify a diverse set of cases (Pettersson and Öberg 2020)[5]. The first selection criterion delimits the population of cases based on the aim of this study, namely cases of Western support to regimes fighting a non-international armed conflict (in the parlance of international humanitarian law) since 1990. I add the scope condition of reducing the time frame from 1990 to 2019, to exclude cases from the Cold War. In that period, the regimes were able to switch alignments between the two superpowers to avoid demands for reforms (David 1991). UN-operations are included in this population if they have a mandate for peace-building or peace-enforcement and are driven by Western powers. In accordance with the research question, the second criterion is that the regime must have faced an existential threat. To avoid making the criterion too subjective, the selection of cases is based on whether the insurgents were able to occupy land beyond their initial area of operation. The regime must also have survived without Western combat troops for at least a brief period when the regime faced an existential threat. Regime strategies cannot be examined if the regimes are not forced to make use of them. This clearly excludes cases such as Iraq 2003 to 2008, when American combat troops were decisive on the battlefield for the entire period. The gradual drawback of Western troops from Afghanistan (2002-present) makes it difficult to delimit the period when the Afghan regime faced an existential threat. The third criterion is that the case must include demands for reforms set by the West for providing military aid.

Based on the three criteria, the bounded universe of cases consists of Afghanistan (2002-present), Algeria (1991–2000), Chad (2005–2010), El Salvador (pre-1990–1991), Guatemala (pre-1990–1996), Iraq (2011–2018), Mali (2011-present), Sierra Leone (1991–2002), Somalia (2006-present). To select among the nine cases, the cases of El Salvador and Guatemala are excluded from the study, because they primarily took place during the Cold War.

40 *Informal politics and regime strategy*

Somalia offers a very interesting case, but was eliminated due to the regime's extremely low degree of autonomy, which makes it more an example of the interaction between subnational actors – clans – and external actors (Menkhaus 2014, pp. 162–163). Afghanistan would provide valuable insights into the dynamics between a withdrawing intervener and a regime, but the most crucial period after the US withdrawal was yet to come at the time of the writing of this book. Finally, the case of Mali is chosen instead of Sierra Leone as a case of combined Western and UN intervention, because of its actuality and exemplarity of a wider pattern of conflict in the Sahel region. From a geographical viewpoint, the five remaining cases are skewed towards Africa, the Middle East, and North Africa, which marginalizes, e.g., Asian or Latin American perspectives. On the other hand, since 2001 Western interventions have mostly taken place in the highlighted three regions.

The four selected cases represent a considerable assortment of Western intervention practices. In the cases of Chad (2005–2010) and Mali (2011–2020), the two political settlements dominated by informal politics, Western practices varied from the minimal military engagement in Chad that delegated demands for reforms to international organizations to the large-scale involvement in Mali that included peacebuilding, counterinsurgency, and –terrorism, as well as wide-ranging demands for reforms. The two cases of Algeria (1991–2000) and Iraq (2011–2018) represent cases of political settlements with important elements of formal politics, but different degrees of Western involvement. Western practices spanned the narrow economic and intelligence assistance to Algeria, which came with demands for reforms, and the broad involvement of Western powers in Iraq in the fight against the Islamic State that included air power, special forces, and ground troops in an advice and assist role in addition to political interaction that included demands for reforms. Although the four cases may not capture the entirety of the evolution in Western intervention practices – and the particular political dilemma for each – they nonetheless add an empirical variation in terms of the key concepts informing this book, namely informal politics and Western intervention practices.

Three out of the four selected cases are former French colonies, which may raise a concern that the findings will be biased by the peculiarities of French post-colonial politics. As chapter eight discusses, France and its former African colonies are often referred to as the domain of *Francafrique*, meant to imply the continuation of close personal contact, hidden political and economic interests, as well as a very active use of the French military to keep African regimes in power (Bovcon 2013). An uncommonly personal and partly hidden relationship between a Western power and a smaller group of regimes in Africa would in itself provide an explanation of the undermining of formal reforms. As chapter three will show, this was arguably the case in Chad, but France had not been involved militarily in Mali prior to the intervention in 2013. And Algeria's war of independence from France led to hostile relations between the two states that were far from the image of Francafrique.

Informal politics and regime strategy 41

The reliance on oil and gas income in Algeria, Chad, and Iraq, as well as Mali's reliance on its gold export, is another potential bias in the case selection. The 'oil curse' literature considers the connection between reliance on natural resources and conflict, corruption, and authoritarianism (Badeeb et al. 2017). It would seem probable that off-budget money fueled by rents from natural resources would allow funds for both the ruling coalition and co-opted insurgent groups. However, a build-up of the formal, repressive capacity of the security institutions may be just as likely an outcome. Indeed in a study of authoritarian regimes, Phoebe Ishak finds little difference in the choice of survival strategies among rentier and non-rentier regimes when facing a major internal, violent threat (2019). Nevertheless, the case studies need to take into account the political impact of natural resources in order to limit the potential impact of this bias. Despite the potential biases, the four cases allow a broad and varied examination of the ways that informal politics limits regime strategy and how the different configurations of external intervention and state- and peacebuilding initiatives shape the conflict dynamic.

Conclusion

Examining informal politics and regime strategies in states dominated by informal politics is a tall order. This chapter reduces the challenge by establishing and operationalizing a theoretical framework that links informal politics in political settlements with a certain kind of regime survival strategies during existential crises. In political settlements with strong non-productive elites specialized in violence, the regime depends on informal politics to uphold the ruling coalition, even when a political settlement is collapsing. This dependency shapes the strategic choices available to the regime that must devise ways to protect itself against a coup and align with elites specialized in violence inside and outside the state. The result is that the basic distribution of power forces the regime to utilize and reinforce informal politics, even when Western powers demand reforms. Moreover, the chapter lays out the methodological considerations behind the choice of four single-case studies and a cross-case comparison. This concludes the theoretical part of the study. All the next four chapters are single case studies that unfold the relationship between informal politics, the three proposed regime survival strategies, and different Western intervention practices.

Notes

1 Power is defined as the capability of an individual or group to engage and survive in conflict, which is in line with the concept of holding power in political settlement theory (Khan 2010, 6).
2 Khan argues that the productive, capitalist sector remains too small in developmental states to generate enough state income to satisfy the demands of elites in the ruling coalition.

42 *Informal politics and regime strategy*

3 Clientelism is defined as a form of non-programmatic political mobilization where individual benefits are conditional on the recipient returning the favor with a vote or other forms of political support (Stokes et al. 2013, 13). Favors are privileges, such as access to an office or the concession of mining rights, or direct payment of public funds to one individual, together labelled patronage.
4 The number of coups have declined since the 1960s, but the frequency of successful coups was constant from 2000 to 2010 (Powell and Thyne 2011, 255). Recent coups and coup attempts in, for example, Burkina Faso 2015, Egypt 2013, Gabon 2019, Guinea-Bissau 2012, Mali 2012 & 2020, Mauritania 2008, Myanmar 2021, Niger 2010, Sudan 2019, Turkey 2016, and Zimbabwe 2017, show that regimes still need to protect themselves from the sudden loss of power at the hands of factions within the security forces.
5 The population of insurgencies since 1990 is defined as conflicts between the government of a state and one or more internal opposition groups (labelled as category 3 and 4 of the variable "type"). This study excludes cases where governmental authority is not established when independence is declared or at any point after (such as Libya 2011–present). Cases with very low levels of violence are excluded, which means that the conflict must have resulted in at least 1,000 battle deaths since its onset. Cases in which an insurgency manages to replace the government, but faces other insurgencies afterwards, are treated as two separate cases.

References

Allen, Nathaniel. 2020. "Interrogating Ethnic Stacking: The Uses and Abuses of Security Force Ethnicity in Sudan" *Civil War*, 22 (2–3): 243–265. 10.1080/1369824 9.2020.1693191

Ahram, Ariel. 2016. "Pro-Government Militias and the Repertoires of Illicit State Violence." *Studies in Conflict & Terrorism* 39 (3): 207–226. 10.1080/1057610X.2015.11 04025

Aliyev, Huseyn. 2020. "Pro-government Anti-government Armed Groups? Toward Theorizing Pro-government 'Government Challengers'." *Terrorism and Political Violence, online.* 10.1080/09546553.2020.1785877

Andrews, Matt. 2013. *The Limits of Institutional Reform in Development: Changing Rules for Realistic Solutions.* Cambridge: Cambridge University Press. 10.1017/ CBO9781139060974

Ash, Konstantin. 2016. "Threats to Leaders' Political Survival and Pro-Government Militia Formation." *International Interactions* 42 (5): 703–728. 10.1080/03050629.2 016.1138108

Badeeb, Ramez Abubakr, Hooi Hooi Lean, and Jeremy Clark. 2017. "The Evolution of the Natural Resource Curse Thesis: A Critical Literature Survey." *Resources Policy* 51: 123–134. 10.1016/j.resourpol.2016.10.015

Bareebe, Gerald. 2020. "Predators or Protectors? Military Corruption as a Pillar of Regime Survival in Uganda." *Civil Wars* 22 (2–3): 313–332. 10.1080/13698249.202 0.1730640

Bayart, Jean-François. 2000. "Africa in the World: A History of Extraversion." *African Affairs* 99 (395): 217–267. 10.1093/afraf/99.395.217

Behuria, Pritish, Lars Buur, and Hazel Gray. 2017. "Studying Political Settlements in Africa." *African Affairs* 116 (464): 508–525. 10.1093/afraf/adx019

Informal politics and regime strategy   43

Berlingozzi, Laura, and Stoddard (eds). 2020. "Assessing Misaligned Counterinsurgency Practice in Niger and Nigeria." *International Spectator* 55 (4): 37–53. 10.1080/0393272 9.2020.1833472

Bierschenk, Thomas, and Jean-Pierre Olivier de Sardan. 2014. "Ethnographies of Public Services in Africa: An Emerging Research Paradigm." In *States at Work*, edited by Thomas Bierschenk and Jean-Pierre Olivier de Sardan, 35–65. Leiden: Brill.

Bierschenk, Thomas, and Jean-Pierre Olivier de Sardan. 2019. "How To Study Bureaucracies Ethnographically?" *Critique of Anthropology* 39 (2): 243–257. 10.11 77/0308275X19842918

Bovcon, Maja. 2013. "Françafrique and Regime Theory." *European Journal of International Relations* 19 (1): 5–26. 10.1177/1354066111413309

Brooks, Risa. 1998. *Political-Military Relations and the Stability of Arab Regimes.* Adelphi Paper 324. Oxford: Oxford University Press.

Bruin, Erica De. 2018. "Preventing Coups D'état: How Counterbalancing Works." *Journal of Conflict Resolution* 62 (7): 1433–1458. 10.1177/0022002717692652

Byman, Daniel. 2006. "Friends Like These: Counterinsurgency and the War on Terrorism." *International Security* 31 (2): 79–115. 10.1162/isec.2006.31.2.79

Byman, Daniel. 2016. "'Death Solves All Problems': The Authoritarian Model of Counterinsurgency." *Journal of Strategic Studies* 39 (1): 62–93. 10.1080/014023 90.2015.1068166

Casey, Adam. 2020. "The Durability of Client Regimes: Foreign Sponsorship and Military Loyalty, 1946–2010." *World Politics* 72 (3): 411–447. 10.1017/S004388712 0000039

Chabal, Patrick, and Jean-Pascal Daloz. 1999. *Africa Works: Disorder as Political Instrument.* Oxford: James Currey Publishers.

Clapham, Christopher. 1996. *Africa and the International System: The Politics of State Survival.* Cambridge: Cambridge University Press.

David, Stephen R. 1991. *Choosing Sides: Alignment and Realignment in the Third World.* Baltimore: Johns Hopkins University Press.

Day, Christopher R., and William Reno. 2014. "In Harm's Way: African Counter-Insurgency and Patronage Politics." *Civil Wars* 16 (2): 105–126. 10.1080/1369824 9.2014.927699

Elias, Barbara and Alex Weisiger. 2020. "Influence through Absence in U.S. Counterinsurgency Interventions? Coercing Local Allies through Threats to Withdraw". *Civil Wars*, online. 10.1080/13698249.2020.1809193

Erdmann, Gero, and Ulf Engel. 2007. "Neopatrimonialism Reconsidered: Critical Review and Elaboration of an Elusive Concept." *Commonwealth & Comparative Politics* 45 (1): 95–119. 10.1080/14662040601135813

Feaver, Peter D. 1996. "The Civil-Military Problematique: Huntington, Janowitz, and the Question of Civilian Control." *Armed Forces & Society* 23 (2): 149–178. 10.1177/0095327X9602300203

Fisher, Jonathan, and David M Anderson. 2017. *Africa's New Authoritarians: Aid, Securitisation and State-Building.* London: Hurst Publishers.

Freedman, Lawrence. 2013. *Strategy: A History.* Oxford: Oxford University Press.

George, Alexander L., and Andrew Bennett. 2005. *Case Studies and Theory Development in the Social Sciences.* Cambridge: The MIT Press.

44 *Informal politics and regime strategy*

Gillies, Alexandra. 2020. *Crude Intentions: How Oil Corruption Contaminates the World*. New York: Oxford University Press. 10.1093/oso/9780190940706.001.0001

Hagmann, Tobias, and Filip Reynthens. 2016. *Aid and Authoritarianism in Africa: Development without democracy*. London: Zed Books.

Hazelton, Jacqueline L. 2017. "The 'Hearts and Minds' Fallacy: Violence, Coercion, and Success in Counterinsurgency Warfare." *International Security* 42 (1): 80–113. 10.1162/ISEC_a_00283

Hoffman, Frank G. 2020. "The Missing Element in Crafting National Strategy: A Theory of Success." *Joint Force Quarterly* 97 (2): 55–64.

Ishak, Phoebe W. 2019. "Autocratic Survival Strategies: Does Oil Make a Difference?" *Peace Economics, Peace Science and Public Policy* 25 (2): 1–22. 10.1515/peps-201 8-0043

Jackson, Robert H, and Carl G Rosberg. 1984. "Personal Rule: Theory and Practice in Africa." *Comparative Politics* 16 (4): 421–442. 10.2307/421948

Käihkö, Ilmari. 2012. "Big Man Bargaining in African Conflicts." In *African Conflicts and Informal Power: Big Men and Networks*, edited by Mats Utas, 181–204. London: Zed Books.

Khan, Mushtaq. 2010. *"Political Settlements and the Governance of Growth-Enhancing Institutions."* Governance for Growth. London School of Economics.

Khan, Mushtaq. 2018a. "Political Settlements and the Analysis of Institutions: An Introduction", *African Affairs* 117 (469): 636–655, 10.1093/afraf/adx044

Knowles, Emily, and Jahara Matisek. 2019. "Western Security Force Assistance in Weak States Time for a Peacebuilding Approach." *RUSI Journal* 164 (3): 10–21. 10.1080/03071847.2019.1643258

Kuo, Didi. 2018. *Clientelism, Capitalism, and Democracy: The Rise of Programmatic Politics in the United States and Britain*. Cambridge: Cambridge University Press. 10.1017/9781108679923

Ladwig III, Walter C. 2017. *The Forgotten Front: Patron-Client Relationships in Counter Insurgency*. Cambridge: Cambridge University Press. 10.1017/978131 6756805

Lemarchand, René. 1972, "Political Clientelism and Ethnicity in Tropical Africa: Competing Solidarities in Nation-Building", *American Political Science Review* 66, 68–90. 10.2307/1959279

Malejacq, Romain. 2016. "Warlords, Intervention, and State Consolidation: A Typology of Political Orders in Weak and Failed States." *Security Studies* 25 (1): 85–110. 10.1080/09636412.2016.1134191

Malejacq, Romain. 2019. *Warlord Survival: The Delusion of State Building in Afghanistan*. Itchaca: Cornell University Press. 10.1515/9781501746437

Marten, Kimberly. 2015. *Warlords, Strong-Arm Brokers in Weak States*. Ithaca: Cornell University Press. 10.7591/9780801464119

Menkhaus, K. 2014. "State Failure, State-Building, and Prospects for a 'Functional Failed State' in Somalia." *The Annals of the American Academy of Political and Social Science* 656 (1): 154–172. 10.1177/0002716214547002

Migdal, Joel S. 1988. *Strong Societies and Weak States*. Princeton: Princeton University Press. 10.2307/j.ctvzsmdzz

Migdal, Joel S. 2001. *State in Society: Studying How States and Societies Transform and Constitute One Another*. Cambridge: Cambridge University Press. 10.1017/ CBO9780511613067

Morency-Laflamme, Julien, and Theodore McLauchlin. 2020. "The Efficacy of Ethnic Stacking: Military Defection during Uprisings in Africa." *Journal of Global Security Studies* 5 (4): 695–702. 10.1093/jogss/ogz015

North, Douglass C. 1991. "Institutions." *Journal of Economic Perspectives* 5 (1): 97–112. 10.1257/jep.5.1.97

Oliveira, Ricardo Soares De, and Harry Verhoeven. 2018. "Taming Intervention: Sovereignty, Statehood and Political Order in Africa." *Survival* 60 (2): 7–32. 10.1080/00396338.2018.1448558

Pettersson, Therese, and Magnus Öberg. 2020. "Organized Violence, 1989-2019." *Journal of Peace Research*, 57 (4): 597–613. 10.1177/0022343320934986

Phillips, Sarah G. 2016. "When Less Was More: External Assistance and the Political Settlement in Somaliland." *International Affairs* 92 (3): 629–645. 10.1111/1468-2346.12601

Pitcher, Anne, Mary H. Moran, and Michael Johnston. 2009. "Rethinking Patrimonialism and Neopatrimonialism in Africa." *African Studies Review* 52 (2009): 125–156. 10.1353/arw.0.0163

Powell, Jonathan M. 2019. "Leader Survival Strategies and the Onset of Civil Conflict: A Coup-Proofing Paradox." *Armed Forces and Societies* 45 (1): 27–44. 10.1177/0095327X17728493

Powell, Jonathan M., and Clayton L. Thyne. 2011. "Global Instances of Coups from 1950 to 2010: A New Dataset." *Journal of Peace Research* 48 (2): 249–259. 10.1177/0022343310397436

Quirk, Patrick W. 2017. *Great Powers, Weak States, and Insurgency*. Cham: Springer International Publishing. 10.1007/978-3-319-47419-9

Reno, William. 2019. "The Importance of Context When Comparing Civil Wars." *Civil Wars* 21 (4): 448–467. 10.1080/13698249.2019.1642614

Roessler, Philip. 2016. *Ethnic Politics and State Power in Africa: The Logic of the Coup-civil War Trap*. Cambridge: Cambridge University Press. 10.1017/9781316809877

Seymour, Lee J M. 2014. "Why Factions Switch Sides in Civil Wars." *International Security* 39 (2): 92–131. 10.1162/ISEC

Silve, Arthur, and Verdier, Thierry. 2018. "A Theory of Regional Conflict Complexes." *Journal of Development Economics* 133: 434–447. 10.1016/j.jdeveco.2018.03.002

Staniland, Paul. 2012. "States, Insurgents, and Wartime Political Orders." *Perspectives on Politics* 10 (2): 243–264. 10.1017/S1537592712000655

Stokes, Susan, Thad Dunning, Marcelo Nazareno, and Valerie Brusco. 2013. *Brokers, Voters and Clientelism: The Puzzle of Distributive Politics*. Cambridge: Cambridge University Press. 10.1017/CBO9781107324909

Tadros, Mariz, and Jeremy Allouche. 2017. "Political Settlements as a Violent Process: Deconstructing the Relationship between Political Settlements and Intrinsic, Instrumental and Resultant Forms of Violence." *Conflict, Security and Development* 17 (3): 187–204. 10.1080/14678802.2017.1319699

Talmadge, Caitlin. 2015. *The Dictator's Army: Battlefield Effectiveness in Authoritarian Regimes*. Ithaca: Cornell University Press. 10.7591/9781501701764

Tangri, Roger. 1999. *The Politics of Patronage in Africa*. Oxford: Oxford University Press.

46 *Informal politics and regime strategy*

Tenenbaum, Élie. 2017. "French Exception or Western Variation? A Historical Look at the French Irregular Way of War." *Journal of Strategic Studies* 40 (4): 554–576. 10.1080/01402390.2016.1220368

Van de Walle, Nicolas. 2001. "The Impact of Multi-party Politics in sub-Saharan Africa." *Forum for Development Studies* 28 (1): 5–42. 10.1080/08039410.2001.9666154

Van de Walle, Nicolas. 2012. "The Path from Neopatrimonialism: Democracy and Clientelism in Africa Today." In *Neopatrimonialism in Africa and Beyond*, edited by Daniel C. Bach and Mamoudou Gazib, 111–123. London: Routledge.

Waal, Alex de. 2015. *The Real Politics of the Horn of Africa: Money, War and the Business of Power*. London: Polity.

Waterman, A. 2021. Counterinsurgents' Use of Force and "Armed Orders" in Naga Northeast India. *Asian Security* 17 (1): 119–137. 10.1080/14799855.2020.1724099

Whitfield, Lindsay. 2009. *The Politics of Aid: African Strategies for Dealing with Donors*. Oxford: Oxford University Press.

3 Chad: turning friends into enemies and enemies into friends

The history of Chad is one of violence. Periods of insurgency wars have alternated with somewhat stable periods that have seen several occurrences of repression and violence among non-regime elites. From 2005 to 2010, the Chadian regime fought to stay in power during the Sudanese supported insurgency. In that period, President Idriss Déby's regime faced an existential threat resulting in two direct attacks on N'djamena, the capital, one of which ended a few blocks from the presidential palace. The militarization of the most important Chadian elites provides an opportunity to study the strategic choices of a regime acting in a political settlement with a wide distribution of military power and a high degree of informal accommodation. Although Déby has pictured Chad as a stable power in the regional fight against Islamist militant groups since 2013, his death on the battlefield in yet another insurgency war in April 2021 is a vivid illustration of the violent and volatile character of Chadian elite politics. The purpose of this case study is, therefore, to examine a case that is most likely to correspond to the theoretical propositions. Not only did the political settlement of Chad resemble the ideal type of informal politics, but the deep French involvement in Chadian politics and permanent deployment of military forces in the country would make it very likely that France would have accepted simulated statebuilding when the EU and the World Bank demanded reforms. However, Chad also represents a facetted case, because the conflict in Chad had deep ties to the violence in Darfur, which caused Sudanese involvement in Chad in the examined period. The intricate interplay between domestic militarized elites, the prospect of an oil boom, regional powers, and Western interveners, thus, offers a case that is far from the model of liberal statebuilding, yet demonstrates the multifaceted impact of informal politics at national and international political levels.

The first section assesses the importance of informal politics in Chad's political settlement prior to the outbreak of the insurgency, while the second section examines to what extent the praetorian protection proposition explains the choices made by the Déby regime. The third section evaluates the proposition of risk-averse alignment, by studying the regime's use of alignment in the complicated mix of militias and insurgents in eastern Chad and

DOI: 10.4324/9781003204978-3

48 *Chad*

the Darfur region in Sudan, as well as its alignment with the external powers of France and Sudan. The fourth section considers the extent to which the proposition of simulated statebuilding explains the regime's behaviour.

The dominance of informal politics in Chad

Since gaining independence from France in 1960, Chad's political life has oscillated between periods of insurgency and periods of repression and political violence. Only excruciating poverty and a small productive sector have remained constants in the volatile state. Non-productive, militarized elites have dominated Chadian politics and distributed funds and privileges to informal networks to secure their loose grip on power. Political parties and ideological declarations have mostly been fronts for personal or kinship-based networks. Chad is an example of a state almost entirely dominated by informal politics.

The dominance of the militarized northern elites

Until 1982, Southern tribes, most notably the Sara tribe, upheld the dominant position they enjoyed during the French colonial period. However, the pastoral, Christian or animistic Southern tribes excluded the Northern and Eastern nomadic, Muslim tribes (Burr and Collins 2008, 32–41) The result was a civil war from 1965 to 1982 with shifting alliances, which ultimately led to the transfer of power to the Northern and Eastern elites under the leadership of Hissène Habré from the Toubou tribe (Schulhofer-Wohl 2020, 191ff). After 1982, a political settlement took shape that relied on the transfer of funds to the many non-productive Northern and Eastern elites in the ruling coalition. The southern part of Chad remained the most productive due to the favourable climate for agriculture, which meant that the economic viability of the political settlement depended on the extraction of resources from cash crops, mostly cotton, for the non-productive ruling coalition (Nolutshungu 1996, 39ff). A distribution of funds that remained in place for the rest of the examined period.

In the period 1982-90, the ruling coalition that supported President Habré became increasingly narrow as elites were excluded. The first exclusion was that of the Arab elites, who became subject to violent oppression in the 1980s, resulting in at least 40,000 Arabs fleeing to Darfur in Sudan, and the ongoing incursions on both sides of the border in that period destabilized the relationship between the two states (Flint and De Waal 2008, 53). Arab refugees played a major role in the Janjaweed movement in Darfur, which began to form in the late 1980s. Surprisingly, the fatal threat to the regime came, not from the populous Chadian Arabs, who made up 15 to 20 percent of the population, but from a coup attempt in 1989 by soldiers from the small Zaghawa tribe that only constituted 1–3 percent of the population (Maio 2010, 34–37). In 1989 Umar al-Bashir took power in Sudan, and welcomed the leader of the attempted coup, Idriss Déby, a Zaghawa who

Chad 49

had previously been the Chief of Staff for Habré in his war with Libya in the mid-1980s (ibid, 32). Déby and his 2,000 insurgents used Darfur as the staging area for a successful lightning attack against N'djamena in 1990 that led to his seizure of power (Nolutshungu 1996, 218–219).

Déby's regime relied heavily on Northern and Eastern tribes, but in a different configuration to Habré's (Prunier 2008, 7). The Arab tribes again joined the ruling coalition and became beneficiaries of the distribution of funds and privileges, although on a small scale. Zaghawa clans, on the other hand, benefited disproportionally considering the small size of the clans. Déby belonged to the Bideyat clan of the Zaghawa tribe, and recruited a great number of Bideyats to fill senior positions within the military, state-owned companies as well as state institutions (Marchal 2006, 475). One example is the high number of Bideyats among the multitude of senior military officers – 60 generals and 256 colonels. Several of the colonels of Bideyat descent were minors who had not even finished high school (Debos 2016, 127). During the conflict, the heavy reliance on the Bideyat clan became a liability to President Déby as they formed the nucleus of the armed resistance.

Since 1982, the elites' expertise in violence and ability to secure weapons had given them access to the ruling coalition in Chad, but not to public legitimacy or influence in the formal political institutions. The degree of influence of societal actors, such as tribes, on the distribution of patronage is dictated by their potential to threaten the regime militarily However, although tribes command important social control, they are not coherent actors. The regime co-opted elite members of the tribes into its client network, while others chose to join the insurgency movements. Still, the overall result was an overwhelming need to use informal politics to accommodate the demands of the non-productive and militarized elites.

Clientelism as the hub of political transactions

Clientelism was the most important instrument of power for the Déby regime. Most public funds and positions were used to distribute money and privileges to members of the ruling coalition. Even before 2003, when oil revenues began pouring in, the structure of the Chadian economy gave several opportunities to reward client networks. The private sector offered little possibility for wealth creation, and the elites within the ruling coalition seemed mostly occupied with access to the client network as the road to economic opportunities (Frank and Guesnet 2009, 49). One example was the second largest exporting company, the state-owned Cotontchad, that bought, processed, and distributed cotton from small-scale farmers in the southern parts of the country (Nako 2012). Little energy was spent on making the company profitable. On the contrary, Cotontchad employed a large number of persons with little responsibility and high wages. In addition to awarding contracts to companies owned by clients of the regime, the

50   *Chad*

main purpose of public companies such as Cotontchad was to allow the patronage to pay for its extensive client networks (International Crisis Group 2016, 16).

In addition to providing direct opportunities for enrichment, the Déby regime most likely used a complicated arrangement of public and private transactions to garner off-budget funds. After Chad became an oil exporting state in 2003, oil income boosted the construction of grand projects, such as stadiums, hospitals, and paved roads, most of which were low quality, built at exorbitant prices, and rarely used afterwards (Bertelsmann 2014, 6, Frank and Guesnet 2009, 48). The Ministry of Infrastructure was the hub of all capital expenditure allocations of other ministries. The ministry devised a system whereby contracts were split into smaller parts, not subject to public oversight, and the prices were set to ensure artificially high profits (International Crisis Group 2009a, 10). Furthermore, in that period the company that won most contracts was SNER owned by the President's older brother, who then hired smaller companies to carry out the work. Companies owned by political clients.

In many cases, petty crime and corruption were linked to the lower end of the factions' client networks. One example was border customs, where armed, self-appointed customs control groups had authority over official customs officers. The official customs system and ordinary citizens and traders accepted the self-appointed groups, because they were under the protection of patrons within the Chadian state (Iocchi 2019). This practice created jobs for many insurgents, who had seen their leaders being included in the regime's client network. By upholding a grey area of crime and corruption, the Chadian regime and its intermediate patrons within the state were able to provide for their clients at a low cost – at least from the perspective of the regime.

Finally, the addition of oil income in 2003 demonstrated the all-encompassing importance of clientelism. Déby decided to distribute the oil money primarily to his closest family without providing sufficient patronage to the ruling coalition (International Crisis Group 2016, 16). The decision to favour a narrow part of the ruling coalition created animosity, because the widespread clientelistic practices had created expectations among the other factions that the payment for political loyalty would increase, once oil began to flow. The high expectations of clientelistic payment was very likely one of the main explanations for the insurgency crisis in 2005. Clientelism was at the heart of Chadian politics.

The illusion of programmatic politics

"I publicly make the following commitment: I will not be a candidate for the 2006 presidential elections. I will not change the Constitution, even if I have 100 percent majority!" (President Déby 2001, quoted in Toïngar 2014, 150). President Idriss Déby did not deliver on his unabashed declaration of adherence to the Chadian constitution by stepping down after the end of his second election period in 2006. Like most African regimes after the end of the Cold

Chad 51

War, the Déby regime established a democratic constitution in 1996. In 2004, Déby backtracked and forced through a constitutional change to allow an indefinite number of reelections, which he legitimized by referring to the failed coup attempt in May 2004 (Boggero 2009, 22). Moreover, Déby announced to his extended family that his son, Brahim Déby, would take over when his father decided to resign, which was a further sign of his ambition to pursue narrow regime interests at the cost of formal democratic rules such as term limits (Wax 2006)[1]. The announcement caused widespread protests in the President's inner circle, which in turn led to the defection of Mahamat Nouri, former Minister and Ambassador, and Timani Erdimi, Déby's cousin and Chief of Staff. These two persons would later become key leaders in the insurgent movements. However, the protests had little to do with the lack of democratic principles, but were about a struggle for power or access to patronage.

Before the insurgency in Chad in 2005, formal political institutions had little or no influence on any decisions except the most mundane ones. The Chadian parliament was heavily dominated by the President's party, the *Mouvement Patriotique du Salut* (MPS), which won a majority in all elections. Manipulation mostly took place in the northern and eastern regions, where the rival parties from the President's own Zaghawa tribe and other Muslim tribes had been banned from standing for election (Debos 2014). By contrast, the regime allowed the election of non-MPS politicians from the Sara tribe, the most populous tribe in southern Chad. Moreover, a practice of appointing prime ministers from the southern region provided excluded elites with nominal political influence. The result was an apparent democracy that included public debate and opposition, but only from – mostly southern – non-militarized elites that did not pose a threat to the political settlement.

President Déby and the dominant MPS party seemed to be guided by a very low degree of programmatic politics, if any at all. Arguably, the MPS party served mostly as a vehicle for clientelism, or even as a "crony network" (Tubiana and Debos 2017, 136). Déby's political trajectory bears witness to a non-ideological and pragmatic approach. The defection from the Habré regime appears to be unrelated to any political questions. Nevertheless, the new Islamist Sudanese regime decided to support Déby, and relations between Sudan and Chad remained warm throughout the 1990s, despite the fact that Déby did not have an Islamist political agenda. In parallel, Déby maintained good relations with France, even when it became clear that he was not genuinely pursuing a democratization of Chad. Moreover, he made very little effort to reform the state administration or address Chad's extreme poverty during the 1990s (van Dijk 2007, 700). In all likelihood, the Déby regime's approach reflects its need to cater to the interests of the ruling coalition, whose primary need was non-programmatic patronage.

To sum up, on the spectrum of political settlements Chad is positioned closely to the purely informal end of the spectrum. For the political settlement in Chad to be viable, funds and privileges had to be distributed

52   *Chad*

according to informal, clientelistic rules. The power held by militarized, non-productive elites translated into a grip on the state institutions and public companies that the ruling coalition used for enrichment. Programmatic politics was hardly detectable, because the regime and the dominant MPS party upheld few, if any, principal ideas. In fact, the conflict between 2005 and 2010 only makes sense when we consider it as a struggle within the ruling coalition related to the distribution of patronage.

Praetorian protection: the problem of Zaghawa loyalty

In 2005, the financial windfall from oil production in theory gave the regime the opportunity to create stronger and more autonomous security forces that could carry out a strategy of elimination against internal threats. President Déby faced a coup- and insurgency threat, because clientelistic bonds had broken within the ruling coalition, and most critically among the trusted Zaghawa Bidyat clan members. Yet, this section argues that the regime pursued a strategy of praetorian protection. New measures for coup-proofing were adopted. And the regime applied a strategy of punishment, though not in the way theoretically expected, but mainly by using private military companies to provide air power to punish the insurgents.

Who in the security institutions benefited from the new oil income?

In 2004, three events that affected the security institutions in Chad provide us with a glimpse into the strategies adopted by the Déby regime. First, oil income began to bolster the regime, allowing for increased military spending. Second, the Bideyat initiated coup within the presidential guard led to a re-structuring of the unit and renaming it *Direction générale des services de sécurité des institutions de l'État* (DGSSIE). The failed coup was part of a widespread defection and mutiny that took place in the regular Chadian Army (Meerpohl 2013, 4). Finally, in June 2004, President Déby founded the Special Anti-Terrorist Group (SATG), as a project under the new Trans-Saharan Counter-Terrorism Initiative launched by the United States. These changes in the security institutions happened at a critical juncture, when the insurgent groups began to receive weapons from the Sudanese government, which also allowed them to use Darfur as a staging ground for incursions into Chad (Tubiana 2008, 34–35). This provides an opportunity to examine the prioritization among the security institutions at a time when the insurgency existentially threatened the regime.

In addition to changing the name of the presidential guard, President Déby changed the ethnic composition of the unit without compromising its competence. According to the estimate of the United States State Department, Bideyat Zaghawas still dominated the officer corps in DGSSIE, but less so than before the reforms, and the group of non-commissioned officers, as well as

Chad 53

enlisted personnel, became ethnically diversified (Author interview 14 March 2016 with a United States Army Special Forces officer with experience from Chad). DGSSIE continued to be a light infantry unit and maintained its primary position near the capital. The unit was under the direct control of the President, and received a payment twice as high as the regular units (Debos 2016, 124–125). After being founded in June 2004, the SATG battalions soon became the regime's preferential unit. Recruitment for the unit primarily took place near N'djamena, an area with a higher number of mixed ethnic groups than the eastern or northern parts of Chad, still the Zaghawas were the most numerous and dominant group among the officers (Author interview 14 March 2016). The two elite units were directed in person by President Déby and were the backbone of the defence of N'djamena in April 2006 and February 2008, which indicates that SATG and DGSSIE were the most trusted as well as the most capable units in Chad.

Unlike guerrilla tactics of slow movement and concealment among the population, Chadian insurgents were highly mobile and visible. They attacked in columns of land cruisers to navigate the vast Chadian desert and savannah, making them vulnerable to air strikes. However, building a capacity to exploit their visibility by using air interdiction or close air support would take years and demanded a proficient force of pilots and ground crew. This, or the difficulty of identifying a loyal cadre, might explain why Chad turned to private companies from Switzerland and Ukraine to provide that capacity. From 2006 to 2008, Chad relied on refitted propeller aircraft and MI-17 and MI-24 attack helicopters operated by Griffon, a Swiss company. The aircraft were manned by Algerian, French, and Mexican ground crews and pilots, which proved vital in the defence of N'djamena in February 2008 (Aherne et al. 2011, 64, Fontanellaz and Cooper 2016). In July 2008, Chad bought a package of six SU-25 attack aircraft and four MI-25 attack helicopters, including pilots and ground crews from Ukraine (Allison 2015, 93). They made a decisive contribution in the last major battle in May 2009, when a column of 400 pick-up trucks was interdicted and many trucks destroyed (Lewis and Gelfand 2009).

The reliance on two elite units personally directed by President Déby, as well as a mercenary air force, supports the proposition of praetorian protection. However, from 2005, the additional income from oil also increased the regime's spending on the regular army, the *Armée Nationale Tchadienne* (ANT). Also, the acquisition of well over 100 armed vehicles as well as advanced anti-tank weapons, such as the MILAN-system, gave ANT mobility, protection, and fire power against an enemy armed with small arms and light weapons. Some of the new vehicles merely replaced others lost in battle, but the net effect was an upgrade of the units that received the weapons (International Crisis Group 2021, 6–7). Still, we cannot know the exact distribution of the weapons among DGSSIE, SATG, and ANT. In addition, ANT handed over substantial parts of the newly acquired small arms and ammunition to insurgent groups in Darfur as part of the regime's

54 *Chad*

alignment with the two insurgent groups Justice and Equality Movement and Sudan Liberation Army (Toïngar 2014, 53).

More importantly, at least half of the increase in the funding of ANT was spent on paying for the rapid influx of new soldiers – or more accurately, to pay for a disproportionally high share of new officers and non-commissioned officers, as well as for expenses for "services to support the troops" (International Monetary Fund 2009, 7). Seen in the light of the absolute uncertainty surrounding the actual number of soldiers in ANT, this suggests that much of the payment went towards including former insurgents in ANT. The Chadian regime traditionally gives co-opted insurgents the rank of officer or non-commissioned officer to provide them with a high salary (Debos 2016, 122). Wadal Abdelkader, the Chadian Minister of Defence, estimated that in 2008 ANT consisted of 50,000 to 80,000 soldiers, seemingly without knowing the exact number (2008). The World Bank data estimated that ANT rose from 34,000 soldiers in 2004 to 35,000 in 2008. When the figures are compared to a 2009 French intelligence estimate of 14,000 active members of ANT, the most apparent explanation is that ANT largely consisted of "ghost soldiers", i.e., soldiers paid without being active, to secure proper patronage for new clients (International Crisis Group 2021, 7). As Roland Marchal concludes, the regime faced a trade-off between efficiency and co-optation in ANT, and chose the latter (2006, 474).

The Déby regime mostly relied on the two elite units, DGSSIE and SATG, after they became more ethnically balanced. During the period when the insurgents existentially threatened the regime, it still favoured elite units, and critical air power capacity was delivered by private companies with no stake in the internal Chadian conflict. Regular forces also received additional funds, but a large part of the extra funding was used for purposes other than increasing the efficiency of ANT.

France and the United States' attempts to professionalize the security forces

The Chadian regime's coup-proofing efforts undermined Western military assistance towards increasing the general efficiency of the Chadian security forces. The regime did not take advantage of Western training of the regular forces, whereas they did when the United States trained praetorian units. In the early 1990s, France undertook an ambitious programme of demobilizing, disarming, and reintegrating the various militiamen and insurgents that had been co-opted into ANT. The idea was to develop ANT into a much smaller, but more professional force. The programme largely failed, as fraudulent practices were abundant, such as demobilizing the same soldiers several times (Debos 2016, 138–139). In a conversation with a US general visiting Chad in 2006, President Déby argued that the army was still an "amalgamation of the opposition groups that came to power in 1990" (United States Embassy N'Djamena 2005). In 2004, the United States had

Chad 55

launched a new programme to professionalize ANT as part of their International Military Education and Training programme. However, unlike the building of SATG, the attempts to professionalize the force from battalion-level to the Ministry of Defence were unsuccessful. Marielle Debos reports that Chadian officials were not even able to produce a chart of the active battalions in ANT, or the names of the commanders (2016, 130). The inability to professionalize the senior level of ANT was at least partly due to political motives. The fact that President Déby replaced the Chief of Staff almost yearly showed that he preferred a disorganized army to a professional and coherent force (Author interview 14 March 2016). Moreover, funding for counter-terrorism exceeded that for general military education and training. From an American perspective, the most important aspect of the Chadian military was the tactical and operational proficiency of its elite units that added to the value of comparable units in the other Sahelian states.

France took a different approach, which hardly constituted an attempt to improve the professionalization of ANT. Besides French units deployed in Chad, French military advisors took an active role during the two attacks on N'djamena in 2006 and 2008. French officers coordinated logistics, intelligence, and possibly drew up a plan of defence for the city, all of which points to the wilful lack of professionalism in the Chadian officer corps (Tubiana 2008, 55). Several high-ranking Chadian officers had attended French military academies, yet they could not, or were not allowed to use their knowledge from France (Hansen 2013, 589). In general, Western pressure for professionalization of the security institutions had a mixed level of success. The tactical proficiency of selected elite units increased, whereas the attempt to strengthen the formal administration of the security forces largely failed (International Crisis Group 2021, 8). In a conversation with French parliamentarians in 2014, President Déby characterized the regular forces of ANT as "warriors, rather than soldiers" ("Compte-rendu d'un déplacement au Tchad" 2014, 8) – i.e., warriors loyal to elites outside the state.

Did the Déby regime employ a strategy of punishment against the insurgents?

The theoretical expectation is that a regime in an informal setting will rely on a punishment strategy of indiscriminate and inefficient violence as a bargaining tool, rather than an elimination strategy. Most confrontations took place in eastern Chad, where the insurgents operated and at times took control of territory. Evidence of indiscriminate violence in eastern Chad is unreliable, as independent media hardly covered the violence in the eastern regions, and the regime and the insurgents obviously had opposite interests in reporting patterns of violence. There are a few identifiable cases of indiscriminate violence, but ANT seems to have applied force in an incoherent way, rather than as part of a strategy. However, one part of ANT, the air

56   *Chad*

force, systematically applied indiscriminate violence in eastern Chad, and even in Darfur, to punish the insurgents, which is why the actions of the Chadian military can be considered a punishment strategy.

In 2006 and onwards, ANT was concentrated in the few large cities in eastern Chad, and could not provide security for the Darfur-refugees in the area (Human Rights Watch 2007, 22–23). The operational choices probably reflected the low level of professionalism in the ordinary ANT units, but also the strategy of exploiting tribal factions. When ANT units were not present, local militias were forced to defend their tribes against the insurgents. One example is the Dadjo militias, who fought local Arab tribes as well as incursions from the Janjaweed militia in Darfur, and gradually received more weapons from ANT. Some Dadjo fighters were subsequently integrated into ANT (Tubiana 2008, 52). Meanwhile, the elite units of DGSSIE and SATG were mainly stationed in N'djamena, although they took part in some of the battles in eastern Chad.

Data from the Armed Conflict Location & Event Data Project have recorded several incidents where Janjaweed, Chadian insurgent groups, as well as ANT, committed violence against civilians. However, from 2005 to 2010, the database only documents 15 incidents of violence by ANT out of 240 entries, with 66 fatalities, which hardly represents a systematic use of indiscriminate force (numbers from Raleigh et al. 2010). In comparison, Janjaweed or tribal militias carried out 105 incidents of violence against civilians. More likely, the factional make-up of ANT made some military units participate in the tribal conflicts in that period. Having been recruited as wholesale units in eastern Chad, ANT units had little motivation for carrying out punitive actions against their kin. General Ganascia, the commander of the EU mission in eastern Chad to protect refugees from Darfur, concluded that the EU forces mainly dealt with "predation, criminality and racketeering" directed against civilians by insurgents, government forces, and criminal groups, not a systematic use of violence to punish the insurgents and the societal groups supporting them (cited in Styan 2012, 662).

Still, the argument that the Chadian regime applied a punishment strategy stands for two reasons. First, the State Department of the United States released a human rights report on Chad that listed several incidents of violence against and torture of civilians suspected of supporting the insurgency, and reported extra-juridical killings of civilians and insurgents, although the report is vague on exact numbers and probably reflects the lack of independent news reports from eastern Chad (United States Department of State 2010). Second, the Chadian air force bombarded insurgent positions in eastern Chad and Darfur, which inflicted damage on the insurgents, but was not supported by land operations to destroy the bases of the insurgents (Dougueli 2009). Overall, the regime raised the cost of continued violence, albeit in a highly inefficient manner.

The Chadian regime acted as the praetorian protection proposition expected of a regime navigating informal politics. The regime mostly reserved

Chad 57

elite forces for coup-protection, which affected the impact of Western training. Moreover, regular forces received relatively fewer resources and their primary purpose was co-optation. As a consequence, the regime relied on a strategy of punishment primarily executed by private military companies. Moreover, the section made empirical observations on how the decision taken by the Zaghawa elites to join the insurgency caused Déby to reorganize the elite forces to ensure their loyalty. The section also identified several instances of elites actively seeking co-optation. Finally, the section argued that the inefficient use of violence in eastern Chad was due to the strong kinship loyalty. The reluctance of the regime to organize and apply forces in a more effective manner caused the regime to rely on alignment-based strategies to overcome the existential threat to the regime.

Risk-averse alignment: winning by alignment

Despite the proficiency of the regime's elite forces, the attack on N'djamena in April 2006 demonstrated the vulnerability of relying on security forces alone. Moreover, the widespread use of co-optation in the security forces begs the question of what alignment strategies underlie co-optation. This section explores the proposition of risk-averse alignment in relation to the actions of the Déby regime, when it utilized the divided and militarized Chadian elites to align and realign with militias and insurgents alike. Moreover, in the end, the regime chose to realign with Sudan to put a stop to the insurgency, since the insurgency was not viable without Sudanese support. The section is structured in two parts that address domestic and external alignment, respectively.

Aligning with militias and insurgents

Exactly what caused the mutinies, the coup, and the insurgency to happen through 2004 and 2005 remains contested. Besides Déby's decision to continue as President after 2006, and the quarrels over the distribution of oil patronage, the Darfur conflict caused clashes among the Chadian Zaghawas (Tubiana 2008, 10). Zaghawa clans in Darfur were organized within the Justice and Equality Movement (JEM) and Sudan Liberation Army (SLA) that fought the Janjaweed militia and the Sudanese regime. After an initial attempt to clamp down on JEM and SLA in 2003 and 2004, Déby changed his mind and began supporting the movements with weapons and logistics from July 2005. Two weeks later the Sudanese regime gave the go-ahead for an uneasy alliance between Tama, Zaghawa, Arab, and Toubou insurgents to launch a campaign against Déby, with Sudanese weapons and staging areas (Marchal 2007, 20).

In response, President Déby initially consolidated his alignment with Chadian Arabs in addition to the regime's alignment with JEM. Given JEM's fighting against Arab tribes in Darfur, the dual alignment appears

58   *Chad*

odd, but shows the flexibility of the regime. The alignment with JEM came off in spite of their mistrust of Déby, who in 2004 positioned himself as a neutral mediator between JEM and the Sudanese regime, even though Déby had tried to arrest JEM's leader Khalil Ibrahim in Chad, and possibly attacked JEM inside Sudan in 2003 (Berg 2008, 77–78). Whereas SLA chose to be co-opted by the Sudanese regime, JEM was in dire need of weapons and safe havens inside Chad, and became more trustful of Déby when the split between Chad and Sudan became obvious. For the Chadian regime, the benefits of the alignment lay in the presence of JEM in both Darfur and eastern Chad. The group provided the regime with an instant ability to harass the rear bases of the insurgents as well as provide more manpower in eastern Chad. Supporting JEM might have been an attempt to shore up the Zaghawa factions of the ruling coalition, though not a very successful one. The immediate cost was acceptable, because oil money could fund arms and training bases. Moreover, the political cost vis-à-vis Sudan was most likely inevitable, because President Déby was still unable to stop the transfer of weapons from disaffected Zaghawa officers to JEM.

The populous Arab tribes played a central role in the insurgency wars of the 1970s and early 1980s, and Arab militias enjoyed supreme positions in the Wadai region under the leadership of Ahmat Acyl (Burr and Collins 2008, 159). In the years leading up to the insurgency Chadian Arabs had been mobilized by the Sudanese regime to fight a counterinsurgency war by proxy in Darfur. Considering the Sudanese regime's general support for the Chadian insurgency and the incursions of Janjaweed militias into Chad, the Chadian regime must have feared an Arab uprising. President Déby managed to keep several Arab tribes at bay because he quickly reaffirmed a political alliance with the leaders in the Wadai region. In September 2005, Déby married his fourth wife Hinda Acyl, a relative of Ahmat Acyl. The Acyl family was still powerful among the Arabs, and an alliance with them secured the support of large parts of the Arab elites in the Wadai region (Tubiana and Debos 2017, 136, Marchal 2013, 218). The domestic alignment with a number of Arab tribes was confirmed in May 2006, when President Déby appointed an Arab general to succeed his son as the commander of ANT forces in eastern Chad (Ayangafac 2009, 6).

In fairness, the alignment did not entirely keep Arab factions out of the insurgency. The Arab movement *Conseil Démocratique Révolutionnaire* (CDR) was part of the different insurgency alliances from 2005 to 2010. In 2009, Albadour Acyl Ahmat Aghbach, Hinda Acyl's cousin, became the leader of CDR (Hansen 2011, 3). CDR, however, only constituted a rather small portion of both the insurgency alliances compared to the large Arab population in Chad, and the Arabs were in general more passive in the insurgency than might have been expected (International Crisis Group 2019, 4–5).

The co-optation of the Acyl family was an immediate cost of the alignment. According to a critic of the regime, Hinda Acyl's father was appointed ambassador, and two of her brothers were given lucrative positions in state-owned

Chad 59

companies (Sandouk 2010). However, the cost of co-opting other Chadian Arabs fell due to the increased mistrust between Khartoum and the Chadian Arabs. Sudanese mistrust of Chadian Arab groups was aggravated after 2006, when Darfurian Arabs began to turn against Sudan, encouraged by Chadian Arabs allied with Déby (Tubiana 2011, 13). Just as other tribes were utilized to balance the Bideyats in the praetorian units, so were Arab elites utilized to serve as a balancing faction within the ruling coalition.

After the attack on N'djamena in April 2006, the quick-strike war changed into a war of skirmishes in eastern Chad. The result was a series of attacks on the largest towns and garrisons. On November 25, the capital in Biltine was briefly occupied by the Zaghawa insurgent group led by Timani Erdemi, the nephew of the President, and insurgents loyal to Mahamat Nuri occupied Abéché, the capital of the Wadai region. They withdrew shortly afterwards, but the incidents bear witness to the relative strength of the insurgent alliance. The French did not officially participate in the fighting, but used reconnaissance aircraft to survey the Sudanese involvement. To turn the tide, Déby needed more than limited French assistance, support of JEM, and the relative passivity of the Chadian Arabs. The uneasiness of the insurgency alliance provided the regime with an opportunity to use patronage to weaken the alliance.

In a matter of ten months, President Déby managed to cause a split among the insurgents. In December 2006, Déby struck a deal with Mahamat Nour from the Tama tribe, who had lost the leadership of the insurgency alliance after the failed attack on N'djamena. In return for Nour leaving the insurgency, the Déby regime integrated Nour's *Rassemblement pour la Démocratie et la Liberté* into the security forces and appointed Nour Minister of Defence in March 2007. Insurgent manpower immediately dropped around 40 percent, and turned the Tama militants against the Toubous and Zaghawas in Biltine and Wadai as well as the northern Province of Tibesti (van Dijk 2007, 702). However, the inclusion of Tamas in ANT was a dangerous and unstable strategy. Zaghawa fractions of ANT turned to violence against Tama militias, because of the general hostilities between Tamas and Zaghawas (Reader 2007). The cost of co-opting Tamas was thus a further erosion of the Zaghawa factions in the ruling coalition, especially among the Bidiyat clan. Furthermore, the lack of common interests between Déby and Nour made the strategy risky. Nour was known for his anti-Zaghawa sentiments and strong connections to Sudan. Indeed, the co-optation strategy was probably so costly and risky that the addition of unreliable Tama militias could not make up for the loss of Bideyat factions.

Within a few months the first co-optation strategy was superseded by a second, which targeted the Zaghawa- and Arab-dominated insurgent groups. A peace agreement was signed in Sirte, Libya, 25 October 2007. No peace ensued, and the agreement was rather an arrangement made for the leader of an Arab insurgency faction, Hassan Al Djineidi, to switch from the insurgents' ranks to becoming Minister of Defence. As a result Nour was

60　*Chad*

sacked 30 November. Djineidi's men were incorporated into the army in the aftermath of the agreement (Debos 2013, 139). Also, Yaya Dillo Djerou, a Beri Zaghawa, was co-opted by the regime and joined the government on 10 November 2007. As discussed earlier, the regime did probably not expect the insurgents actually to be active within the army, so the benefit was primarily a weakening of the insurgency.

The co-optation of parts of the insurgency alliance had the benefit of increasing distrust and fragmentation among the insurgents. The cost of the concessions for the insurgent groups was modest and reversible. Mahamet Nour quickly lost his position, Djineidi was rotated to Chief of Staff in the army – a position he held less than a year – and Djerou only took up junior positions within the government until 2016. In comparison, co-optation of insurgency groups caused distrust and fragmentation within the insurgency alliance. According to the International Crisis Group, each rebel group accused members of other groups of receiving money from the regime as an inducement to abandon the armed struggle (2008, 13). In February 2008, distrust was also a decisive factor in staving off the attack on N'djamena. Insurgency columns stopped when they reached the outskirts of the city, because of a disagreement about the political arrangement after the expected removal of President Déby (International Crisis Group 2009b, 16–17)

However, domestic alignment proved to be a limited strategy, because the insurgent threat of launching a quick attack against N'djamena persisted. The fluid loyalty of all groups as well as the constant influx of weapons from Sudan meant that the remaining insurgency leaders could continue to pose a considerable threat to the regime. In this situation, President Déby proved willing to put regime survival above client relations or fear of external influence in Chad. Chad realigned with Sudan.

Rapprochement with Sudan to end the insurgency

France supported President Déby before, during, and after the crisis in 2005–2010. However, French support was discreet and had not prevented a coup and two attacks on N'djamena from almost toppling the regime. Since 1986, the French operation *Épervier* stationed aircraft and army units in Chad to protect Chadian sovereignty. However, the current insurgency war spanned the categories of domestic affairs and external intrusion on Chadian sovereignty. Given the lack of political differences between the insurgents and the regime, President Déby is likely to have concluded that France could not guarantee the survival of his regime and would cooperate with a potential new regime. Deby explicitly requested 'a sign of U.S. support for the regime' (United States Embassy N'Djamena 2008). US support had become vital because France had responded ambiguously to the attack: they waited for two days to see who might be the victor, having on the first day offered to help Déby leave the country (United States Department of State 2008). On the other hand, support from Sudan was the necessary

Chad 61

condition for the insurgency in Chad from 2005 to 2010. A rapprochement with Sudan was, therefore, the strategy with the least risk to the survival of the Déby regime. However, it only became feasible when the balance of power between the two states changed, and the strategy was still a risky step that again demonstrated that Déby was willing to go against any religious or tribal loyalty to secure his own survival in a period of crisis.

Numerous diplomatic openings preceded the rapprochement in 2009 and 2010, but were always followed by a breach of the agreements. As early as August 2006 diplomatic relations were reestablished following the first attack on N'Djamena, though they did not put an end to the external supply of weapons. The two last major peace agreements in February 2008 and May 2009 seem to have served the tactical purpose of luring the Chadian regime into lowering its guard, as the agreements were both followed by major *razzia*-like attacks by the insurgents from their bases inside Sudan.

Changes in the power asymmetry between Sudan and Chad might have affected the seriousness of the negotiations. In Darfur, the activity of the Janjaweed had declined. JEM had received equipment from the Chadian regime, which allowed the insurgents to launch a raid on Khartoum in May 2008 (Bono 2012, 192). Even though the attack was primarily a symbolic gesture, it demonstrated that Chad took a more assertive role following the 2008 attack on N'Djamena. In addition to the defeat of an insurgency column in the town of Am-Dam on May 2009, which marked the last major insurgent incursion, Chadian aircraft bombed insurgent bases inside Darfur in the same month (Dougueli 2009). In addition, the Sudanese regime faced diplomatic pressure after the International Criminal Court indicted Omar al-Bashir for war crimes at the same time as violence in Darfur actually dropped. Finally, the regime was negotiating the terms for South Sudanese independence. On 5 February 2010, a far-reaching agreement was made that included shared border control, the expelling of key insurgent leaders on both sides of the border, and an end to the supply of weapons and logistics to insurgents.

From the perspective of the Déby regime, the agreement with Sudan was an external balancing of the insurgents, but one that took away their supplies, military equipment, and rear bases. Without Sudanese support, the insurgents would have had to launch an entirely different kind of insurgency, a war amongst the people, for which they were not prepared. As Jeremy Weinstein argues, an insurgency with an early abundance of resources risks losing coherence if resources are taken away, because the necessary discipline has not been built at the earlier stages, and the rank-and-file insurgents do not expect the leadership to remain loyal (Weinstein 2006, 260ff). Rank-and-file insurgents certainly lacked the kind of ideological indoctrination that could have held the insurgency together, albeit small groups of survivors carried on in Darfur and later Libya, and in April 2021 a splinter group launched the attack that killed President Déby. The cost of the rapprochement was to let go of the alignment with JEM. With the abandonment, Déby had come full circle since the outbreak of the main

62   *Chad*

hostilities in 2005. Especially JEM had proven loyal to the regime, but was forced to sign a peace agreement with the Sudanese regime on 24 February 2010 (AFP 2010). Khalil Ibrahim's death in December 2011 removed one of the last points of tension between Chad and Sudan.

In the examined period, the Déby regime favoured alignment with domestic elites rather than reconciliation with Sudan from a position of weakness or a request for more direct French support. To secure domestic alignment the regime showed an absolute willingness to co-opt former rivals and enemies. In the span of five years Déby had aligned with the Islamist Zaghawa-dominated JEM-group, aligned with and fought against Zaghawas from the Bideyat clan, the Tamas, the Toubous, and various Arab tribes. The abandonment of JEM in 2010 was the final demonstration of the regime's lack of any tribal, religious, or ideological considerations. In the end, the regime turned to Sudan, the least risky alignment at the time. Several empirical observations showed how the acceptance of co-optation among the domestic elites made the negotiations of realignments a fairly easy business for the regime. The willingness of domestic – as well as Sudanese – elites to be co-opted was again demonstrated in 2012. President Déby, the self-declared bulwark against Arabism, married Amani Moussa Hilal, the daughter of Musa Hilal, the infamous Arab supremacist and Janjaweed leader. Only the interest of ensuring the regime's survival seems to explain the absence of loyalty towards any group inside or outside Chad.

Avoiding reforms by offering regime stability

Support of the Chadian regime caused controversy among Western powers and international donors, and most aid was either conditional or aimed at addressing what donors considered problematic areas, such as democracy or justice. Based on the informal character of Chadian politics, the theoretical expectation would be that the Chadian regime would secretly undermine reforms while publicly supporting them. The following examination shows that the Déby regime informally undermined three demands for reforms, but openly resisted one reform. The explanation of the public defiance seems to be that France and the United States prioritized regime survival above political and administrative reforms, and the two states put pressure on the international organizations to accept non-compliance. The structure of this section is based on the four demands on the regime. The first interaction relates to the regime's distribution of oil income, while the other three revolve around the demands for good governance and democratization made by France and the EU.

Breaking the deal with the World Bank

Before the crisis unfolded in Chad in 2005, the country was supposed to be a showcase of how external demands made by the World Bank could

Chad 63

discourage a mismanagement of the new oil income. The World Bank and the International Monetary Fund (IMF) imposed conditions on granting loans for building a $4.2 billion pipeline to transport oil from Chad to a harbour in Cameroon. Eighty percent of the oil royalties were supposed to be spent on poverty reduction, whereas 10 percent of the oil revenue for the Chadian state had to be invested in a future generation fund (Reyna 2007, 81). In October 2005, the regime publicly demanded that the so-called future generation fund was to be used for weapon acquisition. The alteration would also give the regime a much freer hand to distribute oil income. In the winter of 2005 Paul Wolfowitz, then President of the World Bank, negotiated with the Déby regime in vain.

President Déby proceeded to undermine the conditions of the use of oil income in public and in private. In January 2006 the Chadian parliament passed a bill to change the legislative framework of the distribution of oil. After the bill was passed, Wolfowitz took a hard stance and suspended all World Bank and IMF programmes, and froze most of the Chadian oil royalties (Pegg 2009 313). In May 2006, shortly before the first attack on N'djamena, Déby declared that "The self-righteous might be outraged. [But] I cannot save the money for future generations, risking to hand over a country dismembered and occupied by rebel factions. I bought weapons and I shall continue to buy them with oil money" (author's translation from Seck 2009). More so, in the wake of the attack on N'djamena Déby escalated the conflict by declaring that he would expel 200,000 Darfur refugees if the World Bank did not release the royalties and the international community did not assist in the counterinsurgency efforts. The threat was never realized, neither was the World Bank able to alter the use of oil royalties.

From 2007, Déby resorted to more private and discrete ways to hide the use of oil income as informal accommodation of factions and clients. As described earlier, infrastructure projects served as vehicles for turning oil income into off-budget funds to reward factions and clients. An independent control organ was supposed to monitor the distribution of oil income, but gradually Déby replaced the members of the committee and cut the funding for their work (Pegg 2009, 315-216). Nonetheless, Déby's choice to fight the agreement openly goes against the expectation of simulated statebuilding, which states that the regime would publicly accept international demands. Gould and Winther explain the outcome as a result of the unfavourable negotiation position of the World Bank, who had already made the investment in Chad and had consequently run out of bargaining chips (2011, 333–334). The World Bank initially agreed to a new deal with vague terms, as it was increasingly aware of the regime's embezzlement and manipulation of the control mechanisms. The World Bank chose to leave the oil project entirely in 2008.

Another explanation of Déby's choice of public confrontation is the split between the World Bank on the one hand, and France and the United States on the other. The primary interest of both states was stability. The primary

64   *Chad*

focus of the French policy was stability, which meant preventing the spread of violence from the conflict in Darfur. Regime stability would allow France to preserve Chad as a base for French troops to monitor a region considered to be of national interest. Consequently, France put considerable pressure on the World Bank to accommodate the Chadian regime (Pegg 2009, 314). The United States also pressured Paul Wolfowitz to accommodate Chadian demands (Massey and May 2006, 446). As the Iraqi insurgency culminated in 2005–2006 and soaked up many of the military resources, the United States could not allow the situation in Sudan and Chad to deteriorate any further. American oil companies also had considerable economic interests in Chad, which overlapped with the United States' ambition to become independent of Middle East oil.

The move away from controlled to uncontrolled use of oil money followed a pattern of both formal and informal undermining of the World Bank's reform attempt. The regime's public use of diplomatic brinkmanship to change the deal deviated from the expected simulated statebuilding, but was supported by the two most important Western powers.

Simulating democratic and administrative reforms

In 2006, France proposed a military mission to protect Chad from the instability produced in Darfur. This proposal came after the first attack on N'djamena in April 2006. However, unlike in previous unilateral French military actions the French government promoted the agenda within the Security Council and the EU (Bono 2012, 188). The Chadian regime was reluctant to accept an international mission with a political mandate, which forced the French government to accept a weak UN resolution 1778 that only mandated a humanitarian mission to protect the refugees from Darfur and internally displaced Chadians. The EU mission in eastern Chad and the Central African Republic – EUFOR Chad/CAR – delivered the initial military contribution. France's unwillingness to pressure Déby led the United Kingdom and Germany to refuse to contribute to the EU mission (Dijkstra 2010, 398). However, the EU initiated parallel programmes to address what they perceived to be the root causes of the conflict, namely a programme for good governance focusing on justice and security sector reforms, and a programme for political negotiations.

From 2006, the EU increasingly supported state institutions related to security and justice over traditional development issues, such as poverty reduction or health care (Orbie and Del Biondo 2015, 253). The EU increased funding to support anti-corruption and to improve impartiality and professional standards. One example is a €25 million programme to improve the workings of the juridical sector in eastern Chad. However, in an internal evaluation of the governance programmes in Chad in 2009, the European Commission found that they had little effect and that no conditions had been made to punish the lack of results (European Commission 2009, 75ff).

One reason for the ineffectiveness of the EU's approach might be that the development programmes and the military mission were uncoordinated (Orbie and Del Biondo 2015). However, in the light of the disinterest of France and the importance of informal politics in Chad, even a well-coordinated initiative would most likely have failed anyway.

Politically, the EU was even more ambitious. From the outset, the EU wanted to initiate political negotiations among the armed parties and the civilian opposition. However, through backdoor discussions between the Déby regime, France, and the EU, the negotiations ultimately included the civilian opposition only, not the leaders of the insurgency groups (Tubiana 2008, 59). Compared to the regime's MPS party, the over 200 oppositional parties were small and only 14 of them were represented in the parliament between 2002 and 2009. The opposition tried to overcome internal disagreement by forming the *Coordination des Partis Politiques pour la Défense de la Constitution* (CPDC). CPDC appointed the widely respected Ibni Oumar Mahamat Saleh as spokesman (ibid 2008, 58). Dealing with the regime limited the opposition's legitimacy after Déby had forced through the constitutional change and the opposition had boycotted the presidential election in May 2006 (Leymarie 2006, 6–7). The regime and CPDC reached an agreement – the political platform of 13 August 2007. The agreement included technical and procedural reforms, such as the establishment of an electoral board and biometric control of voters, but no changes in the political institutional setup were agreed upon, other than a vague mentioning of the intention to depoliticize the state institutions (Article 4.1, "Accord politique en vue du renforcement du processus democratique au Tchad" 2007).

Déby achieved two political gains from the deal. Seemingly, the expectations of the civilian opposition were mainly to take up positions within the government in order to benefit from state resources and strengthen their own clientelistic networks, even at the cost of losing legitimacy in the eyes of the population (International Crisis Group 2008, 8). By pretending to carry out political reforms, the regime managed to provide an international alibi for continuing its struggle for regime survival. Given France's intimate knowledge of Déby's regime and its interest in stability, French diplomats were likely to have taken a cynical stance on the prospects of free and fair elections in 2009 (which were eventually postponed to 2011). However, even in confidential conversations, French officials touted the potential of the 13 August agreement as a possibility to create lasting democratic reforms (United States Embassy Paris 2008). Whether the French officials genuinely believed in the political platform, it legitimized French support for the regime, as well as the EUFOR Chad mission.

The implementation of the agreement was slow, and Déby effectively undermined it in February 2008. Three key oppositional leaders were abducted in the midst of the fighting in the streets of N'djamena. The most notable of them was the above mentioned Ibni Saleh. He was the most popular person among the oppositional politicians, and had the ability to

66   *Chad*

unite factions across the traditional cleavages in Chadian society (Marchal 2013, 216). It seems highly unlikely that DGSSIE would make a coordinated arrest of three oppositional leaders, and that the most prominent of them would die in custody without Deby's knowledge. Still, the EU and France settled for an "independent investigation" of the murder, which did not produce any answers (Human Rights Watch 2011, 2, Rolley 2010).

In the aftermath of the rapprochement with Sudan in 2010, the EU continued to pressure the Chadian regime to keep the political agreement from 2007 on track. In particular, the EU pushed for elections to be held in 2011, and was successful in the sense that both a parliamentary and a presidential election were held that year (Orbie and Del Biondo 2015, 253). However, the presidential election was marred by problems, as the three major rival candidates boycotted it in protest against the delay in the issuing of poll cards. Furthermore, MPS was the only party with the necessary economy and structure to compete in every region in Chad (Dickow 2012). Unsurprisingly, President Déby was reelected and his party, MPS, maintained its majority in the parliament. The regime began to take a more reserved approach to international presence in the country. The MINURCAT operation was forced to close down before time, and President Déby even challenged France in August 2010, when he questioned the importance of the Épervier operation and demanded French payment for future basing rights (Thedrel 2010).

Practices associated with simulated statebuilding dominated most of the relations between the Chadian regime and the Western powers. The regime undermined the EU's inducement-based demands for democratization, good governance, and the resumption of elections in 2011, which had no consequences. One exception was the public confrontation with the World Bank on the distribution of oil income, which was surprising considering the regime's ability to undermine the agreement informally. Still, the Worlds Bank's withdrawal had few consequences for the regime, which was backed by France and the United States. The use of simulated statebuilding is in accordance with the theoretical expectations. However, the very limited reaction of the external actors, besides the World Bank, might indicate that concern for regime survival deterred Western powers from using conditionality.

Conclusion

The informal character of Chadian politics influenced the Déby regime's survival strategies that closely resembled the theoretical expectations of praetorian protection, risk-averse alignment, and simulated statebuilding. Not only did Déby make use of the informal strategies, but the deep pragmatism and flexibility of the regime were mirrored in the choices made by the militant elites inside and outside the ruling coalition. For example the hostile militant elites' acceptance of co-optation demonstrated their absorbance in informal politics. Oil was an important factor in the outbreak of the

Chad 67

conflict, and oil income allowed the regime to spend on both co-optation and security forces. However, the mechanisms of informal politics and regime survival did go beyond oil, which mostly inflated expectations and prices of co-optation.

What stands out from the case study is the distance between the EU's and the World Bank's demands for formal reforms and the logic of informal politics in a time of existential threat and upheaval. The notion that the regime would accept a truly pluralistic political reform or strong and independent state institutions is far from the conception of politics among the regime and most elites inside and outside the ruling coalition. Moreover, the state- and peacebuilding initiatives of the international organizations were disconnected from the military intervention of France and the United States, who sought short term regime stability above long-ranging reforms. The next case, the intervention in Mali, exemplifies a concerted effort of peace- and statebuilding that aimed to coordinate civilian and military instruments to address the conflict comprehensively. The next chapter, therefore, offers an opportunity to study the importance of a comprehensive Western intervention practice in an informal setting.

Note

1 Brahim Déby was killed in Paris in 2007. A former Foreign Legionnaire was convicted, but the political motives were not proven. Afterwards, Idriss Déby's son Mahammat Déby prepared to take over by controlling, for example, the presidential guard. Mahammat Déby took power in April 2021 following his father's death.

References

Abdelkader, Kamougué Waldal. 2008. "J'ai La Caution Du Chef de l'Etat Pour Réorganiser L'armée Nationale." *Tchad et Culture* 67, 2008.

2007 *"Accord Politique En Vue Du Renforcement Du Processus Democratique Au Tchad."* 2007. http://aceproject.org/ero-en/regions/africa/TD/tchad-accord-politique-en-vue-du-renforcement-du/view (Accessed 9 March 2019).

AFP. 2010. "Khartoum Signe Une Trève Avec Les Rebelles Du JEM." *Jeune Afrique*, 24 February 2010. https://www.jeuneafrique.com/156338/politique/darfour-khartoum-signe-une-tr-ve-avec-les-rebelles-du-jem/

Aherne, Gerald, Walter Feichtinger, Norbert Feldhofer, Gerald Hainzl, Ute Kollies, David Lanz, Roland Marchal, et al. 2011. "EUFOR Tchad-RCA Revisited." *Schriftenreihe Der Landesverteidigungsakademie*, 190. https://www.bundesheer.at/wissen-forschung/publikationen/publikation.php?id=562

Allison, Olivia (2015). 'Informal but Diverse: The Market for Exported Force from Russia and Ukraine'. In *The Markets For Force: Privatization of Security Across World Regions*, edited by M. Dunigan, and U. Petersohn. Philadelphia: University of Pennsylvania Press.

Author interview. 2016a. "Author Interview with Special Forces Officer, 3rd Group", Monterey, 14 March 2016.

68   *Chad*

Ayangafac, Chrysantus. 2009. *"Resolving the Chadian Political Epilepsy: An Assessment of Intervention Efforts."* Pretoria: Institute for Security Studies. https://www.africaportal.org/publications/resolving-the-chadian-political-epilepsy-an-assessment-of-intervention-efforts/ (Accessed 18 November 2018)

Berg, Patrick. 2008. "A Crisis-Complex, Not Complex Crises: Conflict Dynamics in the Sudan, Chad, and Central African Republic Tri-Border Area." *Internationale Politik und Gesellschaft, no. 4.* Bonn: Friedrich Ebert Stiftung. https://library.fes.de/pdf-files/ipg/ipg-2008-4/08_a_berg_gb.pdf (Accessed 20 February 2020).

Bertelsmann Stiftung. 2014. *"Chad Country Report 2014."* Berlin: Bertelsmann Stiftung. https://bti-project.org/content/en/downloads/reports/country_report_2014_TCD.pdf (Accessed 18 February 2020).

Boggero, Marco. 2009. "Darfur and Chad: A Fragmented Ethnic Mosaic." *Journal of Contemporary African Studies* 27 (1): 21–35. 10.1080/02589000802576673

Bono, Giovanna. 2012. "The Impact of the Discourse of the 'Politics of Protection': The Case of the EU and UN Policing and Military Missions to Chad (2007–2010)." *African Security* 5 (3–4): 179–198. 10.1080/19392206.2012.732889

Burr, J. Millard, and Robert O. Collins. 2008. *The Long Road to Disaster.* Princeton: Markus Wiener Publishers.

Commission de la défense nationale et des forces armées. 2014. *"Compte-rendu d'un déplacement au Tchad".* Hearing, 10 February. Paris: Assemblée Nationale.

Debos, Marielle. 2013. "La Guerre Des Préfets." *Politix* 104 (4): 47-65. 10.3917/pox.104.0047

Debos, Marielle. 2014. "International Interventions and the Human Cost of a Militarized Political Marketplace in Chad." *Reinventing Peace.* 2014. http://sites.tufts.edu/reinventingpeace/2014/07/17/international-interventions-and-the-human-cost-of-a-militarized-political-marketplace-in-chad/

Debos, Marielle. 2016. "Living by the Gun in Chad: Combatants," In *Impunity and State Formation.* London: Zed Books. 10.5040/9781350221147

Dickow, Helga. 2012. *"Die Hoffnung Auf Den Arabischen Frühling Versandete in Der Sahara."* Forum Weltkirche. http://www.forum-weltkirche.de/de/artikel/13248.die-hoffnung-auf-den-arabischen-fruehling-versandete-in-der-sahara.html (Accessed 10 May 2020).

Dijk, Han van. 2007. "Political Deadlock in Chad." *African Affairs* 106 (425): 697–703. 10.1093/afraf/adm067

Dijkstra, Hylke. 2010. "The Military Operation of the EU in Chad and the Central African Republic: Good Policy, Bad Politics." *International Peacekeeping* 17 (3): 395–407. 10.1080/13533312.2010.500150

Dougueli, Georges. 2009. "La Rébellion Tchadienne Est-Elle En Perdition?" *Jeune Afrique*, 2009 (only available at https://www.makaila.fr/article-32044654.html).

European Commission. 2009. *"Evaluation de La Coopération de La Commission de l'Union Européenne Avec La République Du République Du Tchad."* Brussels: European Commission. https://www.oecd.org/countries/chad/42837929.pdf

Flint, Julie, and Alexander De Waal. 2008. *Darfur: A New History of a Long War.* London: Zed Books. 10.5040/9781350219489

Fontanellaz, Adrien and Tom Cooper. 2016. *"Two Men Built an Air Force From Scratch in Chad."* 2016. https://medium.com/war-is-boring/two-men-built-an-air-force-from-scratch-in-chad-afb3eac4d78 (Accessed 23 September 2020).

Chad 69

Frank, Claudia and Lena Guesnet. 2009. *"'We Were Promised Development and All We Got Is Misery'— The Influence of Petroleum on Conflict Dynamics in Chad."* 41. Bonn: Internationales Konversionszentrum Bonn. https://www.files.ethz.ch/isn/112372/brief41.pdf

Gould, John A., and Matthew S. Winters. 2011. "Petroleum Blues: The Political Economy of Resources and Conflict in Chad." In *High-Value Natural Resources and Peacebuilding*, edited by Päivi Lujala and Siri Aas Rustad, 313–336. New York: Routledge.

Hansen, Ketil Fred. 2011. *"Military Rebels in Chad – Changes since 2008."* Oslo: Norwegian Peacebuilding Ressource Centre. https://www.files.ethz.ch/isn/137779/Military%20rebels%20in%20Chad.pdf

Hansen, Ketil Fred. 2013. "A Democratic Dictator's Success: How Chad's President Deby Defeated the Military Opposition in Three Years (2008–2011)." *Journal of Contemporary African Studies* 31 (4): 583–599. 10.1080/02589001.2013.840974

Human Rights Watch. 2007. *"'They Came Here to Kill Us.'"* 19, 1(A). New York: Human Rights Watch. https://www.hrw.org/reports/2007/chad0107/

Human Rights Watch. 2011. *"World Report Chapter: Chad."* New York: Human Rights Watch. https://www.hrw.org/world-report/2011/country-chapters/chad

International Crisis Group. 2008. *"Chad: A New Conflict Resolution Framework."* Brussels: International Crisis Group. https://www.crisisgroup.org/africa/central-africa/chad/chad-new-conflict-resolution-framework

International Crisis Group. 2009a. *"Chad: Escaping from the Oil Trap."* Brussels: International Crisis Group. https://www.crisisgroup.org/africa/central-africa/chad/chad-escaping-oil-trap (Accessed 1 September 2020)

International Crisis Group. 2009b. *"Chad: Powder Keg in the East."* Brussels: International Crisis Group. https://www.crisisgroup.org/africa/central-africa/chad/chad-powder-keg-east (Accessed 28 August 2020)

International Crisis Group. 2016. *"Tchad: Entre Ambitions et Fragilités."* Brussels: International Crisis Group. https://www.crisisgroup.org/fr/africa/central-africa/chad/chad-between-ambition-and-fragility (Accessed 4 February 2019)

International Crisis Group. 2019. *"Avoiding the Resurgence of Intercommunal Violence in Eastern Chad"*. Brussels: International Crisis Group. https://www.crisisgroup.org/africa/central-africa/chad/284-eviter-la-reprise-des-violences-communautaires-lest-du-tchad (Accessed 4 April 2020)

International Crisis Group. 2021. *"Les défis de l'armée tchadienne"*. Brussels: International Crisis Group. https://www.crisisgroup.org/fr/africa/central-africa/chad/298-les-defis-de-larmee-tchadienne (Accessed 25 May 2021)

International Monetary Fund. 2009. *"Chad: Selected Issues."* Washington D.C.: International Monetary Fund. https://ideas.repec.org/p/imf/imfscr/2009-067.html (Accessed 23 November 2020)

Iocchi, Alessio. 2019. "Informality, Regulation and Predation: Governing Déby's Chad." *Politique africaine* 154 (2): 179–197. 10.3917/polaf.154.0179

Leymarie, Philippe. 2006. "Ingérence À L'ancienne Au Tchad." *Le Monde Diplomatique*, June 2006. https://www.monde-diplomatique.fr/2006/06/LEYMARIE/13568

Lewis, J A C, and Lauren Gelfand. 2009. *"Chadian Army Crushes Rebel Advance."* 12 May. London: Jane's Defence Weekly.

Maio, Jennifer L. De. 2010. "Is War Contagious? The Transnationalization of Conflict in Darfur." *African Studies Quarterly* 11 (4): 25–44. https://sites.clas.ufl.edu/africanquarterly/files/Maio-Vol11Is4.pdf

70   Chad

Marchal, Roland. 2006. "Chad / Darfur: Two Crises Merge." *Review of African Political Economy* 33 (109): 467–482. 10.1080/03056240601000879

Marchal, Roland. 2007. "Creeping Conflict." *The World Today* 63 (4): 20–21. https://www.chathamhouse.org/publications/the-world-today/2007-04/chad-sudan-and-darfur-creeping-conflict

Marchal, Roland. 2013. "Le Tchad Entre Deux Guerres? Remarques Sur Un Présumé Complot." *Politique Africaine* 130: 213–223. 10.3917/polaf.130.0213

Massey, Simon, and Roy May. 2006. "Commentary: The Crisis in Chad." *African Affairs* 105 (420): 443–449. 10.1093/afraf/adl007

Meerpohl, Meike. 2013. *"Libya, Chad and Sudan – An Ambiguous Triangle?"* 5. Bochum: Zentrum für Mittelmeerstudien. https://omp.ub.rub.de/index.php/ZMS/catalog/book/52

Nako, Madjiasra. 2012. "Tchad: Le Phénix Du Coton." *Jeune Afrique*, 28 March 2012. https://www.jeuneafrique.com/206895/economie/tchad-le-ph-nix-du-coton/ (Accessed 10 December 2019)

Nolutshungu, Sam C. 1996. *Limits of Anarchy: Intervention and State Formation in Chad*. Charlottesville: University of Virginia Press.

Orbie, Jan, and Karen Del Biondo. 2015. "The European Union's 'Comprehensive Approach' in Chad: Securitisation And/or Compartmentalisation?" *Global Society* 29 (2): 243–259. 10.1080/13600826.2015.1024620

Pegg, Scott. 2009. "Briefing: Chronicle of a Death Foretold: The Collapse of the Chad-Cameroon Pipeline Project." *African Affairs* 108 (431): 311–320. 10.1093/afraf/adp003

Prunier, Gérard. 2008. *"Armed Movements in Sudan, Chad, CAR, Somalia, Eritrea and Ethiopia."* Berlin: Zentrum für Internationale Friedenseinsätze. https://gsdrc.org/document-library/armed-movements-in-sudan-chad-central-african-republic-somalia-eritrea-and-ethiopia/

Raleigh, Clionadh, Andrew Linke, Havard Hegre, and Joakim Karlsen. 2010. "Introducing ACLED-Armed Conflict Location and Event Data." *Journal of Peace Research* 47 (5): 1–10. 10.1177/0022343310378914

Reader, Nicholas. 2007. "Good Year for President Deby, Bad Year for Chad." *IRIN Africa*, 28 May 2007. (only available at https://www.thenewhumanitarian.org/feature/2007/05/28/good-year-president-deby-bad-year-chad)

Reyna, Stephen P. 2007. "The Traveling Model That Would Not Travel: Oil, Empire, and Patrimonialism in Contemporary Chad." *Social Analysis* 51 (3): 78–102. 10.3167/sa.2007.510304

Rolley, Sonia. 2010. *Retour Du Tchad: Carnet D'une Correspondance*. Paris: Livres.

Sandouk, Alhadj Botouni ma. 2010. *"Un Succès Story À La Tchadienne: The Hinda Family's."* 2010. http://makaila.over-blog.com/article-un-succes-story-a-la-tchadienne-the-hinda-family-s-45922398.html

Schulhofer-Wohl, Jonah. 2020. *Quagmire in Civil Wars*. Cambridge: Cambridge University Press. 10.1017/9781108762465

Seck, Cheikh Yerim. 2009. "Où va L'argent Du Pétrole?" *Jeune Afrique*, 1 June 2009. https://www.jeuneafrique.com/203159/politique/o-va-l-argent-du-p-trole/ (Accessed 18 November 2019)

Styan, David. 2012. "EU Power and Armed Humanitarianism in Africa: Evaluating ESDP in Chad." *Cambridge Review of International Affairs* 25 (4): 651–668. 10.1080/09557571.2012.678293

Chad 71

Thedrel, Arielle. 2010. "Le Tchad Remet En Cause La Présence Militaire Française." *Le Figaro*, 11 August 2010. https://www.lefigaro.fr/international/2010/08/11/01003–201 00811ARTFIG00509-le-tchad-remet-en-cause-la-presence-militaire-francaise.php (Accessed 19 March 2020).

Toïngar, Ésaïe. 2014. *Idriss Deby and the Darfur Conflict*. Jefferson: McFarland & Company Inc, Publishers.

Tubiana, Jérôme. 2008. "The Chad-Sudan Proxy War and The 'darfurization' of Chad: Myths and Reality." 12. *Human Security Baseline Assessment*. Geneva: Small Arms Survey. http://www.smallarmssurveysudan.org/fileadmin/docs/working-papers/HSBA-WP-12-Chad-Sudan-Proxy-War.pdf

Tubiana, Jérôme. 2011. "Renouncing the Rebels: Local and Regional Dimensions of Chad – Sudan Rapprochement." 25. *Human Security Baseline Assessment*. Geneva: Small Arms Survey. http://www.smallarmssurvey.org/about-us/highlights/highlights-hsba-wp-25-renouncing-the-rebels.html

Tubiana, Jérôme and Debos, Marielle. 2017. *Déby's Chad: Political Manipulation at Home, Military Intervention Abroad, Challenging Times Ahead*. United States Institute of Peace. https://www.usip.org/sites/default/files/2017-12/pw136-debys-chad-political-manipulation-at-home-military-intervention-abroad-challenging-times-ahead-v2.pdf

United States Department of State. 2010. *"2009 Country Reports on Human Rights Practices, Chad."* Washington D.C.: United States Department of State, Bureau of Democracy, Human Rights, and Labor. https://2009-2017.state.gov/j/drl/rls/hrrpt/2009/af/135945.htm

United States Embassy (N'Djamena). 2005. *"General Wald Comes to Chad"*, 13 April, ref 06NDJAMENA737. https://wikileaks.org/plusd/cables/05NDJAMENA589_a.html

United States Embassy (Paris). 2008. *"Continued High French Engagement is Key to Chad's Stability and the International Community's Goals in Chad and for The Darfur Exodus"*, 08PARIS1936_a. https://wikileaks.org/plusd/cables/08PARIS 1936_a.html

United States Embassy (N'Djamena). 2008. *"NDJAMENA 006: DAS SWAN meeting with President Deby"*, 27 February, ref. 08FESTTWO14_a. https://wikileaks.org/plusd/cables/08FESTTWO14_a.html

United States Department of State (2008)'MGCD01: Chad monitoring group situation report no. 3', 2 February, ref. 08STATE10826_a. https://wikileaks.org/plusd/cables/08STATE10826_a.html

Wax, Emily. 2006. "New First Lady Captivates Chad." *The Washington Post*, 16 May 2006. https://www.washingtonpost.com/archive/politics/2006/05/02/new-first-lady-captivates-chad-span-classbankheadembattled-leader-at-odds-even-with-family-finds-a-helpmatespan/378fa60c-cdcf-473e-a414-2b69ebb74118/

Weinstein, Jeremy M. 2006. *Inside Rebellion: The Politics of Insurgent Violence*. Cambridge: Cambridge University Press. 10.1017/CBO9780511808654

4 Mali: counterinsurgency by clients and patrons

In August 2020, Mali witnessed a military coup carried out by officers frustrated by years of increased insecurity and blatant corruption. The motive resembled that of the putschists behind the March 2012 coup, which displaced the former President Amadou Toumani Touré. In the tumultuous spring of 2012, an insurgency offensive had almost broken down the Malian army and controlled large parts of northern Mali. In the time between the two coups, the French military intervention *Serval* had rolled back the insurgents territorial gain, and under the leadership of France and the United Nations an array of external interventions pursued an ambitious state- and peacebuilding agenda to stabilize Mali. The interveners made military and economic support conditional on the reintroduction of democracy, the implementation of a comprehensive peace agreement, and the strengthening of the formal state institutions. However, the coup in 2020 suggests that the political dynamics of Mali differed from the interveners' visions.

The purpose of this chapter is to examine the survival strategies of the Malian regimes in order to understand the case of a regime placed in a political settlement dominated by informal politics, where Western powers made comprehensive demands for administrative and political reforms. Examining Mali in the period 2011–2020 should demonstrate the extent to which informal politics is persistent and guides the strategic choices of the Malian regimes under such circumstances. In itself, the 2020 coup does not demonstrate that informal politics persisted and the regimes pursued a strategy of simulated statebuilding, nor that the regimes did not make an effort to coup proof. On the contrary, the coup might have been an outcome of a process of formalization of the Malian state.

The first section assesses the existing political settlement before the insurgency crisis with regard to the importance of informal politics. The second section analyses the extent to which the praetorian protection proposition explains the regimes' choices vis-à-vis Mali's security institutions and military strategy. The third section evaluates the proposition of risk-averse alignment by studying the three regimes' alignments with militias as well as external powers from 2011 to 2020. The fourth section examines the

DOI: 10.4324/9781003204978-4

Mali 73

power of the proposition of simulated statebuilding to explain the regimes' handling of international demands for administrative and political reforms 2013–2020.

Informal politics held uneasy alliances together

If informal politics and corruption dictate the regimes' choice of strategies, the first task is to establish the importance of those factors in Mali prior to the outbreak of the insurgency crisis in 2011. Even though Mali has often been portrayed as an example of a functioning democratic state in Africa, this section argues that informal politics was crucial to the functioning of politics in Mali. In southern Mali, a de facto clientelistic system rewarded otherwise non-productive elites for mobilizing voters and supporting a "consensus democracy" with few public expressions of disagreements. In the central and northern parts of Mali, militias and drug-smuggling armed groups received informal privileges to engage in criminal activities in return for supporting the regime against excluded militant groups.

The increased need for informal privileges in the political settlement

In 1963, three years after Mali's independence, the first Tuareg insurgency broke out. The insurgency was a visible sign of the exclusion of Arab and Tuareg tribes in northern Mali, who had expected a separate political arrangement for the region after the end of colonial rule (Lecocq 2010, 50ff). Demography allowed southern tribes to dominate Malian politics, and Tuaregs were a minority, even in northern Mali, compared to the Arab and "black" tribes of Songhais and Fulanis (Bøås 2015, 304). In combination with a strong movement for independence among the Arab and Tuareg tribes, the result was that the ruling coalition left a large part of northern Mali to regulate itself (Mann 2015, 168). From 1968 to 1991, the ruling coalition in the capital of Bamako consisted of a military dictatorship supported by elites from the different Mandé tribes, especially the Bambara, and established Muslim religious networks in southern Mali (Pezard and Shurkin 2015, 8). The continued exclusion of the northern tribes meant that economic growth and development aid mostly benefited the southern parts, which was one major reason for the Tuareg insurgencies in 1990–1996 and 2007–2009.

In 1991, Amadou Toumani Touré (ATT), the later President, organized a coup against the military junta. He oversaw a quick transition to democracy and handed over power to a new, elected leader, earning ATT the name of "the Soldier of Democracy" (Wing 2013, 477). From one perspective democracy mattered as the elected Presidents peacefully took over power. ATT was elected in 2002 when the previous President resigned after serving the two terms allowed in the Malian constitution. In parallel, ATT seemed prepared to stand down in 2012, when his second term expired but lost

74   *Mali*

power a few months before the election due to a military coup. However, from a political settlement perspective the democratic transition mattered less, as the military junta had relied on a political settlement with almost the same ruling coalition of Bamako-based elites that President Alpha Oumar Konaré and President ATT ruled over after 1991 (Fay 1995,Wing 2008). These elites were non-productive and relied on access to patronage in return for mobilizing voters and political support for the regime.

In the 1990s new economic opportunities in northern Mali distributed more power to northern elites as well as elites from the Mopti Region in the central part of Mali. The smuggling business increasingly profited from transporting migrant workers, state-subsidized goods, and Moroccan cannabis through the Sahara. In the early 2000s, South American drug cartels established new routes through West and North Africa that relied on local groups to get the cocaine for Europe through Mali (Scheele 2011). The new drug economy caused the ATT regime to cooperate with previously excluded elites, who were used as a balance against the traditional elites. Low-caste clans such as the Lemhar Arabs and Imghad Tuaregs, enriched by drug-trading, challenged the authority of the dominating clans (Desgraiset al. 2018, 672). Elites from both clans became part of the ruling coalition, initially as clients of the regime, and gained a free hand to pursue their criminal business.

Finally, Al Qaeda in the Maghreb (AQIM) profited from smuggling and the new hostage business. The region's extreme poverty, in combination with the wealth generated from the illicit economy, increased the ability of elites within AQIM and the Tuareg and Arab tribes to recruit from the local population. AQIM managed to build close relations with Arab clans around Timbuktu and became a part of the social fabric despite the Algerian origin of the organization (Henningsen 2021). AQIM was outside the ruling elite, though not entirely excluded by the regime. It is most likely that the Lemhar Arab clan, which was ATT's client, also cooperated with AQIM. In the aftermath of the intervention in 2013, an Army commander in the North claimed that AQIM did not carry out attacks on Malian soil until 2011 and gave government officials a cut of the ransoms paid for the release of AQIM hostages in return for being left alone (Boeke and Tisseron 2014, 37).

Since 1960, the political settlement in Mali had built on a ruling coalition of non-productive elites in Bamako, who benefited from the clientelist arrangement. However, the increased relative strength of northern elites caused the regime to gradually include Arab and Tuareg elites in the ruling coalition as clients. Unlike the southern elites, the northern elites were in some respects productive but needed informal privileges for their criminal business to thrive.

Clientelism, consensus democracy, and drugs

Since his election in 2002 President ATT had promoted the idea of democracy based on consensus as a particular Malian political idea with roots in the country's history (Hagberg and Körling 2012). The idea of a consensus-based political system initially generated external legitimacy, because Western donors promoted inclusiveness at the same time. However, after a decade of this system, few Malians mistook consensus politics for anything but a clientelistic system to reward political clients for political support. A survey of the Malian population identified the "lack of patriotism" among the political elite as the most important cause of the crisis in 2012 (Coulibaly and Bratton 2013, 7). Moreover, even before the offensive of the insurgents in 2012, demonstrators in cities in southern Mali protested against the widespread corruption among the political elites.

Clientelism was a way to reconcile the economic composition of Mali with the distribution of power. Most of the Malian population engaged in subsistence farming or small-scale cotton crop farming. Elites in Bamako benefited little from formal rules to protect property rights or promote economic growth, because they had few or no productive economic activities, nor did they engage in building any. Instead, they were dependent on access to patronage from the few centralized incomes in Mali. Economic means came primarily from the large state-owned businesses, taxation of the gold mining industry, and foreign aid. Since 2002 foreign aid had constituted more than half of the state budget and approximately 15 percent of the BNI (Van De Walle 2012, 1). A large proportion was budget support, which immediately placed aid money at the disposal of the regime. Furthermore, taxes on gold mining and partial state-ownership of mining companies also provided the state with 15–20 percent of the government revenue, although artisan mining outside state control had become more common (Raineri 2020, 103).

President ATT had no political party to absorb political clients and build relations with societal elites. Instead, he relied on the political parties with connections to influential families, religious leaders, and others with power in their local constituencies. To a great extent, the political parties accepted their role as a ruling coalition that supported ATT in return for self-enrichment and the expansion of their client networks (Van Vliet 2014,Wing 2013b). They became gatekeepers that could place their clients in profitable positions within the state and state-owned companies, or the regime allowed them to bid for projects funded by external donors. Mali's economic growth mainly benefited factions within the ruling coalition, and the political factions co-opted by ATT lost touch with the concerns and needs of the majority of Malians outside the client networks in the years leading up to the outbreak of hostilities (Wing 2013, Cramon 2019).

In northern Mali, clientelism became a key method for the regime to – temporarily – control the increased power of the northern elites (Bøås and Strazzari 2020). Instead of distributing funds and access to positions within the state, informal rules of lax law enforcement and collusion became a way of accommodating the northern elites' newfound power within the institutions of the political settlement. More precisely, the regime informally condoned smuggling

76 *Mali*

by the low-caste clans and influenced the workings of formal state institutions, e.g. by giving key persons within the smuggling networks favourable treatment in the juridical system or releasing them shortly after their imprisonment. In return, the low-caste clans aligned with the regime, at least until the distribution of power changed once again in 2011.

Clientelism reflected the relative power of the non-productive southern elites and the newfound power of northern elites through illegal economic activities. In order to ensure the stability of the political settlement, and thereby remain in power, the ATT regime used clientelism in different variants to satisfy the demands of powerful elites.

Consensus due to the lack of programmatic politics

On paper, Mali symbolized the democratization of Africa in the 1990s, with free elections, an inclusive form of politics, a free press, and somewhat functioning political parties (Bergamaschi 2014). Consequently, international donors flocked to Mali to support its democratic development. In fact, Mali received a higher share of foreign aid than comparable states such as Burkina Faso or Niger. However, Malian politics had few, if any, elements of programmatic politics, which allowed for "consensus politics" and reduced the ability of the Malian democracy to connect the needs of voters with the policies of the regime (Boeke and Valk 2019).

The lack of voter mobilization was probably more pronounced in Mali than in comparable clientelistic states. Since 1991, voter turnouts had been between 22–37 percent[1]. More importantly, none of the parties campaigned on an ideological programme or other systematic ideas. Still, in theory, the parliament could have controlled President ATT to limit clientelism, and discuss the broader needs of the population. Based on interviews with 15 parliamentarians, Martin van de Vliet identifies mechanisms that explain why informal politics became so dominating. The Minister of Finance, appointed by the President, controlled most of the state budget, and MPs used informal channels to gain resources for their constituencies (Bleck and Michelitch 2015, Van Vliet 2014). Being part of the regime's ruling coalition in the parliament provided the parties with such informal channels. By contrast, MPs that publicly criticized a minister were cut off from resources. Excluded parties were left without access to public funds or influence, and were delegitimized by a political system that publicly lauded consensus.

In general, the political parties focused on acquiring enough benefits for their clients to secure their own election. Only in rare cases did societal actors mobilize to protest the legislation. The most crucial protest was against a liberal family law that drew heavy criticism from the High Islamic Council and the protest was organized by Mahmoud Dicko, one of the organizers behind the public protests in 2019 and 2020 that eventually led to the military coup. The result of the generally non-programmatic and informal character of

Malian politics was an apathetic reaction among the Malian population when the military coup removed President ATT in 2012.

To sum up, the regime relied on support from the ruling coalition of non-productive, Bamako-based elites. These elites accepted the arrangement due to the lack of programmatic politics and their enrolment in the regime's client network. However, previously excluded northern elites became increasingly powerful due to the surge in drug smuggling. To accommodate the change in power distribution, the ATT regime established informal practices of impunity in return for support. The overall conclusion is that informal politics was central to the workings of the political settlement in Mali, and the regimes would therefore be expected to choose strategies adapted to the realm of informal politics.

Praetorian protection: coup-proofing to no avail

The conjunction of the insurgency war in northern Mali and the coups in 2012 and 2020 allows not only an examination of the prioritization between counterinsurgency and coup-proofing but also a comparison of the ATT regime and the Ibrahim Boubacar Keïta (IBK) regime to find out if there is a continued use of praetorian protection. The military junta is excluded from the analysis, as it only held power in a few months after the 2012 coup. This section argues that the ATT regime acted in line with the expectations of the propositions and that the IBK regime continued most of the practices despite external interference. To compare the two regimes the section is structured into three parts. The first and second parts examine the structure and strategy of the security forces during the ATT regime, whereas the third part tracks changes during the IBK regime.

An anti-terror or coup-proofing organization?

In order to understand the organization of the security forces, the historical backdrop is important. President ATT himself had served as commander of the presidential guard in the years prior to his military coup in 1991. Mali was led by a military dictatorship from 1968 to 1991, and that historical experience, arguably, induced the regimes of Alpha Oumar Konaré and ATT to isolate and counterbalance the army. More specifically, since 1968 the 33rd Parachute Regiment (33rd Para) had performed the function of presidential guard. In return, the regiment received lavish funding including higher salaries and better equipment[2]. In addition, the neighbouring countries of Niger and Mauritania witnessed successful military coups in 2009 and 2012, respectively. The threat of coups was both a historical experience in Mali as well as a contemporary occurrence in the region.

In 2011, the Malian army consisted of only 7,300 men, which furthermore was balanced by paramilitary forces totalling 4,800 men, including the 33rd Para (Powell 2014, 337). The regular Malian army suffered from insufficient

78   Mali

manpower and materiel, which severely limited its mobility and, thereby, ability to operate in the desert terrain of northern Mali (Boisbouvier and Groga-Bada 2012). In 2010, President ATT fired a number of officers stationed in northern Mali, for fear that they were cooperating with Algeria to launch a coup. Moreover, the political loyalty of senior officers was more important than their military professionalism, and most generals were part of the President's client network (Solomon 2015, 71). Separately, the organization of the security forces and ATT's actions could be explained by low levels of professionalism, but together they suggest a focus on coup-proofing.

As part of the Trans-Sahara Counter Terrorism Partnership, the United States provided military assistance to Mali. The United States' forces chose two lines of effort: one, in 2010, to raise, train, and equip a counterterrorism unit within the 33rd Para; another to train and equip the mobile units named Echelons Tactiques Inter-Armes (ETIA) operating in northern Mali. Even though the two units were both part of a train and equip programme, their core tasks differed. Stationed just outside Bamako, most of the activities of the 33rd Para took place near the capital, even though the President only tasked part of the regiment with the role of presidential guard (Boisvert 2019, 110). By contrast, ETIA units were ethnically mixed and operated in northern Mali as an outcome of the peace agreement after the latest Tuareg insurgency. Their task was to maintain order in the northern region and combat renewed insurgencies. The Touré regime clearly prioritized coup-proofing. ETIA units lacked equipment, the army constantly rotated personnel and did not allow ETIA to receive training at the unit level. According to officials at the United States Embassy in Bamako, the regime chose to give ETIA unfavourable treatment for fear of a coup (Warner 2014, 75). In contrast, the regime expanded the 33rd Para and allowed the new elite company to train as a unit with US instructors.

Ultimately, years of coup-proofing did not protect President Touré against the military coup in Bamako in March 2012. Disgruntled units from the regular army joined the spontaneous and successful coup led by Captain Amadou Sanogo. The coup was not an indication that the regime had not made an effort to coup-proof. For 21 years President Touré had avoided coups. After the coup, the 33rd Para managed to evacuate President Touré and even launched an unsuccessful counter-coup only days after the first coup pushing the new military junta to dismantle the 33rd Para and to execute at least 21 officers (International Crisis Group 2014, 7). Once the insurgent threat rose, organizing for coup-proofing had devastating consequences.

Inconsistent and sporadic use of force during the initial crisis

In the years before the crisis, violence increased in northern Mali, mostly due to AQIM's use of terror. In the autumn of 2011, violence escalated as Tuareg fighters returned from Libya, after having fought for the Gaddafi regime in the Libyan civil war. They spurred the secessionist sentiments among elite Tuareg

Mali 79

leaders. One of the returning soldiers, Mohammed Ag Najim, became the leader of the newly founded secessionist *Mouvement National pour la Libération de l'Azawad* (MNLA). The returning fighters brought with them tactical knowledge as well as vehicles, heavy machine guns, and rockets that could be fitted onto 4x4 vehicles. Simultaneously, AQIM stepped up its attacks on civilians and military installations in northern Mali.

After a previous peace agreement between Tuareg secessionists and the ATT regime in 2006, the Malian security forces had very little presence in northern Mali. As a response to the violence, the ATT regime spent few resources on tackling the lack of public services and more on strengthening the repressive apparatus. The result was a weak form of punishment strategy that failed to change the calculation of the insurgent groups. Since the summer of 2010, after years of neglect as well as regional and global criticism of its inactivity, the ATT regime launched the $60 million *Programme spécial pour la paix, la sécurité et le développement au Nord-Mali* (PSPSDN), which was almost exclusively paid for by donors. Originally, the programme intended to bring development and security to the northern regions, but the ATT regime chose to spend most of the money on military infrastructure (Chauzal and Damme 2015, 31).

The Imghad Tuaregs in the security forces benefited from the new military installations and were active in suppressing the growing discontent among the other Tuareg clans (Ahmed 2011, Lebovich 2017, 10). Far from stemming the insurgency, the favours provided for one clan only spurred the insurgency. From November 2011, once the insurgents began attacking the military installations, the regular forces crumbled. Most army units failed utterly when faced with the insurgents. Even units occasionally trained by US Special Forces fought without any tactical acumen and lacked supplies. Most soldiers recruited among the northern tribes chose to defect to the insurgent groups. Only privileged units with strong ties to the regime proved tactically proficient. The first one was the ETIA unit that recruited from the Imghad Tuaregs under the leadership of Colonel El haj Gamou Imghad[3]. The second unit was the *compagnie forces spéciales* unit recruited from the praetorian 33rd Para. In conjunction with combat helicopters, these two units achieved the only two tactical successes in Meneka and Tessalit in the spring of 2012 (Powelson 2013). In conversations with French civil servants in May 2012, interim President Traoré confidentially described the Malian Army as good for parades and coups, but not wars (Chivvis 2016, 77). The security institutions offered the interim regime few means for a military strategy and the military junta had to rely on additional strategies to survive.

The impact of the security sector reforms since 2013

On 18 August 2020, history repeated itself when units from the largest army base in Kita near Bamako launched a coup that led to the resignation of the President and the government. The similar trajectories of the ATT and IBK

80 *Mali*

regimes might lead to a foregone conclusion that the regimes organized and applied the security institutions in similar manners. Nonetheless, the circumstances were different. After 2013, Malian forces were under the supervision of international training missions, and international forces mostly exempted the Malian army of the responsibility to uphold security in northern Mali, due to the presence of the United Nations Multidimensional Integrated Stabilization Mission (MINUSMA) and the French counter-terror operation *Barkhane,* which superseded the Serval operation in August 2014. The scale of the external military training changed in February 2013, when approximately 600 instructors from the EU Training Mission (EUTM) arrived in Mali. In 2015, the EU launched the European Union's Civilian Mission in Support of The Malian Internal Security Forces (EUCAP Sahel Mali), which trained the gendarmerie and the National Guard. This footprint made the EU training mission the largest security sector initiative in Mali in the examined period. At a glance the output of the EUTM is impressive, having trained more than 14,000 soldiers and paramilitary forces at the end of 2019 (Erforth 2020, 576). In addition, the EU focused on the thorny question of instilling a norm of rule of law into the security institutions. Besides the EU's initiative, several countries, most importantly the United States and Morocco, provided bilateral counter-terrorism training (Schmitt 2014,Touchard 2014).

Despite the increased external effort, the main issues in the security institutions are comparable to those the ATT-period. The presidential guard was dissolved in 2012, but the IBK regime pushed for a strict separation between elite units and regular units, and the elite units were mainly directed against non-armed political opponents. Initially, IBK chose an elite unit from the National Guard as the primary counter-terrorism unit and presidential guard. In 2014, the President, without informing the Minister of Defence, allowed a French company with personal relations to former French intelligence officers to pay for the training of parts of the presidential guard in return for unknown favours (Carayol 2015). Apparently displeased with the National Guard unit, IBK chose a counter-terrorism unit from the gendarmerie.

When demonstrations erupted against the lack of security and corruption in Bamako in 2019, the IBK regime augmented the riot control units with the elite counterterrorism unit called FORSAT to restore order, which resulted in the death of at least 14 civilians (Human Rights Watch 2020a). The targeted use of violence against the opposition created widespread anger, and is an important indication that the elite unit's primary responsibility was protection of the regime in the capital against the opposition rather than fighting terror groups in northern Mali. Another indicator is the timing of the coup that happened only hours after the President fired Lieutenant-Colonel Ibrahim Traoré from his position as head of presidential security, which demonstrates that the survival of the regime was highly dependent on the support of elite units (Diallo and Soumaré 2020). In the summer of 2020, IBK ordered

Mali 81

Colonel Assimi Goïta, who eventually came to lead the coup, to redeploy his special forces to quell the demonstrations Bamako (Diallo 2020).

Efforts in Bamako to secure a regime-loyal force hampered regular army units and ETIA units which faced the same deficiencies as during the ATT-regime. The impressive number of Malian security forces trained by EUTM hid the regime's undermining of the training by only allowing soldiers to participate as individuals, not as units (Cold-Ravnkilde and Nissen 2020). In addition, the Algiers peace accord stipulated that the ETIA units were to consist of equal shares of soldiers from the regular army, pro-government militias, and demobilized separatists. In reality, the regime undermined the efficiency of the newly trained ETIA units by rotating individuals, and slowing down the integration of the former insurgents (Carter Center 2020, 22–24).

On the battlefield, the regular units had little control and relied on indiscriminate violence and local and international actors. They lacked basic military equipment and supplies (Tull 2019). Moreover, despite a war bonus paid to the front soldiers, the incompetence of the regular army and ETIA left soldiers demoralized and frustrated by the political level, especially as attacks on their garrisons became increasingly deadly throughout the examined period (Diallo and Soumaré 2020). Internationally assisted security sector reforms only created meagre improvements in military efficiency and the security situation degenerated between 2013 and 2020. As to military efficiency, a team of analysts from RAND analysed the first units which had gone through the EU training, and found that their tactical performance was far below that of the militias in northern Mali (Shurkin et al. 2017, 99–101).

The same fundamental problem that plagued the Malian Army before 2012 seems to have shaped the period from 2013 to 2020. Multiple client networks reduced the IBK regime's control of the regular army, of which the coup in August 2020 was but the last indication. A telling example of the strength of the client networks happened in July 2016. The Chief of Staff, General Mahamane Touré, refused to order General El Haj Ag Gamou (the former leader of the Imghad militia) to return his forces from Kidal to their base in Gao. General Gamou was in Kidal to coerce one of his clients into the position of President of the Regional Assembly in Kidal. As a reaction, IBK fired the Chief of Staff and replaced him with Didier Dacko. However, Dacko and Gamou apparently had a common understanding that allowed Gamou to stay in Kidal (Ahmed 2016). The episode is an illustration of the wider split into clientelistic networks within the armed forces. The example also illustrates the level of involvement of client networks within the army in communal conflicts in especially the Mopti region.

International actors, most notably France and the EU, pushed for an army relying on ethnically integrated mobile units suited for the conditions in northern Mali. However, the Malian security forces, as well as the regime, did not support the efforts wholeheartedly. The coup in August 2020 demonstrated how the regime tried to use elite forces as a protection against

82 *Mali*

the political opposition in Bamako, leaving the regular forces disadvantaged in the middle and northern parts of Mali.

The IBK regime's negligible military strategy

Having an independent Malian strategy in the wake of operation Serval proved difficult for the IBK regime. The bilateral relations with France, the multidimensional strategy of MINUSMA, and the EU's comprehensive strategy all set a direction that limited the freedom to chart a Malian strategy. Furthermore, the IBK regime put very little effort into creating an official counterinsurgency strategy, as the parliament spent two years adopting a plan for the development of the security forces. The plan concerned acquisitions and personnel until 2020, but only spoke vaguely of promoting stability (Shurkin et al. 2017, 48). The lack of an official strategy for northern Mali and the failure to develop sufficient military units capable of being stationed in the North undermined the French plan of a quick handover of security responsibility to the Malian security forces. Instead, the protection of civilians was left to the MINUSMA forces.

The lack of an official strategy did not equal tactical inactivity. In the North and in the central Mopti region, the IBK regime applied indiscriminate violence to punish militant groups. In the North, the application of indiscriminate violence was politically sensitive, because there was a fundamental disagreement between, on the one side, the UN and France, and on the other side the ruling coalition in Bamako. The UN brought non-Jihadist Tuareg insurgent groups into an inclusive peace process. Conversely, public demonstrations and Bamako-based elites pressured the regime to take a hard stance and to consider Jihadist and non-Jihadist groups one threat (Charbonneau 2017, 418). In the eyes of the ruling coalition, the peace process now protected them. The regime's willingness but inability to combat the non-Jihadist Tuaregs makes sense of the haphazard and self-defeating military operations in Kidal from November 2013 to May 2014. Despite French warnings and with no political or economic plan for the city, 30 November 2013 Prime Minister Moussa Mara in vain visited Kidal, which was held by Tuareg separatists. 21 May 2014, the Malian forces attempted to attack Kidal deploying an ETIA unit trained by the EU mission, but were routed, and at least 70 soldiers were killed (Carayol 2014). Kidal was the centre of the non-Jihadist Tuareg movement, whereas the Jihadists considered Timbuktu and Gao their operational centres. By attacking Kidal, the regime tried to harass and punish the non-Jihadist insurgents. However, the defeat led to a wider Tuareg offensive that forced the regime to accept the peace negotiations.

By contrast, the Malian security forces only initiated 51 clashes against Jihadist groups of the 1025 armed clashes between 2014 and 2020 recorded in the ACLED database (numbers from Raleigh et al. 2010). Most of these took place in the Mopti region, where the IBK regime pursued an ineffective

Mali   83

punishment strategy, but one that primarily targeted Fulani militias and civilians, who were subject to indiscriminate violence, intimidation, and killings, often under the guise of counter-terrorism according to reports issued by MINUSMA (MINUSMA 2020). The spread of inter-communal violence in the Mopti region led to several instances of army units targeting Fulani civilians, although militias were the most common perpetrators (ibid).

To sum up, both regimes saw to it that the security forces remained disorganized, and both regimes privileged small, but trusted elite forces, which became the primary beneficiaries of Western training. Moreover, regular forces did not receive sufficient resources, and the question of co-optation was clearly linked to the political position of the militias. Strategically, the regimes relied on ineffective and symbolic operations not coordinated with its external allies. This is noticeable in the light of how external interventions gave the security forces a breathing space to focus its efforts. The case study observed that the regime accommodated elites within the ruling coalition as part of its strategy. The co-optation of Imghad Tuaregs in the ETIA units was a reflection of the Imghads' newfound power. In addition, the IBK regime used a punishment strategy as a result of pressure from Bamako-based elites. The next section will examine the ways in which the regimes became even more dependent on domestic elites and external actors.

Risk-averse alignment: relying on militias and the old colonial power

The passivity and tactical deficiency of the security institutions are in contrast to the regimes' high level of activity and skilful negotiations of alignments to balance the threat of the insurgents. This section argues that the three regimes favoured internal alignment with militias in northern and central Mali and co-opted them through the distribution of funds and privileges. The regimes chose domestic rather than external alignment and continued to favour the domestic elites after external actors provided security in Mali from 2013. The regimes only reluctantly aligned with France, favouring a regional intervention. The first part of the section examines the hasty attempts by the ATT regime and the military junta to co-opt parts of the insurgency groups. The second part analyses the debate within the military junta with regard to external alignment. The third part examines the continued reliance on internal alignment from 2013 to 2020.

ATT tried to use the blueprint from 2006 to 2009

The early negotiations between the ATT regime and the Tuareg and Arab secessionists in the autumn of 2011 provide a glimpse into the alignment-based strategies in the final months of the ATT regime. The regime offered several concessions to the negotiators representing Ifogha Tuareg (Ahmed 2012). Negotiating with elite Tuaregs in the autumn of 2011 was an attempt

84 *Mali*

to co-opt the elites that were likely to support an insurgency. The level of violence in the Kidal area was rising, which makes it probable that the ATT regime knew of the Tuareg elites' hostile intentions (International Crisis Group 2012, 10). Furthermore, the inclusion of returning Tuareg fighters also indicates that the regime was aware of the increased level of threat generated by the fallout of the Libyan war. Therefore, it was most likely an attempt to separate the Tuareg insurgents from AQIM and its offshoots among the Arabs, Fulanis, and Songhays. AQIM backtracked from its tacit agreement with the government and began to conduct several attacks on the Malian Army. Yet, there were no parallel efforts to negotiate with AQIM. It seems reasonable to conclude that the ATT regime was trying to split a potential insurgent alliance by offering targeted inducement.

Targeted inducement was a blueprint from the insurgency 2006–2009. In fact, the regime still had two of the alliances left. As already mentioned, the Imghad Tuaregs were mobilized into an ETIA unit and the Lemhar Arabs were given a free hand by the regime to smuggle drugs in return for abstaining from joining secessionist movements. Moreover, the regime had important allies among senior Ifogha Tuaregs, such as Agatam Ag Alhassane, who was Minister of Agriculture. More surprisingly, Iyad Ag Ghali, the uncompromising leader of Anser Dine, the Al Qaeda affiliated Tuareg movement, had served as consul to the Malian Embassy in Saudi Arabia from 2007 until 2010. The fragmentation of the Tuareg movement paints the Tuaregs as less of a monolithic force and more as a set of diverse actors that pursued autonomy, secession, or simply self-enrichment. What is more, President ATT did not mobilize accessible support from Algeria and France (Marchal 2012). Based on this behaviour, ATT most likely preferred domestic to external alignment, but the coup prevents a clear conclusion.

The regime's attempt to carry out an internal balancing strategy ultimately failed. A succession of rapid defeats on the battlefield as well as the resulting violent protests from soldiers and their families might explain the ensuing paralysis of the regime. After the tumult following the improvised coup, the new military junta and interim President Traoré also settled on a strategy of internal alignment to balance the threat from the insurgency groups. At that point, the Imghad Tuaregs and the Lemhar Arabs had lost their military capacity due to defection and a series of military defeats. Colonel El haj Gamou Imghad decided not to shoot at the Tuareg deserters that swelled the ranks of MNLA and Anser Dine (Boisbouvier and Groga-Bada 2012).

To compensate, the military junta took advantage of old and new self-protection forces that emerged as a result of the increased insurgent threat to the Fulani and Songhay tribes living in the Mopti region in central Mali. Both tribes had connections to the ruling coalition in Bamako, and Songhays were well represented among political leaders and officers. In 1994, Songhay officers from the 33rd Para formed the militia Ganda Koy, whereas Fulanis founded the militia Ganda Iso in 2008 (Cristiani and Fabiani 2013, 88–89, Baldaro 2021). Both militias were active in the counterinsurgency war against Tuaregs from 2006 to 2009 and were perceived by the Tuareg elites as being protected by juridical immunity from the ATT regime. Moreover, a new self-defence militia – the *Forces de libération des régions Nord du Mali* – came into existence in April, with as many as 800 recruits. In July 2012, the three groups founded the umbrella organization *La Coordination des mouvements et forces patriotiques de résistance* (CM-FPR). The intentions of the militias were different from those of the Bamako regime; in 2013 an offshoot of CM-FPR even flipped side to the seperatists, but for a certain period their interests coincided (Desgrais et al. 2018, 667). Captain Sanogo and the military junta promoted and utilized the militias to launch a low-cost internal balancing strategy.

None of the militias were able to change the status quo on the battlefield in the autumn of 2012. Although elements of Ganda Koy and Ganda Iso had taken control of Douentza in July 2012, they were chased away by the insurgents in August without a battle. As soon as the insurgents decided to move south across the Niger River, they were mostly unopposed by the militias. Nonetheless, the regime's decision to arm militias in both southern and northern Mali afterwards created a much more complex internal distribution of power and gave rise to the so-called Political Platform Group in 2014. The ATT regime and the military junta favoured alignment with domestic elites in northern and central Mali and co-opted them through funds and immunity from prosecution, but their efforts failed due to the inefficiency of the militias.

Internal debates about the risk versus the cost of external alignment

With no improvement in sight on the battlefield, the military junta, and interim President Traoré debated external interventions. The negotiations of the regime in the autumn of 2012 with the Economic Community of West African States (ECOWAS) and Western powers, especially France, provide insights into the regime's cost-benefit and risk calculations. The regime was divided between Captain Sanogo, the coup leader who was reluctant to accept external intervention, and interim President Traoré, who secretly negotiated an external intervention with President Hollande from his hospital bed in Paris in May and June 2012[4]. In September, Traoré's position prevailed. Captain Sanogo accepted the more limited role of overseeing army modernization, although he retained influence on political decisions.

On 1 September 2012, Traoré officially asked ECOWAS for military assistance and, 18 September, he officially requested a UN Security Council resolution for an ECOWAS-led stabilization force to stabilize the military situation in Mali. More specifically, Traoré asked for five battalions from ECOWAS and aerial logistical support, which would probably have been provided by France (Boeke and Tisseron 2014, 4–5). For months a regional solution appeared the most likely, as this was the African Union's and

86 *Mali*

France's preference, and a limited intervention would accommodate the scepticism of the former military junta.

A relatively small ECOWAS-led intervention provided the regime with several benefits at a low cost and with limited risk. While a five-battalion force in the bottle-neck region of Mopti would have had strong potential to stop any further advances of the insurgents, it seems unlikely that it could have recaptured northern Mali. The number of insurgents was roughly the same as the number of requested soldiers. Yet, the force would allow the regime time. Furthermore, if militant extremists were to take a firmer grip on power in northern Mali, international military and financial support was almost a matter of course. The cost would have been a divided Mali for an extended period, but with a low risk of demands for substantial political or economic reforms as part of the ECOWAS-mission. Several ECOWAS member states had a very poor democratic record, with several instances of military coups. A greater risk might have been posed by an increase in pressure to enter comprehensive peace negotiations with parts of the insurgents. Captain Sanogo especially had very little room for manoeuvre, due to his faction of black, nationalist leaders that rejected anything but the complete surrender of the insurgents (Bøås and Torheim 2013, 1289). A small ECOWAS intervention would have made it more difficult for external actors to impose a peace agreement on the regime.

In the end, events on the ground convinced France to take a dominant role in the military intervention. 10 January 2013, when insurgents began moving towards the army base in Konna and the cities of Mopti and Ségou further south, Bamako would be within a few weeks' reach of the insurgents. Interim President Traoré immediately asked assistance from France – or rather, he was asked by the French President to request for assistance under article 51 of the UN charter (Chivvis 2016, 94–95). The first French aircraft attacked insurgent columns 11 January. French forces launched a lightning offensive to catch the insurgents on the wrong foot. The French forces received logistical and intelligence support from mainly the United Kingdom and the United States, and combat troops from Chad and ECOWAS member states. Malian security forces, on the other hand, were glaringly missing from the main hostilities.

The benefit of an external alignment with France was a dramatic change in the balance of forces in favour of the Malian state. Even before 11 January, the regime almost certainly had an appreciation of the disruptive effect of French airpower and highly trained and mobile forces in northern Mali – even though the actual pace of the operations came as a surprise to many observers, including the US military. Furthermore, France drafted all three resolutions in relation to Mali in the Security Council, initiated the EU training mission, and finally convinced the United States to support the French mission (Boeke and Schuurman 2015, 808). France proved a very active ally that was able to influence the international environment.

Mali 87

Despite the obvious benefits, French intervention was only viewed as a last resort by members of the Malian regime. The long-term presence of the former colonial power might spark political resistance, create international pressure for democratization, and increase the popular support of Islamist forces. Moreover, the regime faction of Captain Sanogo viewed France as a de facto ally of MNLA and believed that French involvement would force the regime to make substantial concessions to the Tuaregs – a fear not entirely groundless (Harmon 2014, 207–208). The short-term cost of a French-led military intervention might have been rather low, but the long-term political risk stemming from a French intervention would have been appreciably higher.

The IBK regime continued internal alignments

After the end of the main hostilities and the transition of power to the democratically elected President Ibrahim Boubacar Keïta (IBK), the new regime continued and expanded its internal alignments. In the short run, the presence of international forces secured the regime against insurgent threats. Still, besides the theoretical arguments for maintaining domestic alignment, the IBK regime disagreed with France on the status of MNLA. The IBK regime considered MNLA as part of the insurgency alliance, whereas France perceived it as a potential ally after the Islamists had routed MNLA in 2012 (Guichaoua 2020). Even after MNLA and other Arab and Tuareg groups organized in the Coordination Group, which intended to negotiate a peace agreement with the regime, the IBK regime maintained its hostile attitude towards MNLA and the Coordination Group.

A key example demonstrates how the IBK regime used internal alignment to balance and harass the Coordination Group. The Islamist group *Mouvement pour l'Unicité et le Jihad en Afrique Occidentale* (MUJAO) was aligned with AQIM during the offensive in the spring of 2012. However, President IBK selected a number of former MUJAO leaders to run as candidates for his party in the parliamentary election of 2014. They were cleared of all criminal charges, despite being well-known drug smugglers, and became part of IBK's client network. In return, they formed the *Mouvement Arabe de l'Azawad – Bamako* (MAA-Bamako), which broke with AQIM and conquered Ménaka from MNLA in 2015 (Raineri and Strazzari 2015, 266). Ménaka was the hub of drug smuggling in Mali.

Another example is the establishment of the Platform Group by the Imghad Tuareg militia GATIA, MAA-Bamako, Ganda Koy and Ganda Iso in the summer of 2014. In 2015, when President IBK was confronted with claims that the government secretly supported the Platform Group militias, IBK declared that "They call them governmental vigilantes. That is not true! They are only Malians who refuse to submit" (RFI 2015). By implying that the cause of the Platform Group was patriotic, the President, in reality, legitimized the militant groups. In September 2016, the United States' Ambassador in Bamako

88 *Mali*

publicly urged IBK to "stop all ties both public and private with GATIA" (Boutellis and Zahar 2017, 27–28). The pressure from the United States compelled the regime to reduce its materiel support of the Platform Group, although the regime maintained close links to the pro-government militias.

Moving away from direct support of the Platform Group, General Moussa Diawara, the director of the intelligence service, together with the President and other regime insiders devised a new unofficial approach of forcing a wedge between the members of the Coordination Group (UNSC 2020). In November 2017, the intelligence service helped establish the Coordination des Mouvements de l'Entente (CME), which claimed to be part of the Coordination Group, but in reality only coordinated with the intelligence service and drew valuable funds for disarmament, demobilization, and reintegration away from the Coordination Group. The scheme caused public debate in August 2020, when an expert group reporting to the UN Security Council chose to report the involvement of the regime (ibid, 22).

Pro-government militias and selective alignment with a separatist group obviously undermined the Malian state's monopoly of force. From 2017 and onwards, the state had little control in the northern regions and the growing violence in the Mopti and Liptako regions near Burkina Faso and Niger posed a threat to the security forces. Militant Jihadist groups regrouped in 2015–2017, a period which saw the formation of the Islamic State in Greater Sahara and the fusion of four al-Qaeda affiliated groups into Jama'at Nasr al-Islam wal Muslimin. Importantly, the Fulani elements of the two groups provoked inter-communal conflicts on land use, between the nomadic Fulani communities and sedentary tribes, foremost the Dogon. While operation Barkhane and MINUSMA eventually reoriented their efforts toward the Mopti and Liptako regions, the IBK regime reacted quickly. Since 2016, the self-defence militia Dan Na Ambassagou received weapons, ID cards with the Malian state emblem, and acted as scouts and informants for the security forces (International Crisis Group 2020, 12, Human Rights Watch 2018). Allegedly, in 2017 Prime Minister Soumeylou Boubèye Maïga drew up a plan to counter Fulani militants that would formalize the close coordination between Dan Na Ambassagou and state security forces (International Crisis Group 2020, 14). However, since 2018 a series of massacres on Fulani villages created an outcry from international interveners and NGOs. Publicly, the IBK regime distanced itself from Dan Na Ambassagou, and eventually banned it in March 2019 (Venturi and Toure 2020, 62). In practice, in 2020 the security forces still turned a blind eye to atrocities committed by Dan Na Ambassagou and other self-defence militias of the sedentary tribes, even though the regime initiated dialogues between Dogon and Fulani communal leaders (Human Rights Watch 2020b). Given the empirical evidence the government's continued internal alignment with the Platform Group and use of self-defence groups in the Mopti and Liptako regions, it seems most likely that the regime pursued a deliberate strategy of favouring domestic alignments, even seven years after the end of the main hostilities.

To sum up, the regimes favoured domestic alignments. The ATT regime and the military junta established domestic alignments before negotiating external alignments. Domestic alignments were primarily based on patronage in the form of materiel support or impunity. Moreover, once external alignments were in place, the IBK regime worked hard to retain domestic alignments, even when the domestic allies hurt the peace process and contributed to an increased fragmentation of authority in Mali. The military junta's negotiation of external alignment clearly showed a preference for reducing the risk to regime survival. The practice of continued domestic alignment with militias made it difficult for the IBK regime to cater to international demands for reforms.

Simulated statebuilding: reintroducing consensus politics

Operation Serval was a tactical and operational success that removed the insurgents' territorial control in less than three months. To turn Serval into a strategic success, France and other international aid donors demanded a peace agreement with the non-Jihadist Tuaregs to isolate Jihadists linked to AQIM and demanded a comprehensive plan for development in northern Mali in return for further aid. Despite the IBK regime's public support of both conditions, the resulting standstill reflected the interests of the uneasy ruling coalition of elites from the political establishment associated with the consensus politics of ATT and IBK. As a result, the ends of both regimes were marred by public outcries against corruption within a self-serving "political class". The section is structured into two parts that first analyses the regime's handling of the peace process, and, second, the regime's reaction to demands for administrative reforms in northern Mali.

The regime's dual role in the peace negotiations

France demanded political concessions for undertaking Operation Serval: democracy had to be restored in Mali and the Malian government had to reach a political agreement and reconciliation with the Tuareg and Arab minorities in the North (Charbonneau and Sears 2014, 603–4). Restoring democracy met little resistance outside the regime. The military junta and interim President Traoré had no political experience and were isolated from the political elites in Bamako, who refused to cooperate with them (Lecocq et al. 2013). After French troops arrived in Bamako, the military junta lost its ability to threaten with violence, thus losing its primary tool for gaining influence. On 18 June 2013, the interim President and representatives from MNLA signed the Ouagadougou accord in Burkina Faso, which started the process of peace negotiations and the reestablishment of democracy (Boutellis

90 *Mali*

and Zahar 2017, 10–11). Presidential and parliamentary elections were held in July and November 2013, respectively.

Algeria hosted the peace negotiations between the Malian government and many of the armed groups in northern Mali. From the summer of 2014, the militant groups coalesced into the previously mentioned Coordination Group and the pro-Bamako Platform Group. The Islamist groups linked to Al-Qaeda, such as Anser Dine or the Macina Liberation Front, were excluded from negotiations and their leaders hunted by the French Barkhane operation. In June 2015, the Platform Group, the Coordination Group, and the government signed the Algiers Accord under intense pressure from France as well as international donors (Charbonneau 2017, 11). The UN, in particular, needed the Algiers Accord to have a framework that would guide the work of MINUSMA. Afterwards, the UN saw the implementation of the Algiers Accord as the most salient question in Mali. In May 2019, Antonio Guterres, the UN Secretary-General, claimed that the accord "remains the only valid and viable framework" for the Malian peace process (United Nations Security Council 2019, 16). The accord resembled previous peace agreements made in 1991 and 2006 since its main elements were increased decentralization, restoration of state authority in the North through public investments and service provision, the inclusion of militias in the security forces, disarmament, demobilization, and reintegration, all of which were parts of previous agreements.

There is a marked contrast between the regime's official position and its informal practices. Officially, the regime remained supportive of the peace process and surprisingly saw great progress. Speaking at the United Nation's General Assembly in September 2016, IBK declared: "(…) I can assure you that the hostilities have effectively ceased between the government and the signatory groups. (…) These efforts eloquently demonstrate the will of my government to honour its commitments and have led to tangible progress in all areas." (Keita 2016). Unofficially, the regime took a much less supportive stance. In the view of the Carter Center, which the United Nations chose as an independent observer of the Algiers Accord, the lack of will is a key impediment:

"Five years after its signature, however, the agreement remains far from achieving its objectives and the peace process is not yet irreversible. This reality is largely attributable to the parties' actions, both in Bamako and in the field." (Carter Center 2020, 8). More to the point, the Carter Center supports the findings of the United Nations Security Council's panel of experts, who single out informal derailment as the key to the faltering implementation process (ibid, 13–14):

> (…) high-ranking figures, elected officials, and military actors also have been involved in actions aimed at delaying, blocking, or altering steps in the implementation process. Corrupt practices and schemes to divert

Mali   91

implementation based on political, personal, or financial interests have been a persistent impediment to implementation.

In the Mopti and Liptako regions, the actions of the regime tell a more nuanced story of the shift in the government priorities from the unambiguous alignment with sedentary self-defence militias until 2018 to the sustained effort to foster dialogue and reconciliation among the ethnic groups. The successive Prime Ministers Abdoulaye Maïga and Boubou Cissé have led the so-called Integrated Security Plan for the Central Regions that aimed at elite reconciliation[5]. So far, few tangible results have materialized, which most likely reflects the incapacity, not will, of the Malian state to provide security and other state-services in the regions. Moreover, the punishment strategy of the security forces created hostility among Fulani communities, who still perceived the state as aligned with the sedentary tribal militias (Human Rights Watch 2020b)

Even under the assumption that the IBK regime was serious in its support of the peace agreement, Bamako elites and international interveners severely restricted the strategic freedom of the regime. In contrast to previous agreements, the Algiers peace process left out some of the strongest Islamist militant groups. The views on the Islamist militant groups differed among the most powerful elite networks in Bamako. Whereas IBK held a confrontational 'no dialogue' view, Mahmoud Dicko, the influential leader of the High Islamic Council, met with representatives of MUJAO. Dicko, who had strong links to the opposition party M5-RFP was part of the Conference of National Understanding in 2017 and 2019 that called for a reconciliation process that included the Islamist militant groups (International Crisis Group 2020). At the other end stood the southern-oriented, black nationalists. A telling example is the small Yéléma party led by Moussa Mara, who took a confrontational view of the conflict with the northern tribes. Mara's visit to Kidal in May 2014 in his capacity of Prime Minister was no mistake, but a demonstration of his view of northern Mali as subjugated to Bamako's control (Ba 2015). After the removal of Moussa Mara as Prime Minister, Yéléma remained part of the government's coalition and Mara continued as Mayor of Bamako. The implementation of the peace accord suffered from France's ardent rejection of dialogue with militant Islamists, and the factionalized elite politics in Bamako. In light of the disappointment that led to the military coup in 2020, it remains puzzling why the regime did not aggressively pursue dominance in the North by implementing administrative reforms to make the state institutions more effective.

Insisting on, but undermining administrative reforms

In early 2013, France and the international donor community, most noticeably the EU, made a comprehensive development plan for northern Mali a prerequisite for donor support. France and the international donors

92   *Mali*

perceived security and development as interrelated, and the *Plan pour la Relance Durable du Mali*, adopted by the interim Malian parliament in February 2013, incorporated the language of the donors. Specifically, the plan called for enforcement of rule of law, good governance, and improved public services together with decentralization in the North in order to increase the legitimacy of the Malian state (Republique 2013). The official Malian plan provided international donors with a blueprint for a conference in May 2013, under the leadership of the Presidents of the EU and France, who pledged to help Mali with 3.25 billion Euros (Raineri 2016, 89). However, the actual practices of the IBK regime undermined many of the official intentions, because factions and clients were constantly favoured at the cost of administrative reforms in the North.

In parallel to the regime's position on the peace process, the Malian state officially embraced administrative reforms, as the parliament adopted various plans that demonstrated its commitment to reforms. President IBK was not slow to pick up on the intentions of the Western donors and in his inaugural speech declared that "no longer is anyone going to get rich off the back of the Malian people" (International Crisis Group 2014, 28). In practice, the regime did very little to change the practices of clientelism and informal accommodation of criminal activities that had hindered efficient state administrations in the past. Indeed, the leaders of the gendarmerie and the national police were both fired by the regime because they tried to fight corruption and enhance meritocratic practices (Bleck et al. 2016, 13). Informal channels were still the main way to regulate affairs in northern Mali.

Obviously, little progress can be expected in terms of public welfare output or state authority in a period of increased violence in northern Mali. In general, institutional reforms are long-term investments that may still improve the capacity and legitimacy of the Malian state in the future. Moreover, the deteriorating security situation explains much of the lacking implementation. For example, only 23 and 27 percent of state officials were present at their duty stations in the northern and middle regions respectively in 2019 (UNSC 2020, 20). What can be examined is the ways in which the regime's practices crippled or strengthened the official goal of administrative reforms. In light of the skewed geographical distribution of violence, the regime appeared to contravene the intention of controlling the northern and the middle regions when only 3,200 out of approximately 13,000 national security forces were in the violence-ridden regions in 2019 (United Nations Security Council 2019, 21).

Decentralization was one of the most contentious elements of the development programme. During the ATT regime, decentralization was synonymous with the withdrawal of the state in northern Mali in return for an end to violence by Tuareg insurgents. The Malian parliament and international donors planned a different kind of decentralization, which strengthened the state administration in addition to the inclusion of local elites. In practice, decentralization bore a close resemblance to past practices. The most telling example of the way the regime used decentralization to co-opt militant groups involved in illicit trading was the creation of two new regions, Taoudeni and Ménaka, in 2016. Both regions were sparsely populated, and the state had little presence. In March 2012, when the new regions were first proposed by the ATT regime, the creation of the units was perceived as a way to buy off powerful traffickers by providing them with official posts and control of trade in the provinces (Lebovich 2017, 15). By reintroducing the bill in 2016, the IBK regime merely reproduced the informal accommodation of factions in the North.

In addition to decentralization, the Malian state needed governance reforms to change the practices of the ATT regime. In May 2013, international donors described the conditions for future aid by stating that "international aid will not resume without a meaningful reform of governance and a determined fight against rampant corruption and embezzlement of public funds" (Donor Conference for Development in Mali 2013). However, Transparency International considered the levels of corruption to be higher in 2020 than in 2012, the year of the ATT regime's downfall. High levels of corruption and a lack of rule of law made IMF temporarily suspend aid in 2014. This was particularly triggered by the IBK regime's decision to acquire a presidential jet at $40 million as well as fraudulent contracting. In addition, the United States did not provide direct assistance for the Malian government out of concern about corruption (Brown 2016, 13). Together this suggests that the problem was on a scale beyond petty corruption and disbursement of public funds. Instead corruption was linked to the regime's practice of political clientelism, which was "returning to past patterns" of the ATT regime according to the Bertelsmann Stiftung (2018).

The return to past patterns of political clientelism was paralytic to governance reforms. Political initiatives had to be acceptable to a broad coalition of political elites as well as to numerous clientelistic networks, which in most cases meant serving economic self-interest. A self-enrichment scheme to create stability that resembled the system set up by the ATT regime (Craven-Matthews and Englebert 2018, 6–7). Instead of pursuing reforms, IBK recirculated elites by appointing six different governments from 2013 to 2020. Moreover, most of the ministers and high-ranking officials had close personal connections to IBK. More generally, Moseley and Hoffman conclude that from 2013 governance reforms were built on a shaky foundation because the political elites tried to recreate the old system (2017, 12–13). The result was pressure on the regime to provide benefits for the ruling coalition, which could not be done if administrative reforms had been implemented. In the end, protests against corruption, nepotism, and electoral fraud became the backdrop of the military coup in 2020.

Despite the obvious lack of administrative reforms from 2013 to 2020, international donors did not make good their initial conditions for providing development aid. In September 2016, the EU announced an increase in development aid until 2020, with a focus on humanitarian needs and the

94 *Mali*

strengthening of the Malian state. In 2020, Mali was included in an additional aid package for Sahel. This might not be surprising given the EU member states' concern about terrorism and migration. Nonetheless, the failure to punish non-compliance would remove the Malian regime's incentive to reform. However, the official acceptance of the donors' conditions made it even more difficult for them to cut ties with the Malian regime and might have provided a fig leaf for continued support.

To sum up, the military junta complied to the initial condition of restoring democracy in return for external assistance. After the intervention, the Malian regime faced two sets of conditions for receiving external assistance, namely participating in a peace and reconciliation process with the non-Jihadist northern actors, and carrying out a genuine reform of the state administration to reduce corruption and increase efficiency. Officially, the regime accepted both demands and expressed support. In practice, the regime undermined the peace process and the administrative reforms to protect the interests of the factions of the ruling coalition in both the North and the South, which added to the worsening of the security situation in the Mopti region and the North. The regime's behaviour closely resembles the expected strategy of simulated statebuilding. Western powers and international aid organizations protested against the lack of progress in the implementation of the peace agreement and informal support to the Platform Group, and the United States protested against corruption. Yet, their reaction was ultimately acceptance.

Conclusion

Western intervention in Mali provides us with a case of three regimes placed in a political settlement dominated by informal politics that faced a comprehensive Western state- and peacebuilding intervention that demanded wide-ranging administrative and political reforms. Despite the presence of large UN forces, EU military trainers, and civilian advisers, the IBK regime continued the practices of the ATT regime. Informal politics shaped state security institutions, and the regimes primarily survived the insurgency wars by relying on client militias in the middle and northern Mali, and on its Western "patrons" as providers of military power and underwriters of the economic viability of the political settlement. The case study also observed the way in which the Bamako-based factions and the northern militant factions restricted the ability of the regime to implement Western-imposed reforms – although the willingness of IBK to support the Western initiatives might also be called into question. The insurgency crisis escalated in 2012 and after 2017, but the political settlement remained in place throughout the examined period.

Until January 2012, the ATT regime prioritized elite units reserved for regime protection at the cost of the regular units. Strategically, the regime applied violence sporadically, which hardly constituted a punishment strategy. After 2013, the same pattern of differentiation between trusted and distrusted units was apparent in the security forces, and the regime applied military force in northern Mali in a similar sporadic fashion. Instead, the ATT regime, the military junta, and the IBK regime all relied on internal alignment with militias in central or northern parts of Mali, and the military junta only reluctantly accepted an external alignment. Despite the presence of international troops, the IBK regime continued its alignment with militias organized in the Platform Group. Several factors caused the peace process to stall or even regress, but what is important for the purpose of this study is that the regime's need for accommodating the demands of factions within the ruling coalition contributed to the negative outcome.

Mali's case suggests that not even detailed Western monitoring of the local regime and use of conditionality are able to change the strategies of local regimes and allow for administrative and political reforms because the demands of the ruling coalition put pressure on the regime. The next chapter on Iraq examines a case of a comparable Western engagement, but with a political settlement that made room for formal politics to play a certain role.

References

Ahmed, Baba. 2011. "Mali: Pourquoi Une Nouvelle Rébellion Touarègue Est Sur Le Point d'éclater." Jeune Afrique, 28 October 2011. http://www.jeuneafrique.com/1 78767/politique/mali-pourquoi-une-nouvelle-r-bellion-touar-gue-est-sur-le-point-d-clater/

Ahmed, Baba. 2012. "Mali: Ce Que Bamako Proposait Au MNLA Avant La Rébellion." *Jeune Afrique*, 31 January 2012. https://www.jeuneafrique.com/1 77514/politique/mali-ce-que-bamako-proposait-au-mnla-avant-la-r-bellion/

Ahmed, Baba. 2016. "Mali: IBK, l'armée et Le Dossier Ag Gamou." Jeune Afrique, 18 July 2016. http://www.jeuneafrique.com/342697/politique/mali-ibk-larmee-dossier-ag-gamou/

Ba, Mehdi. 2015. "Moussa Mara: « Mon Horizon, C'est La Mairie de Bamako." *Jeune Afrique*, 4 December 2015.

Baldaro, Edoardo. 2021. "Rashomon in the Sahel: Conflict Dynamics of Security Regionalism." Security Dialogue 52 (3): 266–283. 10.1177/0967010620934061

Bergamaschi, Isaline. 2014. "The Fall of a Donor Darling: The Role of Aid in Mali's Crisis." *The Journal of Modern African Studies* 52 (3): 347–378. 10.1017/S00222 78X14000251

Bertelsmann Stiftung. 2018. "*Mali Country Report 2018.*" Berlin: Bertelsmann Stiftung. https://www.bti-project.org/content/en/downloads/reports/country_report_2018_ TCD.pdf

Bleck, Jaimie, and Kristin Michelitch. 2015. "The 2012 Crisis in Mali: Ongoing Empirical State Failure." *African Affairs* 114 (457): 598–623. 10.1093/afraf/adv038

Bleck, Jaimie, Abdoulaye Dembele, and Sidiki Guindo. 2016. "Malian Crisis and the Lingering Problem of Good Governance." *Stability: International Journal of Security and Development* 5 (1). 10.5334/sta.457

Boeke, Sergei and Giliam de Valk. 2019. "The Unforeseen 2012 Crisis in Mali: The Diverging Outcomes of Risk and Threat Analyses." *Studies in Conflict & Terrorism* 44 (10), 835–854. 10.1080/1057610X.2019.1592356

96 Mali

Boeke, Sergei and Bart Schuurman. 2015. "Operation 'Serval': A Strategic Analysis of the French Intervention in Mali, 2013–2014." *Journal of Strategic Studies* 38 (6): 801–882. 10.1080/01402390.2015.1045494

Boeke, Sergei and Antonin Tisseron. 2014. "Mali's Long Road Ahead." *The RUSI Journal* 159 (5): 32–40. 10.1080/03071847.2014.969942

Boisbouvier, Christophe, and Malika Groga-Bada. 2012. "Coup d'État Au Mali: Le Jour Où ATT a Été Renversé." *Jeune Afrique*, 30 March 2012. http://www.jeuneafrique.com/142284/politique/coup-d-tat-au-mali-le-jour-o-att-a-t-renvers/ (Accessed 30 August 2019).

Boisvert, Marc-André. 2019. *The Malian Armed Forces and its discontents: civil-military relations, cohesion and the resilience of a postcolonial military institution in the aftermath of the 2012 crisis.* PhD dissertation, University of East Anglia, https://ueaeprints.uea.ac.uk/id/eprint/77807/1/2020BoisvertMAPhD.pdf

Boutellis, Arthur, and Marie-Joëlle Zahar. 2017. *"A Process in Search of Peace: Lessons from the Inter-Malian Agreement."* New York: International Peace Institute. https://css.ethz.ch/en/services/digital-library/publications/publication.html/2e538b3c-6ca2-4 94d-9fe8-fa9b65c70729

Brown, Stephen. 2016. "Putting Paris into Practice: Foreign Aid, National Ownership, and Donor Alignment in Mali and Ghana." 145. Helsinki: United Nations University. https://www.wider.unu.edu/publication/putting-paris-practice

Bøås, Morten, and Strazzari, Francesco. 2020. "Governance, Fragility and Insurgency in the Sahel: A Hybrid Political Order in the Making". *International Spectator* 55 (4): 1–17. 10.1080/03932729.2020.1835324

Bøås, Morten. 2015. "Crime, Coping, and Resistance in the Mali-Sahel Periphery." *African Security* 8 (4): 299–319. 10.1080/19392206.2015.1100506

Bøås, Morten, and Liv Elin Torheim. 2013. "The Trouble in Mali—Corruption, Collusion, Resistance." *Third World Quarterly* 34 (7): 1279–1292. 10.1080/014365 97.2013.824647

Carayol, Par Rémi. 2014. "La Bataille de Kidal, Un Mal Pour Un Bien?" *Jeune Afrique*, 9 June 2014. https://www.jeuneafrique.com/52733/politique/la-bataille-de-kidal-un-mal-pour-un-bien/

Carayol, Par Rémi. 2015. "Sécurité Au Mali: Pour Ibrahim Boubacar Keïta, Une Garantie Nommée Michel Tomi." *Jeune Afrique*, 16 November 2015. https://www.jeuneafrique.com/mag/276036/politique/securite-au-mali-pour-ibrahim-bou-bacar-keita-une-garantie-nommee-michel-tomi/

Carter Center, 2020. *Report of the Independent Observer: Observations on the Implementation of Agreement on Peace and Reconciliation in Mali, Resulting from the Algiers Process.* Atlanta: Carter Center. https://pubhtml5.com/qpno/wlre/

Charbonneau, Bruno. 2017. "Intervention in Mali: building peace between peace-keeping and counterterrorism." *Journal of Contemporary African Studies* 35 (4): 415–431. 10.1080/02589001.2017.1363383

Charbonneau, Bruno, and Jonathan Sears. 2014. "Faire La Guerre Pour Un Mali Démocratique: L'intervention Militaire Française et La Gestion Des Possibilités Politiques Contestées." *Canadian Journal of Political Science* 47 (3): 597–619. 10.1 017/S0008423914000924

Chauzal, Grégory, and Thibault van Damme. 2015. *"The Roots of Mali's Conflict - Moving beyond the 2012 Crisis." The Hague: Netherland's Institute of International*

Relations, Clingendael. https://www.clingendael.org/sites/default/files/pdfs/The_roots_of_Malis_conflict.pdf

Chivvis, Christopher S. 2016. *The French War on Al Qa'ida in Africa.* Cambridge: Cambridge University Press. 10.1017/CBO9781316343388

Cold-Ravnkilde, Signe Marie and Christine Nissen. 2020. "Schizophrenic Agendas in the EU's external actions in Mali." *International Affairs* 96 (4): 935–953. 10.1093/ia/iiaa053

Coulibaly, Massa, and Michael Bratton. 2013. "Crisis in Mali: Ambivalent Popular Attitudes on the Way Forward." *International Journal of Security and Development* 2 (2): 1–10. 10.5334/sta.bn

Cramon, Eric. 2019. "Ethnic Group Institutions and Electoral Clientelism." *Party Politics* 25 (3): 435–447. 10.1177/1354068817728212

Craven-Matthews, Catriona and Pierre Englebert. 2018. "A Potemkin State in the Sahel? The Empirical and the Fictional in Malian State Reconstruction." *African Security* 11 (1): 1–31. 10.1080/19392206.2017.1419634

Cristiani, Dario, and Riccardo Fabiani. 2013. "The Malian Crisis and Its Actors." *The International Spectator: Italian Journal of International Affairs* 48 (3): 78–97. 10.1080/03932729.2013.823731

Desgrais, N., Guichaoua, Y., and Lebovich, A. 2018. Unity Is the Exception. Alliance Formation and de-formation among armed actors in Northern Mali. Small Wars and Insurgencies 29 (4): 654–679. 10.1080/09592318.2018.1488403

Diallo, Aïssatou. 2020. "*Ce qu'il faut savoir sur Assimi Goïta, le nouvel homme fort du Mali*". Jeune Afrique. https://www.jeuneafrique.com/1031853/politique/ce-quil-faut-savoir-sur-assimi-goita-le-nouvel-homme-fort-du-mali/ (Accessed 20 August 2020)

Diallo, Aïssatou and Marième Soumaré. 2020. "*Mali Coup d'État: The Soldiers Who Brought Down IBK*". The Africa Report. https://www.theafricareport.com/38414/mali-coup-detat-the-soldiers-who-brought-down-ibk/ (Accessed 20 August 2020)

Donor Conference for Development in Mali. 2013. "*Together for a New Mali.*" www.donor-conference-mali.eu (Accessed 2 May 2016).

Erforth, Benedikt. 2020. "Multilateralism as a Tool: Exploring French Military Cooperation in the Sahel." *Journal of Strategic Studies* 43 (4): 560–582. 10.1080/01402390.2020.1733986

Fay, Claude. 1995. "La Démocratie Au Mali, Ou Le Pouvoir En Pâture." *Cahiers D'études Africaines* 35 (137): 19–53. 10.3406/cea.1995.2022

Guichaoua, Yvan. 2020. "The Bitter Harvest of French Interventionism in the Sahel". *International Affairs* 96 (4): 895–911. 10.1093/ia/iiaa094

Hagberg, Sten, and Gabriella Körling. 2012. "Socio-Political Turmoil in Mali: The Public Debate Following the Coup D'État on 22 March 2012." *Africa Spectrum* 2 (3): 111–125. 10.1177/000203971204702-306

Harmon, Stephen A. 2014. *Terror and Insurgency in the Sahara-Sahel Region: Corruption, Contraband, Jihad and the Mali War of 2012-2013.* London: Routledge. 10.4324/9781315612096

Henningsen, Troels B. 2021. "The Crafting of Alliance Cohesion Among Insurgents: The Case of al-Qaeda Affiliated Groups in the Sahel Region". *Contemporary Security Policy*, online version. 10.1080/13523260.2021.1876455

Human Rights Watch. 2018. ""We Used to Be Brothers": Self-Defense Group Abuses in Central Mali." New York: Human Rights Watch. https://www.hrw.org/report/2018/12/07/we-used-be-brothers/self-defense-group-abuses-central-mali.

98 *Mali*

Human Rights Watch. 2020a. *"Mali: Security Forces Use Excessive Force at Protests"*. New York: Human Rights Watch. https://www.hrw.org/news/2020/08/12/mali-security-forces-use-excessive-force-protests (Accessed 18 March 2021).

Human Rights Watch. 2020b. *"Army, UN Fail to Stop Massacre"*. New York: Human Rights Watch. https://www.hrw.org/news/2020/03/18/mali-army-un-fail-stop-massacre (Accessed 18 March 2021).

International Crisis Group. 2012. *"Mali: Avoiding Escalation."* Brussels: International Crisis Group. https://www.crisisgroup.org/africa/west-africa/mali/mali-avoiding-escalation (Accessed 24 October 2019).

International Crisis Group. 2014. *"Mali: Last Chance in Algiers."* Brussels: International Crisis Group. https://www.crisisgroup.org/africa/west-africa/mali/mali-last-chance-algiers (Accessed 10 February 2018).

International Crisis Group. 2020. *"Reversing Central Mali's Descent into Communal Violence"*. Brussels: International Crisis Group. https://www.crisisgroup.org/africa/sahel/mali/293-enrayer-la-communautarisation-de-la-violence-au-centre-du-mali (Accessed 3 March 2021).

Keita, Ibrahim Boubacar. 2016. "President of the Republic of Mali Delivers Remarks at the United Nations General Assembly, General Debate of the 71st Assembly." New York: Political Transcript Wire.

Lebovich, Andrew. 2017. "Reconstructing Local Orders in Mali: Historical Perspectives and Future Challenges." 7. *Local Orders Paper Series*. Washington D.C.: Brookings Institute. https://www.brookings.edu/research/reconstructing-local-orders-in-mali-historical-perspectives-and-future-challenges/

Lecocq, Baz. 2010. *Disputed Desert Decolonisation, Competing Nationalisms and Tuareg Rebellions in Northern Mali*. Boston: Brill. 10.1163/ej.9789004139831.i-433

Lecocq, Baz, Gregory Mann, Bruce Whitehouse, Dida Badi, Lotte Pelckmans, Nadia Belalimat, Bruce Hall, and Wolfram Lacher. 2013. "One Hippopotamus and Eight Blind Analysts: A Multivocal Analysis of the 2012 Political Crisis in the Divided Republic of Mali." *Review of African Political Economy* 40 (137): 343–357. 10.1080/03056244.2013.799063

Mann, Gregory. 2015. From Empires to NGOs in the West African Sahel - The Road to Nongovernmentality. Cambridge: Cambridge University Press. 10.1017/CBO9781139061209

Marchal, Roland. 2012. *The Coup in Mali: The Result of a Long-Term Crisis or Spillover from the Libyan Civil War?* Oslo: Norwegian Peacebuilding ressource centre. https://reliefweb.int/sites/reliefweb.int/files/resources/3a582f1883e8809a0e18cd2d58a09a81.pdf

McGregor, Andrew. 2013. "Red Berets, Green Berets: Can Mali's Divided Military Restore Order and Stability?" *Terrorism Monitor* 11 (4): 1–10. https://jamestown.org/program/red-berets-green-berets-can-malis-divided-military-restore-order-and-stability/

MINUSMA. 2020. *"Note sur les tendances des violations et abus de droits de l'homme au Mali 1ᵉʳ avril – 30 juin 2020"*. Bamako: MINUSMA. https://minusma.unmissions.org/sites/default/files/note_trimestrielle_tendances_des_violations_et_abus_de_dh_avril-juin_2020_final_version.pdf

Moseley, William G., and Barbara G. Hoffman. 2017. "Introduction: Hope, Despair, and the Future of Mali." *African Studies Review* 60 (1): 5–14. 10.1017/asr.2017.12

Pezard, Stephanie, and Michael Shurkin. 2015. *Achieving Peace in Northern Mali: Past Agreements, Local Conflicts, and the Prospects for a Durable Settlement.* Santa Monica: RAND Corporation. https://www.rand.org/pubs/research_reports/RR892.html

Powell, Jonathan M. 2014. "Trading Coups for Civil War." *African Security Review* 23 (4): 329–338. 10.1080/10246029.2014.944196

Powelson, Simon J. 2013. *"Enduring Engagement Yes, Episodic Engagement No: Lessons for SOF From Mali."* Monterey: Naval Postgraduate School, Defense Analysis. https://calhoun.nps.edu/handle/10945/38996

Raineri, Luca. 2016. "Mali: The Short-Sightedness of Donor-Driven Peacebuilding." *Journal of Peacebuilding & Development* 11 (1): 88–92. 10.1080/15423166.2016.1145516

Raineri, Luca. 2020. "Gold Mining in the Sahara-Sahel: The Political Geography of State-making and Unmaking." *The International Spectator* 55 (4): 100–117. 10.1080/03932729.2020.1833475

Raineri, Luca, and Francesco Strazzari. 2015. "State, Secession, and Jihad: The Micropolitical Economy of Conflict in Northern Mali." *African Security* 8 (4): 249–271. 10.1080/19392206.2015.1100501

Raleigh, Clionadh, Andrew Linke, Håvard Hegre, and Joakim Karlsen (2010). Introducing ACLED: An Armed Conflict Location and Event Dataset. *Journal of Peace Research* 47 (5): 1–10. 10.1177/002 2343310378914

Republique du Mali. 2013. *"Plan Pour La Relance Durable Du Mali 2013-2014."* Bamako: Republique du Mali. https://reliefweb.int/report/mali/plan-pour-la-relance-durable-du-mali-2013-2014

RFI. 2015. "Mali: À Gao, IBK Réaffirme Le Rôle de l'ONU Dans Le Pays." *Radio France Internationale*, 30 January 2015. https://www.rfi.fr/fr/afrique/20150130-mali-gao-ibk-reaffirme-le-role-onu-le-pays

Scheele, Judith. 2011. "Circulations Marchandes Au Sahara: Entre Licite et Illicite." *Hérodote* 142 (3): 143. 10.3917/her.142.0143

Schmitt, Eric. 2014. "U.S. Training Elite Antiterror Troops in Four African Nations." *New York Times*, 27 May 2014. https://www.nytimes.com/2014/05/27/world/africa/us-trains-african-commandos-to-fight-terrorism.html (Accessed 7 March 2019).

Shurkin, Michael, Stephanie Pezard, and S Rebecca Zimmerman. 2017. *"Mali's Next Battle Improving Counterterrorism Capabilities."* Los Angeles: RAND Corporation. https://www.rand.org/pubs/research_reports/RR1241.html

Solomon, Hussein. 2015. *Terrorism and Counter-Terrorism in Africa.* New York: Palgrave Macmillan. 10.1057/9781137489890

Touchard, Laurent. 2014. "Défense: Où En Sont Les Forces Armées Maliennes?" *Jeune Afrique*, 11 June 2014. https://www.jeuneafrique.com/52526/politique/d-fense-o-en-sont-les-forces-arm-es-maliennes/

Tull, Denis M. 2019. "Rebuilding Mali's Army: The Dissonant Relationship between Mali and Its International Partners". *International Affairs* 95 (2): 405–422. 10.1093/ia/iiz003

United Nations Security Council. 2019. Situation in Mali: Report of the Secretary-General. New York: United Nations Security Council. https://www.securitycouncilreport.org/atf/cf/%7B65BFCF9B-6D27-4E9C-8CD3-CF6E4FF96FF9%7D/s_2019_454.pdf

100 *Mali*

United Nations Security Council. 2020. *"Final report of the Panel of Experts established pursuant to Security Council resolution 2374 (2017) on Mali and renewed pursuant to resolution 2484 (2019)"*. New York: United Nations Security Council. https://digitallibrary.un.org/record/3876820?ln=en

Venturi, Bernardo and Nana Toure. 2020. "The Great Illusion: Security Sector Reform in the Sahel". *The International Spectator* 55 (4), 54–68. 10.1080/03932729.2020.1835326

Vliet, Martin Van. 2014. "Weak Legislatures, Failing MPs, and the Collapse of Democracy in Mali." *African Affairs* 113 (450): 45–66. 10.1093/afraf/adt071

Walle, Nicolas van de. 2012. "The Path from Neopatrimonialism: Democracy and Clientelism in Africa Today." In *Neopatrimonialism in Africa and Beyond*, edited by Daniel C. Bach and Mamoudou Gazib, 111–123. London: Routledge.

Warner, Lesley Anne. 2014. *"The Trans Sahara Counter Terrorism Partnership: Building Partner Capacity to Counter Terrorism and Violent Extremism."* Washington D.C.: Center for Complex Operation, National Defense University. https://www.cna.org/cna_files/pdf/crm-2014-u-007203-final.pdf

Wing, Susanna D. 2008. *Constructing Democracy in Transitioning Societies of Africa: Constitutionalism and Deliberation in Mali*. New York: Palgrave Macmillan. 10.1057/9780230612075

Wing, Susanna D. 2013. "Mali: Politics of a Crisis." *African Affairs* 112 (448): 476–485. 10.1093/afraf/adt037

5 Iraq: fighting the Islamic State with an unstable alliance

In August 2014, the fall of Mosul and the declaration of the Caliphate marked the culminating point of the dramatic downturn in the stability of Iraq since the withdrawal of the United States' military in December 2011. Against the instincts of President Obama, the United States reengaged, but not until forcing a regime change to increase the likelihood that the Iraqi regime would implement administrative and political reforms. At the end of 2017, the Islamic State (IS) had lost its territorial gains, but for the United States the question of administrative and political reforms was still urgent in order to avoid renewed conflicts and Iranian dominance in Iraq. Even though the Hadr al-Abadi regime managed to hold the anti-IS coalition together and realized a few reforms, it nonetheless lost the parliamentary elections in 2018.

The case of Iraq 2011–2018 is of interest to this study, because, on the one hand, militarized elites dominated the Iraqi society, and, on the other hand, the Iraqi state had formal political institutions able to accommodate some of the demands of the militarized elites. The case, therefore, provides an example that would include different degrees of simulated statebuilding and co-operation, depending on the issue. Iraq is also a case of an intervening power that returns to a site of a former major statebuilding effort. For the United States, it was of national interest to build on its previous statebuilding efforts to create a strong formal state in Iraq. A formal state would be able to counter militant Sunni extremism and counter informal Iranian influence in the Iraqi state, especially the security institutions. Moreover, the US strategy was to aid, advise, and assist the Iraqi forces, which hinged on the (re)establishment of capable security institutions. Prime Minister Al-Abadi had an interest in complying with US demands that would strengthen his powerbase, yet he needed to reconcile US demands with domestic pressure from militarized elites that thrived on informal politics. To study how al-Abadi reconciled formal and informal impetuses offers an opportunity to understand how the political dynamics of Western interventions can unfold in a mixed political settlement.

The first section gauges the importance of informal politics in the political settlement, the second section analyses to what extent the praetorian protection

DOI: 10.4324/9781003204978-5

102   *Iraq*

proposition explains the Iraqi regimes' choices concerning the security institutions and military strategy in the period after the US withdrawal in 2011. The third section examines the proposition of risk-averse alignment by focusing on the regimes' use of alignment in the relatively short period 2014–2017. The fourth section studies the regimes' interaction with Western powers to establish to what extent the proposition of simulated statebuilding explains the behaviour of the regimes.

Formal power-sharing arrangements and informal accommodation

The invasion of Iraq in 2003 was the United States' conscious attempt to redefine Iraq to become a democratic beacon for the Middle East (Belloni and Costantini 2019, 517). The result was a complete reversal of the Iraqi political settlement, so that previously excluded Shia and Kurdish elites now gained power, but it excluded the once powerful Sunni Arab elites. Nevertheless, the factions of the new ruling coalition and the excluded elites were all established militarized elites. The formal power-sharing arrangements in the new Iraqi constitution accommodated many of the militarized elites. Yet, the successive regimes of Nour al-Maliki (2006–2014) and Haider al-Abadi (2014–2018) needed to complement this with informal accommodation through clientelism, which reduced the importance of programmatic ideas in Iraqi party politics.

Invasion, civil war, and the shift in the ruling coalition

The year 2003 is a critical juncture in any analysis of the political settlement in Iraq and the role of informal politics. Before the invasion the regime of Saddam Hussein had relied on a narrow coalition of Sunni Arab elites organized in the Ba'ath Party, which dominated the state institutions and especially the security forces (Haddad 2020, 265ff). Sunni Arabs were a minority of around 20 percent of the Iraqi population. However, the almost exclusive reliance on oil income made it possible for the Hussein regime to fund a vast set of security institutions, many of them tasked with suppressing excluded elites or other dissident voices. Even so, the Ba'ath Party and state institutions were drained of resources due to the loss of loyal Ba'athists during the Iran-Iraq war in the 1980s and the loss of state income as a result of international sanctions in the 1990s. The ruling coalition became increasingly dependent on lower level factions among the Sunni tribes to deliver internal security and to organize the life of ordinary Iraqis (Jabar 2000, Marr 2017, ff. 213).

Not only did the Iraq-Iran war strengthen the Sunni tribes, it also sharpened the definition of the factions among the excluded Shia and Kurdish elites. Initially, the Shia opposition organized in the Islamic Dawa Party, but a pro-Iranian faction split and organized into the Supreme Council of the

Iraq 103

Islamic Revolution, and its Badr-militia, who became clients of the Iranian regime (Gulmohamad 2021, 3ff). The Dawa Party continued its nationalist outlook whilst remaining in Iran. Kurdish elites had splintered before the war, and the Kurdistan Democratic Party (KDP) fought the Patriotic Union of Kurdistan (PUK) in the 1970s. Yet, during the 1980s both groups aligned with Iran and received military assistance in return, which was one the motivations behind the Hussein regime's infamous Anfal genocidal campaign (Gunter 1993, 295–296). The weakening of the Hussein regime in 1991, and the subsequent no-fly zone, allowed the Kurdish elites to establish de facto autonomy in northern Iraq, which they used to force a fait accompli of Kurdish autonomy after the fall of Saddam Hussein.

The readily available elites of the previous decades took advantage of the regime's overthrow in 2003. After the end of the transitional government, a ruling coalition consisting mostly of Islamist Shia-elites took power in 2006. Three factions dominated, namely the nationalist Dawa Party, the Sadr movement under the leadership of Muqtada al-Sadr, and the pro-Iranian Supreme Council of the Islamic Revolution (Grinstead et al. 2017, 17ff). The Kurds also took part in the ruling coalition and held the presidency due to the power-sharing arrangements of the constitution and the political compromises between Kurdish and Shia Arab elites. The United States' recognition of the de facto Kurdish autonomy made it possible to accommodate the Kurdish factions formally. The constitution delegated the Kurdish regional parliament the right to legislate, formally acknowledging the Kurdish Peshmerga, as well as ensuring the economic viability through the transfer of oil income. Therefore, many of the demands of the Kurdish militarized factions were satisfied (Palani et.al. 2019, 6).

Shia factions disagreed internally, and the al-Maliki regime found it harder to accommodate them formally, because by the design of the constitution the United States sought to avoid the complete dominance of the Shia bloc, despite their demographic advantage. The power of the Shia elites grew as violence spiked in 2006, and the Shia militias, most notably the Badr militia and al-Sadr's Mahdi army, proved to be the most efficient in protecting Shia neighbourhoods (Thurber 2014, 911–912). The militias appealed to different social classes, and were able to mobilize certain Shia segments but not to turn their military success into a wider electoral success (ibid, 918).

Suspicion and disagreement broke down the cooperation among the Shia factions, and changes in their relative power meant that informal accommodation had to be renegotiated, often with the assistance of Iran. For example, in 2008, Prime Minister al-Maliki ordered an attack on the Mahdi army to reduce the power of al-Sadr and to enhance his own standing as a non-sectarian leader (Mansour and Jabar 2017, 5). However, the parliamentary elections in 2010 made al-Maliki dependent on the Sadr movement to form a new government. Iranian pressure and mediation alone secured a new al-Maliki government that included the al-Ahrar Party of the Sadr movement and the Supreme Council of the Islamic Revolution. The price

104 *Iraq*

was that al-Sadr now had the power to distribute oil income to his vast network of clients, and the regime had to codify its alignment with the pro-Iranian militia of Hadi al-Ameri, the Badr-militia, to exist formally as a military organization (Eisenstadt et al. 2011, 3). The example also demonstrates Iran's central role in the negotiations of the political settlement, due to its close contact with Shia factions, support for the pro-Iranian parties, ability to create new militant groups, and support for the use of force against the United States (Seliktar and Rezaei 2020, 153). This allowed Iran to limit the factions' ability to threaten with violence, although some of the militarized Shia factions were occasionally at odds with Iran.

In terms of demography and economy, the Shia and Kurdish ruling coalition was much stronger than the excluded Sunni elites. However, because of the retribalization in the last 20 years of Saddam Hussein's rule, the Sunni tribes had considerable capacity to organize militant resistance against the ruling coalition. The decision of the United States' Coalition Provisional Authority to remove all former members of the Ba'ath Party provided the Sunni tribes and the Islamist insurgent groups with organizational and military knowledge, not least from the former officer corps. The result was a devastating insurgency that only declined in 2008 as a result of a surge in the number of United States combat troops, new tactics, and the co-optation of Sunni tribes to combat al-Qaeda (Biddle et al. 2012). However, the inclusion of Sunni tribes in the security forces was short-lived and the Syrian civil war provided the militant Sunni Islamists with a new opportunity to combat the ruling coalition in Iraq.

In summary, the radical shift in the ruling coalition in 2003 meant that those who gained power were readily available elites specialized in violence. In addition, the Sunni insurgency increased the power of the Shia militias, and the al-Maliki regime was forced to informally accommodate them, because the power-sharing arrangement kept in place by the United States prevented the regime from formally catering to all the demands of the militarized Shia elites (Dodge 2018a, 35). However, Iran's influence limited the Shia factions' ability to threaten the regime with violence. The Kurdish factions benefited from the formal power-sharing arrangements and mostly worked peacefully with the regime, whereas most Sunni elites were excluded from the political settlement due to their links to the Ba'ath Party and the former regime.

Oil and the need for clientelism

In 2006 al-Maliki, the newly elected Prime Minister, mostly focused on accommodating the Kurdish and Shia factions of the ruling coalition besides the few Sunni politicians in the government. Oil thoroughly dominated Iraqi economy and enabled both formal and informal accommodation of the ruling coalition's factions. Iraqi oil income constituted around 80 percent of GDP between 2009 and 2013 (World Bank 2014, 8). Taxes and royalties from oil

Iraq 105

production made up 94 percent of the state income in 2014 (International Monetary Fund 2016, 7). Moreover, rents from US foreign aid to the security sector alone amounted to $1.2 billion in 2012. The constitution (article 112) prescribed that oil income was to be distributed fairly among the regions, which was mostly a synonym for the sectarian groups. This provision meant that the Kurdish factions of the ruling coalition could formally receive 17 percent of the total oil income. This is not to say that clientelism did not play a role in Kurdish politics, but it was mainly necessary in order to accommodate lower level factions among the Kurds.

The Shia militias had political wings, and because their parties were part of the government, oil-based clientelism was fixated around the control of ministries. A senior judge explained this as being part of the political culture: "As long as political parties treat ministries as their private bank accounts and as long as courts and law enforcement officials are not given the legal means to prevent this, high-level corruption will continue." (International Crisis Group 2011, 10). Al-Sadr and al-Ameri, two of the actors most crucial in the negotiations with Iran in 2010, gained access to ministries with the potential for grand-scale embezzlement. They both took full advantage. The Sadr movement obtained several ministries, but especially the Ministry of Construction and Housing provided the opportunity for huge economic advantages, which al-Sadr could use to pay his extensive network (Zaid 2014). Al-Ameri became Minister of the Interior, which the Badr organization used to employ numerous members of its militia in the police forces as well as to siphon money to the larger client network (Salehyan 2020, 110). The greatest sums, however, went to al-Maliki's own party, which controlled the Ministry of Oil and the Ministry of Defence.

The Dawa Party and the Prime Minister did not have a strong militia. To avoid becoming too dependent on other Shia-militias, the regime needed to ensure the loyalty of clients in the state institutions. Prime Minister al-Maliki built a strong client network that dominated the executive branch of the Iraqi state. Clients of al-Maliki came to be known as 'Malikiyouns' to signify their personal allegiance (Hoekstra 2020, 693). The Malikiyouns were primarily al-Maliki's family members or Dawa Party functionaries loyal to al-Maliki, not to the party. While most factions used clientelism, al-Maliki took it one step further by removing administrative obstacles to the practice. He was able to push the Supreme Court to rule that the oversight of public spending and the investigation of corruption were to be under the executive rather than the legislative branch (Schmidt and Healy 2011). The use of oil income for clientelism was a way for the Shia factions to secure their power within the ruling coalition, either by placing their clients in the movement's civil and military wings within the state, or by rewarding them with other benefits.

106 *Iraq*

Programmatic politics and the political wings of the militarized elites

Formal political institutions, especially the parliament, were important in Iraqi politics, because the factions within the ruling elite, and even some excluded elites, were organized in political parties. As a result, party politics and negotiations in the parliament reflected the interests of the strongest elites in the Iraqi society (Boduszyński 2016, 114). Political parties used the parliamentary platform to express criticism of the regime, to protect the formal limits to its power, and to promote their political goals (Dodge and Mansour 2020, 66–67). At the same time, political parties also functioned as vessels for clientelism. Hence, the parties often distributed benefits according to narrow, personal criteria rather than their declared programmatic goals. As a result, programmatic and clientelistic practices were intertwined features of Iraqi politics.

A look at the interplay among the Shia factions in the ruling coalition shows that there is more at stake than tactical positioning to increase power and improve access to patronage. The Dawa Party, the Supreme Islamic Iraqi Council (formerly known as the revolutionary council), the Sadr movement's Party all sought an Islamist political order based broadly on the principles of Shia Islam. Al-Sadr, who often made opportunistic choices whether to stay in or leave the government and launch public protests, rested his politics on the activist ideology promoted by his family of Shia clerics since the 1950s. Moreover, the political programme laid out by al-Sadr's father and his father's uncle also pointed to the need to mobilize the lowest social classes in southern Iraq and Baghdad and cooperate with the Shia Arab tribes (Rizvi 2010, 1303–4). The Dawa Party also drew heavily on the teachings of the first two generations of the al-Sadr clerics, and, moreover, gained the support and tacit backing of Ayatollah Ali al-Sistani, the highest Shia authority in Iraq, when the Shia parties united in the electoral coalition in 2006 (ibid, 1310).

Another example of the significance of programmatic politics was the disagreement on the role of pan-Shiism vis-à-vis an Iraqi nationalist Shiism. Besides the mentioned split between the Supreme Islamic Iraqi Council and the Dawa Party, al-Hezbollah and Asa'ib Ahl al-Haq (AAH) broke with al-Sadr once he chose a form of nationalist Shiism. In parallel, the Supreme Islamic Iraqi Council chose a nationalist line, which led the Badr organization to break away from the council. The splinter parties envisioned a pan-Islamist order under the leadership of Iran, whereas the Dawa Party was much closer to the position of al-Sistani, who saw the unity of an Islamist Iraq as the political goal (Isakhan & Mulherin 2020, 370). Still, the parties cooperated in the parliament and accepted Iranian mediation. In parallel, the two centres of power in the Kurdish areas, KDP and PUK, had severe historical and political differences, stemming from reoccurring armed clashes and the contrast between the socialist outlook of PUK and the more

Iraq 107

conservative, nationalist ideology of KDP (Pischedda 2020, 43ff). However, ideological differences had become less important after years of cooperation and the accommodation of lower level factions through clientelism.

Most of the programmatic differences went along sectarian lines. In fact, the role of sectarianism in Iraqi politics became so considerable that in 2015, 95 percent of all Iraqis considered politicians and parties as "very responsible" for creating divisions and obstructing reconciliation (Boduszyński 2016, 115). However, within the sectarian blocs, and even in some cases between the blocs, clientelism diverged the parties away from their religious or ideological goals. The most important Iraqi parties pursued a political agenda that represented a compromise between their programmatic goals, developed over decades, and their acute need to build and maintain vast clientelistic networks.

In summary, the new political settlement in Iraq following the toppling of Saddam Hussein in 2003 formalized a power-sharing arrangement among the major sectarian groups in Iraq. Consequently, the militarized Kurdish factions within the ruling coalition gained formal access to patronage to distribute to their clients and they could formally uphold their Peshmerga militias. Iran's influence allowed the militarized Shia elites to pursue at least some programmatic goals through political representation in the parliament and in the government. However, to keep the ruling coalition together the Iraqi regime used informal, clientelistic practices to accommodate the militarized Shia factions by allowing them access to state institutions. In Iraqi politics, both programmatic and informal considerations influenced the choices of the elites.

Praetorian protection: the hollow army and the politicized elite forces

This study expects regimes in an informal political setting to reserve elite units for praetorian protection, and to use a military strategy of punishment with indiscriminate attacks in order to raise the cost of continuing an insurgency. However, politics in Iraq was not entirely dominated by informal politics. So how did the regimes react to the violent protests in 2012–2013 and to IS's conquest of large parts of western and northern Iraq in 2014 and 2015? This section argues that al-Maliki and al-Abadi organized and applied the security forces in ways caught between the logic of tolerating competing client networks and that of increasing the capacity of the security forces. This section is structured into three parts. The first and second parts examine the structure and strategy of the security forces during the al-Maliki regime, whereas the third part tracks changes during the al-Abadi regime.

Al-Maliki's attempt to take personal control of the security forces

In 2011, the al-Maliki regime's security outlook was auspicious. The Islamic State in Iraq and the Levant was a dormant organization with as few as

108 *Iraq*

1,000 active members (Knights 2014, 3). Seen in that light, the inability of the regime and the United States to reach an agreement to extend the presence of American combat troops carried little military risk. On the contrary, as the United States began its withdrawal from Iraq, the al-Maliki regime had more liberty to alter the organization, functions, and purposes of the Iraqi security forces. A liberty that al-Maliki used to gain personal control of the security forces to increase his power vis-à-vis the other Shia factions. The price was a drop in the efficiency of the security forces and waning acceptance of his regime among the ruling coalition.

At the heart of al-Maliki's security apparatus was the Counter Terrorism Service (CTS), which was trained by the United States Special Forces (Hoekstra 2020, 692). The Prime Minister took control of CTS to such a degree that it became a praetorian guard for al-Maliki. The units were outside the oversight of the Ministry of Defence and the Ministry of the Interior, and was effectively al-Maliki's personal force. Accordingly, after taking personal control in 2006, al-Maliki expanded the CTS from 1600 to 13,000 personnel in late 2013 (ibid). Among Iraqis, CTS was known as "Fedayeen al-Maliki", with a reference to Saddam Hussein's secret police (Yaphe 2012). The net result was the inception of a strong military actor whose purpose and operations were to protect the regime against any legitimate and illegitimate threats to its hold on power.

Organizationally, al-Maliki enhanced the Prime Minister's control of all security forces. To circumvent the power of Abdul Obeidi, the Sunni Minister of Defence, al-Maliki enhanced the role of the Office of the Commander in Chief and moved it into the office of the Prime Minister. The office began giving orders down to battalion level in violation of the chain of command (Dodge 2014, 12–13). Similarly, al-Maliki ordered the formation of and commanded the Provincial Command Centres, which coordinated all military and police activity. Finally, from 2010 Prime Minister al-Maliki avoided appointing a new Minister of Defence or Minister of the Interior, leaving himself in charge. This move reduced the formal accommodation of the Badr movement, who previously controlled the Ministry of the Interior. There is little doubt that the Shia factions still kept clients in the security forces, but the regime attempted to monopolize the control of the forces.

Client networks were the key in al-Maliki's attempt to control the security forces. As early as 2010, nine out of 18 senior commanders in the Iraqi Security Forces were long-time members of the Dawa Party (Salmoni 2011, 18). Professional, capable generals were replaced with persons lacking the same credentials, but loyal to al-Maliki. The most obvious sign of the strife for personal loyalty was the appointment of Ahmed al-Maliki, the son of the Prime Minister, as Deputy Chief of Staff (Hoekstra 2020, 692). Moreover, clientelism had a degrading effect on the regular forces, which suffered from low combat readiness and morale. The breakdown of meritocratic practices – even though they might have been limited previously – led to widespread corruption among division commanders. Generals not handpicked by al-Maliki paid graft to gain commissions as division commanders. Or rather, they

Iraq 109

made investments that were returned by withholding payments, logistics, and keeping deserted soldiers on the official payrolls (Knights 2016, 17–18). The decline in the efficiency of the regular army units was a major explanation for the stunning advances of IS in 2014 and 2015. Moreover, by reducing the ability of other Shia factions to develop their client networks in the security forces, al-Maliki reduced his own political support in the parliament. Nevertheless, in the short term he took full advantage of the small, politicized elite units to carry out strikes against the legitimate political opposition and to punish protestors in 2012 and 2013.

A strategy of punishment against Sunni-protests in 2012–2014

Thousands of Sunni Arabs in the Anbar and Nineveh provinces flooded the streets in December 2012. The immediate cause was the arrest of persons close to Rafi al-Issawi, a Sunni politician, but it was also a reaction to the general marginalization of Sunnis in politics and the public administration. Al-Maliki reacted to the protests by using a strategy of punishment to increase the cost of protesting. Interestingly, al-Maliki primarily relied on CTS units, which we would have expected to be reserved for regime protection. However, the punishment strategy mostly demonstrated the ineptness of the security forces and pushed important Sunni tribes to align with IS after the non-violent protests proved unsuccessful.

Politically, the al-Maliki regime effectively closed the door on negotiations. During an electoral conference in April 2013 in the Shia-dominated city of Nasiriyah, al-Maliki said the ranks of the protestors were "teeming with members of al-Qaeda and the Ba'ath Party" (Abbas 2013). Unsurprisingly, Sunni leaders interpreted al-Maliki's political and military response as a step in al-Maliki's strategy to close yet another channel of influence for the Sunnis. The harshness of al-Maliki's domestic rhetorical stance was reinforced by the actions taken by the Iraqi security forces. From the onset, brigades from the army and CTS units under the direct control of al-Maliki forcefully controlled protestors. The most important turning point was the raid of the Hawija protest camp in April 2013. The Dilja Command, a CTS unit directly controlled by al-Maliki, was behind the killing of at least 50 (more likely hundreds of) protestors, which sparked violent clashes between the security forces and protestors in Mosul and Falluja for example (O'Driscoll 2014, 5). The use of violence against the protestors was part of the regime's strategy to quell Sunni dissent with as little cost as possible.

The tribal uprising demonstrated that the regime was willing to use elite forces to punish the protestors, but also that the personalized security forces, apart from CTS, quickly fell apart when the resistance became organized. Many soldiers and police officers proved more loyal to their tribes or religious leaders than to the regime, and joined rank with the protestors (Jensen 2016, 4). However, the inefficiency of the regular forces was not the

110 *Iraq*

result of the regime's co-optation of former insurgents and militias, but the al-Maliki regime's attempt to take personal control of the security forces.

The military organization and strategy of the al-Abadi regime

In August 2014, new Prime Minister al-Abadi was thrown into acting as commander-in-chief of the Iraqi security forces in the face of the IS advancing forces. The United States' military involvement makes it difficult to determine the independent choices made by the al-Abadi regime. American assistance focused on an indirect by-with-and-through approach (or liquid warfare approach as introduced in the introduction), where the international coalition provided air power, training, special forces, and intelligence. However, the strategy hinged on Iraqi ground forces, although many of them were not part of the armed forces. By tracking how the Iraqi army was rebuilt after its string of initial defeats in 2014–2015, it becomes possible to glimpse the impact of formal politics on security institutions. Furthermore, the section analyses the role of the security institutions in the military strategy that allowed al-Abadi to declare victory on 9 December 2017.

From a personally loyal force to a neutral and capable force?

In August 2014, the quick disintegration of fourteen army brigades and six federal police brigades, as well as massive desertion among the remaining units, resulted in a state of chaos (Knights 2016, 21). To evaluate the behaviour of the regime in relation to the reconstruction of the security institutions, we need to consider it in the context of this chaotic starting point. Inherent Resolve, the US-led mission to fight IS, contributed greatly to the reconstruction. Training took place at a dazzling speed. In 2014–2017 126,500 security forces had been trained by the U.S.-led coalition (Combined Joint Task Force – Operation Inherent Resolve 2017). However, the outcome of the effort was less spectacular. In July 2017 a report to the United States Congress estimated that only two brigades were able to conduct offensive operations (United States Government Accountability Office 2017). Moreover, desertions remained widespread, and recruitment problems plagued the army, as the Shia militias recruited more effectively (Mansour and Jabar 2017, 11). On balance, the type of offensive operations that the reconquering of IS territory required differed from the Iraqi army's previous mission of controlling territory, and the army slowly adapted (Broekhof et al. 2019, 23). For the purposes of the praetorian protection proposition, the main point is that the al-Abadi regime did not obstruct the reconstruction of the army, as the proposition would have expected, had Iraq been purely dominated by informal politics.

Publicly, al-Abadi emphasized the importance and independence of the Iraqi security forces, which must be understood as a political move in the light of the distribution of military power in Iraq. The Prime Minister's office formally directed key elite units, such as CTS, and the three

Iraq 111

presidential brigades. However, the Badr movement controlled the Ministry of the Interior, and its paramilitary federal police forces. Minister of Defence Khaled al-Obeidi, a Sunni and ally with al-Abadi, controlled parts of the army, such as the 6th and 9th army divisions that took part in key battles in the Anbar province and Mosul in 2016–2017 (Rose Dury-Agri et al. 2017). However, other factions of the ruling coalition had de facto leadership of several parts of the Iraqi army. In particular, the Dijla Operations Command and the Fifth Army Division reported to the Badr militias' chain of command rather than to the Ministry of Defence. Remarkably, in 2015 Abdul-Wahhab al-Saadi, the Commander of the Salah al-Din Operations Command, was removed by the pro-Iranian militias during operations to recapture Tikrit, because he insisted on cooperating with the Inherent Resolve coalition (ibid, 22). Other army divisions, such as the 15th Division, were organized along sectarian and ethnic lines, and, e.g., the Turkmen brigade of the Division retook Turkmen cities in cooperation with a co-ethnic militia (ibid, 20). However, for the Prime Minister, picturing the security forces as coherent institutions controlled by the government was a way to gain popular support. In practice, the Iraqi army straddled between institutional independence and informal penetration by the ruling coalition.

From a strategy of punishment to one of elimination?

From August 2014 to December 2017, the strategy of the Iraqi regime and its allies shifted towards one of elimination. However, the strategy mainly relied on the tactical achievements of Kurdish and Shia Arab militias, CTS units, as well as Western intelligence and airpower, although the Iraqi army units became increasingly more important. The character of the war had changed because IS chose to defend territory rather than operate with fluid battle lines. Population-centric approaches became less relevant as a tactical measure, because the clandestine operations of IS in the areas taken by the opposing forces mostly consisted of terrorist attacks. Therefore, a strategy of elimination provided the alliance with visible signs of progress as IS lost territory throughout this period, even though it came at a slow rate considering the favourable force ratio of the alliance against IS.

On the battlefield the small, 10,000 man strong CTS force led the attacks against the fortified cities controlled by IS (Laub 2016). Officially, the Western coalition had a secondary role in the war against IS, but Western air strikes launched as part of Operation Inherent Resolve killed as many as 45,000 IS soldiers in Iraq and Syria from August 2014 to August 2016, which is several times the number killed by local forces (Department of Defense 2016). In the battle of Mosul, which ended in July 2017, regular Iraqi army units (mainly from the 16th Division) played a gradually greater role as the lengthy operation evolved. In the end, regular army units were the primary units in the elimination strategy in Mosul (Broekhof et al. 2019, 15).

112   *Iraq*

In other provinces, such as Diyala, army units were passive and the lack of tactical initiative allowed IS units to melt into the population, once they decided to give up territorial control (Redaelli 2018). Afterwards, PMF units engaged in violence against Sunni civilians, yet those atrocities were not part of a regime-led elimination strategy, but reflected the de facto control of the region by the Badr organization (Isakhan & Mulherrin 2020, 374).

Although the Iraqi regular forces only developed their tactical skills near the end of the conventional war, the sum of the tactical engagement of CTS, the militias, the regular forces, and the Western powers equals a strategy of elimination. The United States' initial strategy of degrading and destroying IS took advantage of the tactics of IS and targeted its front units as well as its staging ground. In parallel, the security forces and the militias could destroy or drive back the units of IS. This might suggest that al-Abadi pursued a systematic elimination strategy. On the other hand, the regime's reliance on militias and Iranian and American assistance probably points to the more modest conclusion that the combined effort of non-state, state, and external forces amounted to a less-than-coherent strategy of elimination.

To sum up, IS exposed the way in which the security forces of the al-Maliki and al-Abadi regimes were organized and applied. Contradictory rationales guided the regimes, namely that of tolerating competing client networks to keep the ruling coalition together, that of increasing personal control of the security institutions, and that of increasing the efficiency of those institutions. As such, when summarizing the answers to the general questions, the differences between the two regimes appear greater than they actually were. None of the regimes reserved CTS units for coup protection but put them at the front of military actions to suppress protest and fight IS. Coup-proofing did not hinder Western training during the al-Abadi regime, but no comparison can be made to the al-Maliki regime. Whereas al-Maliki reduced the efficiency of the regular forces by placing clients in senior positions, al-Abadi did not obstruct the reconstruction of the army. Nevertheless, both regimes accepted militia penetration of the armed forces. In regards to the choice of strategy, the more effective elimination strategy of the al-Abadi period might simply reflect the conventional tactics of IS as well as the availability of US military assets. The limited capacity of the regular security forces made alignment an integral part of both regimes' strategies as the existential threat from IS materialized.

Risk-averse alignment: a vulnerable alliance

In early 2014, the complete collapse of the punishment strategy and the fast-paced IS offensive forced the al-Maliki regime to depend on additional strategies to avoid the collapse of Iraq. In practice, both regimes preferred to align with the militarized factions of the ruling coalition, even though al-Abadi depended on the backing of the United States to seize and retain power. The far-reaching influence of Iran, and to a lesser extent the United

States, allowed the regime to utilize its external alignments to keep the ruling coalition together. Besides the arduous task of keeping the uneasy anti-IS alliance together, the regime had little freedom to choose the strategy for co-optation of Sunni militias, but mostly had to leave it to the Shia militias.

The rise of the Shia militias

10 June 2014, al-Maliki was facing two urgent threats that together defined his predicament. The first threat was the parliamentary election in April that made the State and Law coalition dependent on support from the rest of the Shia parties. Even though the parties ran as a coalition – the National Alliance – the other parties refused to accept al-Maliki as Prime Minister, insisting that the State and Law coalition had to nominate another candidate. Obviously, the second threat came from IS forces positioned just 35 miles from Baghdad, which created a perception among Shia elites that Baghdad might fall (Cockburn 2014a). To balance the threat al-Maliki needed more than the shattered security forces, which in practice meant domestic militias or the military forces of Iran or the United States.

The al-Maliki regime was closest to the pro-Iranian factions, and most easily aligned with their militias. The three largest, the Badr Organization, the Hezbollah Brigades, and the AAH militia, all had a political wing in the parliament. Much of their military capacity came from Iranian financial and materiel support and training, and they provided the regime with more than 20,000 militiamen (Katzman and Humud 2016, 18, Salehyan 2020, 114). The risk of aligning with the pro-Iranian militias of Badr, Hezbollah, and AAH was the lack of shared political goals beyond the fight against IS. Programmatic political goals of pan-Shiism clashed with the regime's attempt to keep Iraq together. Al-Darraji, a Badr commander, boasted that the Badr militia could outgun the official Iraqi Army and set up an alternative system of government (George 2014). In addition to the pro-Iranian militia, PUK was closer to the regime than KDP. PUK pursued the narrow ambition of Kurdish autonomy, but not independence, as well as the consolidation of their power in the Kurdish region in competition with Barzani's KDP. Up to that point, al-Maliki had managed to hold the alignment together, however other forces among the Shias soon added to the confusion of the political goal of the militias.

13 June 2014, the Iraqi Grand Ayatollah Ali al-Sistani issued a fatwa to take up arms against IS. Al-Sistani enjoyed a high degree of legitimacy among the Shia population, which explains why thousands of volunteers joined the militias in the weeks after the fatwa. Al-Sistani combined a nationalistic and Shia rhetoric that called for the defence of the Iraqi nation as well as Shia shrines. In the same week, al-Sadr officially reactivated the Mahdi army under the less sectarian name "the Peace Companies". Al-Sadr was a much more overtly political figure than al-Sistani, however they shared the political goal of reducing Iranian influence in Iraq. As early as

114 *Iraq*

January 2014 al-Sadr spoke of the need to reach out to Sunni Muslims in Iraq to reach national unity. A month later al-Sadr declared that he withdrew from politics denounced al-Maliki as a thief and dictator (Cole 2020). The Shia militias might have united in their fight against IS, but agreed on little else.

Al-Maliki tried to co-opt his pro-Iranian allies and the more nationalistic militias. 15 June, al-Maliki declared that all militias fighting IS were to be organized and paid as part of the umbrella organization of the Popular Mobilization Forces (PMF). However, neither al-Sistani nor al-Sadr had any intentions of realigning with al-Maliki. 25 July, the conflict became public, when Sheik al-Karbalai, the spokesperson of al-Sistani, urged Iraqi politicians to "bear their national responsibilities, which requires sacrifice, and not to cling to their posts" (Bazzi 2014). The declaration increased the split within the Dawa Party, where many members were wary of a confrontation with the highest Shia authority in Iraq. In addition, al-Sadr still refused to accept al-Maliki as Prime Minister, and refused to let the Peace Companies join the Popular Mobilization Forces, thereby openly revealing the split within the Shia groups (Ottaway 2015, 17).

The al-Maliki regime proved willing to co-opt the militias by paying for their services and formally integrating them into the security forces, albeit in separate units. However, the clash of interests among Shia elites as well as confusion over the political and military situation made it difficult for the regime to reconcile the factions. Moreover, the factions insisted on settling the question of regime survival within the formal political institutions.

The fall of the regime

The rapid unfolding of events in 2014 makes it difficult to determine whether the regime preferred internal to external alignments, as the proposition of risk-averse alignment would suggest. However, al-Maliki's actions suggest that he was wary of involving the United States on the ground in Iraq. In November 2013, al-Maliki sought and obtained materiel support from the United States in return for a vague promise to seek the political inclusion of Sunnis (Katzman 2013, 37). However, the regime proceeded with a punishment strategy that made inclusion impossible. The exclusion of Sunni Arabs from the security forces as well as the regime's reliance on strongly sectarian Shia parties made a real compromise with the Sunni factions next to impossible. Consequently, al-Maliki squandered an external alignment with the United States that would have made the threat from IS manageable.

In May 2014, the White House chose to make the resignation of al-Maliki a core demand for providing military aid, despite a shared perception of threat from IS (Cockburn 2014b). Al-Maliki rejected the American terms. Diplomats from the United States met with key political actors in Iraq to build a political consensus and identify candidates to replace al-Maliki as Prime Minister. Only the public outcry against the mass killings of Yazidis in

Iraq 115

Sinjar in the early days of August forced the United States into action. 8 August, the United States allocated airstrikes and Special Forces for the assistance of the Peshmerga Forces, only one day before Obama called Haider al-Abadi to endorse him as a candidate for the office of Prime Minister (Dreazen 2014).

However, the most critical blow to al-Maliki's fragile position came from Teheran. With a hostile United States any hope of resolving the military and political crisis hinged on Iranian cooperation. Military advisors from the Iranian Revolutionary Guard, commanded by General Qasam Soleimani, directed the efforts of the pro-Iranian militias and coordinated the military materiel support. In parallel, senior figures such as former President Hashemi Rafsanjani, closely aligned with the Iranian President Rouhani, criticized al-Maliki's sectarian and authoritarian strategies (Akbarzadeh 2015, 51). The criticism was indicative of Iran's preparation for finding a new candidate to head the Iraqi government. Although leaked cables show that Hassan Danaiefar, the Iranian ambassador in Iraq, considered al-Abadi as "a British man and the Americans' candidate", Iranian officials had no doubt that they could control the regime, because so many of the new ministers would cooperate with Iran (Risen et al. 2019). One day after the United States, Iran formally broke ties with al-Maliki. Without Iranian support, al-Maliki had no chance of breaking the deadlock in the ruling coalition.

Reconciling an uneasy alliance

8 September, Haidar al-Abadi presented a new government. Prime Minister al-Abadi had to reconcile actors with very different interests in an alliance against IS. The internal distribution of power forced al-Abadi to favour domestic elites. The United States played an instrumental role in bringing al-Abadi to power, and had good relations with the Kurdish KDP and their Peshmerga forces. However, the rest of the regime's alignments consisted of actors reluctant or hostile to American influence in Iraq. Al-Abadi retained the internal alignment with the pro-Iranian Badr, Hezbollah, and AAH militias and the external balancing with Iran, personified by Qasem Soleimani, the ever-present Commander of the Quds Force. Even the nationalist Shia groups, personified by al-Sadr and al-Sistani, the two Iraqi Shia clerics, were reluctant to accept too much cooperation with the United States. Al-Abadi might have preferred an alignment with the United States, but he had to favour the domestic ruling coalition in order to keep it together politically and militarily.

Therefore, the regime had to accept that Kurdish and Shia elites pursued parochial goals, which explains why the military campaign against IS took three years. Peshmerga forces pushed IS back to the Sinjar area in the northwest. In 2016–2017, Kurdish forces only reluctantly participated in the battle for Mosul, as their territorial ambitions were fulfilled. In comparison,

116 *Iraq*

Shia militias played a more integral role in the counteroffensive. In general, in 2015 the Shia militias played a highly active role as the most effective fighting force in, e.g., the offensive to retake Tikrit, which al-Abadi praised afterwards (Ambrozik 2019, 894). However, after the army slowly began to recoup in 2016, al-Abadi convinced Shia militias to accept secondary tactical roles, such as establishing cordons or holding territory, which was a US prerequisite to provide airpower, and a political tool to raise the public standing of the Iraqi army (ibid). Nonetheless, during the offensive to take Ramadi, the Badr militia and some Iraqi security forces diverted their efforts towards Fallujah, which is closer to Baghdad (Michaels 2015). Parochialism among militant elites limited the impact of the numerical and materiel superiority of the anti-IS alliance, but did not obstruct the military campaign.

The Shia militias' control of a major part of the strategy towards IS had a surprising effect on the co-optation of Sunni militias. Co-optation took place within PMF, which meant that especially Badr, but also other Kurdish and Shia militias, screened and hand-picked a few Sunni militias, but demobilized most of them (Mansour and Jabar 2017, 12). Co-optation of selected Sunni militias made it easier for the Badr militia to control mixed demographic areas in the north-western parts of Iraq (Gulmohamad 2021). Importantly, the co-optation of former insurgents cannot be considered a part of the regime's strategy, as al-Abadi did not make the decisions about whom to co-opt, or whether to disarm them or integrate them into the security forces.

For al-Abadi the key challenge was to keep the alliance together rather than to achieve a swift, conventional victory over IS. As with most alliances, a decline in the perceived threat from the common enemy made it more difficult to settle discords among alliance members. After 2016, when the threat from IS decreased, the alignment with the Kurdish Peshmerga forces suffered because of the conflict over land and oil income. The Kurdish elites had used the dissolution of the Iraqi army to seize Kirkuk and the major oil fields in northern Iraq (Paasche and Michael 2016, 23–24). In the spring of 2017, even while the Kurds participated in the battle of Mosul along with the other members of the anti-IS alliance, KDP leader Masoud Barzani planned a nonbinding popular vote on Kurdish independence. The 93 percent votes for Kurdish independence resulted in a violent reaction from the remaining part of the ruling coalition. 12 October 2017, CTS, the Iraqi army, and PMF units retook Kirkuk and its major oil fields, and PUK Peshmerga units did not resist, because they had made a secret deal with Iran (Azizi 2020, 173). The question of Kurdish independence lost salience for the remainder of the examined period, but the actions of the Kurds spoke to divergent interests among the factions of the ruling coalition.

Shia factions held the survival of the regime in their hands. Politically, al-Abadi's majority in the parliament depended on continued support from the pro-Iranian parties. Militarily, the pro-Iranian Shia militias remained a considerable threat to the Iraqi security forces throughout the examined

Iraq 117

period. As the United States provided crucial military assistance and Iran kept the pro-Iranian factions together, the al-Abadi regime had no chance of reconfiguring its alignment strategies. What separates Iraq from cases more thoroughly dominated by informal politics is the mirroring of the distribution of military power and parliamentary influence. During the parliamentary election in 2018, AAH, the al-Badr organization, and al-Sadr's faction were able to translate military success into electoral gains. In October 2018, once they compromised on Adil Abdul Mahdi as new Prime Minister, al-Abadi lost power.

To summarize, the political survival of the two regimes depended on the militarized factions of the ruling coalition. To avoid political defeat in the parliament and military defeat at the hands of IS, the regimes made concessions to the other factions to hold the ruling coalition together. In that sense, both regimes favoured domestic alignments from 2014 to 2018, despite al-Abadi's orientation towards the United States. The strength of the militarized factions and the importance of the sectarian divide meant that the regimes relied less on co-optation of former insurgents and more on formal and less formal divisions of labour. Finally, both regimes walked a tightrope in their external alignments with Iran and the United States. Al-Maliki relied on Iran to keep the Shia coalition together, which until the end of his regime was a less risky alignment than the one with the United States. During the intense fighting with IS, al-Abadi leaned towards the United States, which was less intrusive and risky strategy than aligning with Iran, who directed the pro-militias that threatened the regime's grip on power. Largely, the informal negotiation of the anti-IS alliance was mirrored in the political negotiations in the Iraqi parliament. The extent to which the negotiations resulted in formal reforms is the subject of the next section.

Simulated statebuilding to hold the ruling coalition together

After the United States' retreat in 2011, al-Maliki's exclusion of Sunni Arabs and attempt to control the security forces presented a minor nuisance to the Obama administration. However, once IS began its territorial conquest, the United States demanded reforms to include the Sunnis in the political process in return for military support. After August 2014, the question of administrative and political reforms remained part of the US strategy, even after President Donald Trump took office in 2017. But the political aspect of the counter-IS strategy remained underdeveloped, which is most likely an outcome of the lack of an overarching US political strategy for the civil war in Syria and the Obama and Trump administrations' unwillingness to engage in statebuilding efforts in Iraq (Al-Istrabadi and Ganguly 2018, 189ff). Nonetheless, the United States pressured al-Abadi on the three most critical issues in Iraqi politics from 2014 to 2018, which provides the structure of the section, namely the inclusion of Sunnis in the Iraqi state and politics, anti-corruption reforms, and the political control of the militias.

118 *Iraq*

The inclusion of the Sunni minority

In August 2014, when al-Abadi took office, the United States made it clear that military support was conditioned by a more inclusive policy towards the Sunni Arab population (Lake 2016, 147). More specifically, the United States wanted a better representation of Sunni politicians in the government and a reintegration of the Sunni militias in the security institutions, as they were in 2007 as part of the surge. Nominally, al-Abadi met the demands in September, when he presented a new government, which included several Sunni and Kurdish ministers as well as two ministers from al-Sadr's al-Ahrar Party. However, most of the ministers came from the Shia parties and had been part of the governments under the al-Maliki regime. Still, President Obama congratulated al-Abadi on forming an inclusive government (Fahim and Ahmed 2014).

To assist the al-Abadi regime with materiel, training, and air strikes, the United States insisted that al-Abadi rearm the Sunni tribal militias and include them in a national guard. Approximately 120,000 to 200,000 militiamen were supposed to be recruited locally, but within the chain of command of the army. In the eyes of most Shia political and militia leaders, a Sunni force represented a threat. Abu Mahdi al-Muhandis, the leader of Hezbollah, declared that a national guard would lead to the partition of the country (Cigar 2015, 37). As will be discussed shortly, the attempts to create a national guard failed due to the political resistance in the parliament. However, the United States and its Western allies took the inclusion of Sunnis into their own hands. Western forces trained a classified number (probably around 20,000) of Sunni members of the Tribal Mobilization Forces in the examined period. The Iraqi government officially conducted the programme, but in practice the United States provided the funds and support (Gaston 2017).

Yet, the United States' attempt to foster sectarian inclusion was mostly undermined by the factions promoting sectarian exclusion. As mentioned previously, PMF vetted each potential militia, which gave the Badr movement a strong say on the composition of the Sunni militias. Moreover, they recruited small Sunni militias among the tribes that opposed IS rule, which increased the Shia militias' nationalist profile, but resulted in incidents of intra-Sunni atrocities (Rose Dury-Agri et al. 2017, 45ff). Although the programme fostered the inclusion of Sunni militias, these were also used for the benefit of the Shia militias.

In August 2016, the question of the inclusion of Sunni Arabs flared up again, when the parliament fired Khaled al-Obeidi, the Minister of Defence. Al-Abadi's own party, the State and Law coalition, was behind a vote of no-confidence that forced the Minister to resign. In spite of American pressure for keeping al-Obeidi, Al-Abadi chose to accept the resignation just before the offensive against Mosul commenced. The State and Law bloc and the pro-Iranian parties successfully

Iraq 119

charged al-Obeidi with corruption when he negotiated defence procurement contracts, despite al-Sadr's support for the Minister. Al-Obeidi himself accused several members of the parliament of blackmailing him into securing contracts for parliamentary members (Stratfor 2016). However, al-Abadi made no effort to investigate the accusations against the Minister of Defence or against the members of the parliament. Two ministers from the State and Law coalition subsequently held the post, despite the fact that the position was reserved for Sunni politicians under the power-sharing arrangements of 2005.

In the eyes of the Iraqi population, the continued influence of the sectarian Shia parties reduced confidence in al-Abadi's ability to make the government more inclusive. From December 2014 to September 2015, the number of Sunnis who believed that al-Abadi's government was more inclusive than al-Maliki's dropped from 52 percent to 36 percent (Mansour 2016, 10). Sunni politicians shared the view of the lack of inclusiveness. Saleh al-Mutlaq, Sunni leader and Deputy Prime Minister, formulated the lack of Sunni influence as: "it is not like we [the Sunni Arabs] are writing the bylaws." (ibid 2016). During al-Abadi's premiership, he took several steps towards inclusion but was left powerless when the ruling coalition did not support his initiatives. Nevertheless, the opposition of the ruling coalition had to be expressed, at least partly, in public as part of parliamentary debates, which reflects the mixed political character of the Iraqi political settlement.

Institutional reforms and anti-corruption

From August 2015, al-Abadi made a daring attempt to increase the efficiency of the formal political institutions as well as to reduce corruption in order to accommodate the public demands of the United States, Sunni tribes, and the populist discourse of al-Sadr. Pro-Iranian Shia parties frustrated the efforts, which led to a major political crisis at the height of the fight against IS. In August 2015 al-Abadi temporarily got the parliamentary support to impose reforms by removing the three Vice Presidents and reshuffling the cabinet to turn it into a small, technocratic government. However, the State and Law coalition, including factions of al-Abadi's Dawa Party, most notably party leader al-Maliki, thwarted the implementation in the parliament. On the other hand, al-Sadr and al-Sistani publicly derided the Prime Minister for not doing enough to fight corruption. Al-Sadr mobilized his followers into massive street protests in Baghdad that increased the pressure on al-Abadi. Apparently, only the double pressure from General Solaimani and Vice President Joe Biden prevented a vote of no confidence against al-Abadi (Kalin and Chmaytelli 2016).

For six months the parliament was deadlocked, but the confrontation came to a head in March and April 2016, when al-Sadr followers stormed the parliament. Al-Abadi was not able to achieve a compromise over a new technocratic cabinet. Most of the Shia parties closed ranks to protect their access to lucrative ministries. Moreover, in October 2016 the Supreme

120   *Iraq*

Federal Court ruled that the removal of the office of vice president was unconstitutional, and the Vice Presidents – including al-Maliki – were re-instated[1]. The inability to implement fundamental reforms against clientelism is telling of the regime's weakness when faced with opposition from factions within the ruling coalition, but also shows the continued relevance of the parliament, where the pro-Iranian parties had to defend their position publicly.

In place of fundamental reforms, al-Abadi had to settle for small reforms, but also took steps that closely resembled simulated statebuilding. In August 2015, the public promise of fighting corruption translated into two committees to carry out the intent. The first committee, headed by al-Abadi himself, was supposed to increase transparency in Iraqi public administration, but the pro-Iranian Shia parties withdrew their support for the commission after three months (Gunter 2018). The second, the Integrity Committee, was to examine the political parties' use of public property. The committee noted some achievement, despite the despondent, yet honest, assessment by one member, Mishan al-Jabouri, that "Everybody is corrupt, from the top of society to the bottom. Everyone. Including me." (quoted in Chulov 2016). At the senior level, Abdul Falah al-Sudany, a former minister and Qasim Al-Fahadawi, a junior Sunni minister were arrested and convicted, as were three governors. Moreover, many more lower-level civil servants were charged and convicted of corruption. Still, the anti-corruption campaign failed to prosecute those with sufficient political protection. For example, Abu Mazin, the Sunni Arab Governor in Salah al-Din, was closely connected to the pro-Iranian power bloc in the Parliament, who used their influence to acquit the Governor (Saleem 2021, 15).

The lack of fundamental political and administrative reforms against corruption and clientelism was a point of continuous public contestation. In the summer of 2018, Shia Arabs continued to protest against corruption, and state inefficiency, and al-Sistani supported them in his sermons that criticized the sectarian principles of Iraqi politics (Isakhan and Mulherin 2018). Public disaffection with the ruling coalition also manifested itself in the low voter turnout of 45 percent in the parliamentary election in May 2018. The Iraqi Communist Party supported the protest movement, but had to form the Saairun coalition with al-Sadr's party to protect themselves from repression from the security forces and militias (Dodge 2018b, 47). The Saairun coalition won the election and gained 54 out of 329 seats in the parliament. Prime Minister al-Abadi's party, the Victory Alliance, came in third receiving 42 seats. The United States supported and assisted al-Abadi's Victory Alliance, partly due to its pro-Western stance and partly due to its agenda of inclusion of minorities and reforms (Mansour and van den Toorn 2018). In the light of the successful military campaign against IS, al-Abadi's election result was low, but most likely reflected the disaffection among the population with the failed reforms in the previous four years.

Even though the election rewarded protest parties, the distribution of seats in the parliament prevented any political group from carrying out sweeping reforms. The pro-Iranian Shia parties translated the military success of their militias into electoral success. The Fatah Alliance became the second largest party with 45 seats and constituted the political wing of the al-Badr and AAH militias. Moreover, most of the other parties in the new parliament consisted of entrenched elites, such as al-Maliki, the two Kurdish parties, and the Sunni politician al-Nujaifa, former Speaker of the Parliament. As mentioned, the ruling coalition compromised and made the non-elected Adil Abdul Mahdi Prime Minister. Mahdi was an integral part of Iraqi politics as former Vice President, Minister of Oil, and utterly loyal to Iran, hardly a catalyst for reforms. In the examined period, reforms proved elusive because the factions of the ruling coalition jealously guarded the distribution of formal and informal rules. Al-Abadi could not reconcile the demands of al-Sadr and his followers in the "Arab Street" with the interests of the pro-Iranian parties and militias. He was also unable to tackle the political aspects of the endemic corruption when domestic elites protected their informal accommodation of client networks. Instead, al-Abadi lost the election in 2018, because he could not put an end to the informal aspects of the Iraqi political settlement.

The question of political control of the militias

"I remember in some countries with a history of coups d'état, usually leaders are afraid of arming the army…. And the same I think [holds] for this popular mobilization force." (Prime Minister al-Abadi, in Pelham 2015). The desperate move by al-Sistani to call for the formation of militias and the expansion of the pro-Iranian militias further militarized the factions within the ruling coalition. In the quote above, al-Abadi was fully aware of the potential risk of arming and tolerating militias, even under the banner of the popular mobilization force. The regime tried to include the militias under the chain of command of the regular military to gain greater political control of them. The ensuing fight for political control of the militias provides us with a significant glimpse into the power struggle between Iraqi factions aligned with Iran and the elites aligned with al-Abadi.

The United States pursued a two-pronged approach: first, to pressure al-Abadi into organizing the militias in a national guard and bring them under the regular chain of command; second, to work pragmatically with selected militias, such as the Peshmergas, to ensure sufficient ground forces to take advantage of American airpower (Katzman and Humud 2016, 30–31). To pressure the Iraqi elites, including al-Abadi, the United States refused to carry out airstrikes in support of the Popular Mobilization Front as long as it was not organized into a national guard (Mansour and Jabar 2017, 22). And the pressure had an effect on the battlefield, as previously described in the division of labour that mostly moved PMF away from the front line.

122   *Iraq*

Politically, the attempts by al-Abadi to bring the militias under the control of the army proved largely futile. The efforts made to construct a national guard failed due to resistance from Kurds, pro-Iranian militias, as well as al-Sadr. In February 2016, al-Abadi made a more modest attempt to control PMF by passing executive order 91, which placed PMF under the authority of the Prime Minister, with a committee to oversee its day-to-day activities (Eisenstadt and Knights 2017). In November 2016, the executive order was turned into a law, leading Sunni politicians to leave the parliament in protest. They protested that the regulation was close to the one established by al-Maliki, whereby PMF militias retained their independent commands and funding. Moreover, the operational leader of the PMF commission was Abu Mahdi al-Muhandis, a former leader of the Iraqi Hezbollah militia and a member of the Iranian Revolutionary Guard in the 1980s. Al-Muhandis was clearly a part of the pro-Iranian faction, as witnessed in January 2020 when he died alongside Soleimani in an American drone strike. A drone strike that responded to the PMF attacks on US troops (O'Connor and Laporta 2020). After November 2016, the state formally controlled the militias, but in reality, the pro-Iranian militias were loyal to their own political and religious leaders.

It is a reflection of the strong ties between the political parties and the militias that the latter are generally fighting to protect or promote political views. One of the issues dividing the Shia militias was support for the al-Assad regime in Syria. So-called Shrine militias – formed immediately after al-Sistani's fatwa to protect the holy cities of the Shias – and al-Sadr's Peace Companies saw their goal as strictly limited to Iraq. The pro-Iranian militias held the opposite view. Forces from the Badr organization, the AAH, and Hezbollah all fought in Syria to protect the Alawite regime (Gulmohamad 2020). The issue of Syria reflected the deeper-lying question of political loyalty: should the Iraqi Shias be loyal to a transnational Shia community under the leadership of Iran, or should they first and foremost be loyal to the Iraqi nation? The programmatic politics of the Shia factions mattered and undermined reforms to gain national control of the PMFs. The regime's lacking control of the Shia militias again demonstrates its weak position in the ruling coalition. Despite the al-Abadis' successful removal of Shia militias from the frontline against IS, their power and influence remained strong.

In sum, the military success against IS was not equally matched by administrative and political reforms. The inclusion of Sunnis in a national guard and in government, was delayed and partially implemented. Al-Abadi could not keep Defence Minister al-Obedi, despite US pressure, nor was he able to gain control of the Shia militias, which in the examined period led to simulated implementation. Anti-corruption reforms were partially implemented to the extent that it did not threaten the access to patronage for the Shia elites. In Iraq, the Obama and Trump administrations prioritized the destruction of the Islamic State over reforms to address root causes of Sunni extremism. Besides the initial demands for the inclusion of Sunni

Iraq 123

Arabs in the government, the United States only warily held the al-Abadi regime publicly accountable, which might explain the acceptance of partial or simulated implementation.

Conclusion

Neither formal nor informal politics were dominant in Iraq's political settlement. The regimes accommodated the militarized elites of the ruling coalition through formal power-sharing arrangements and inclusion in the government. On the other hand, the strength of the militarized Shia elites forced the regimes to allow the co-existence of competing client networks in the state institutions. When Nour al-Maliki went too far in his attempt to concentrate power and create praetorian protection for his regime, he lost the support of the ruling coalition and the external powers. The al-Abadi regime chose military strategies that carefully avoided challenging the Shia militarized elites. When the threat from IS demanded military action, the regimes brought trusted elite units into battle instead of reserving them for coup-protection. In addition, the regular units of the ISF were not simply vessels of co-optation, because most militias chose to operate within the PMF framework. The legal battle in the parliament to gain state control of the militias also showed the importance of formal politics, although the outcome did little to curb informal politics.

The United States needed formal politics in Iraq. The dual interests of combating the Islamic State and curbing Iranian influence in Iraq could be met by developing a strong and independent Iraqi state. Despite the strong incentive, the United States was far from successful in this endeavour, which is noteworthy in the light of the public outcry against the cronyism of the elites. It is most likely that Al-Abadi had the intention of carrying out reforms to strengthen the political and administrative institutions of Iraq, and lost the popular vote due to his failure to implement them. Although the Iraqi political settlement had formal elements, the militarized Shia elites backed by Iran were so well-entrenched inside and outside the state that even the concerted pressure from parts of the public and a Western superpower proved futile. The next chapter deals with the last case, Algeria, which makes it possible to study regime strategies in a political settlement where formal politics is more dominant than informal politics.

Note

1 The Iraqi Constitution, article 138, clearly states that the offices of Vice Presidents should exist, although the constitution speaks of two vice presidents and does not mention any sectarian distribution of the offices.

124 *Iraq*

References

Abbas, Mushreq. 2013. "Who Is to Blame For the Hawija Violence?" *Al-Monitor*, 25 April. https://www.al-monitor.com/originals/2013/04/iraq-hawija-massacre-politics.html

Akbarzadeh, Shahram. 2015. "Iran and Daesh: The Case of a Reluctant Shia Power." *Middle East Policy* 22 (3): 44–54. 10.1111/mepo.12142

Al-Istrabadi, Feisal and Sumit Ganguly. 2018. *The Future of ISIS: Regional and International Implications*. Washington D.C.: Brookings Institution Press. https://www.jstor.org/stable/10.7864/j.ctt1zctt19

Ambrozik, Caitlin. 2019. Not Whether, But When? Governments' Use of Militias in War, *Security Studies* 28 (5): 870–900. 10.1080/09636412.2019.1662479

Azizi, Arash. 2020. *The Shadow Commander: Soleimani, the US, and Iran's Global Ambitions*. New York: Simon & Schuster.

Bazzi, Mohamad. 2014. "The Sistani Factor." *Boston Review*, August 2014. http://bostonreview.net/world/mohamad-bazzi-sistani-factor-isis-shiism-iraq

Belloni, Roberto, and Irene Costantini. 2019. "From Liberal Statebuilding to Counterinsurgency and Stabilization: The International Intervention in Iraq." *Ethnopolitics* 18 (5): 509–525. 10.1080/17449057.2019.1640964

Biddle, Stephen, Jeffrey A Friedman, and Jacob N Shapiro. 2012. "Testing the Surge: Why Did Violence Decline in Iraq in 2007?" *International Security* 37 (1): 7–40. 10.1162/ISEC_a_00087

Boduszyński, Mieczysław P. 2016. "Iraq's Year of Rage." *Journal of Democracy* 27 (4): 110–124. 10.1353/jod.2016.0067

Broekhof, Maarten P., Martijn W. M. Kitzen, and Frans P. B. Osinga. 2019. "A Tale of Two Mosuls, The resurrection of the Iraqi armed forces and the military defeat of ISIS". *Journal of Strategic Studies*, online publication. 10.1080/01402390.2019.1694912

Chulov, Martin. 2016. "Post-war Iraq: 'Everybody is corrupt, from top to bottom. Including me.'" *The Guardian* 19 February. https://www.theguardian.com/world/2016/feb/19/post-war-iraq-corruption-oil-prices-revenues

Cigar, Norman. 2015. *"Iraq's Shia Warlords and Their Militias: Political and Security Challenges and Options."* Carlisle: The United States Army War College. https://ssi.armywarcollege.edu/2015/pubs/iraqs-shia-warlords-and-their-militias-political-and-security-challenges-and-options/

Cockburn, Patrick. 2014a. "Battle for Baghad." *London Review of Books* 36 (14). https://www.lrb.co.uk/the-paper/v36/n14/patrick-cockburn/battle-for-baghdad

Cockburn, Patrick. 2014b. "Iraq Crisis Exclusive: US Rules out Military Action until Prime Minister Nouri Al-Maliki Stands down." *The Independent*, 19 June 19 2014. https://www.independent.co.uk/news/world/middle-east/iraq-crisis-exclusive-us-rules-out-military-action-until-pm-nouri-al-maliki-stands-down-9547311.html

Combined Joint Task Force - Operation Inherent Resolve 2017 CJTF-OIR reflects on 2017 and looks forward to 2018. Available at: http://www.inherentresolve.mil/News/News-Releases/News-Article-View/Article/1406595/cjtf-oir-reflects-on-2017-and-looks-forward-to-2018/ (Accessed 1 August 2018).

Department of Defense. 2016. *"OIR Campaign Reached Turning Point in Ramadi, Commander Says."* Department of Defense. 2016. https://www.defense.gov/News/Article/Article/910747/oir-campaign-reached-turning-point-in-ramadi-commander-says/

Iraq 125

Dodge, Toby. 2014. "Can Iraq Be Saved?" *Survival* 56 (5): 7–20. 10.1080/00396338. 2014.962795

Dodge, Toby. 2018a. "'Bourdieu Goes to Baghdad': Explaining Hybrid Political Identities in Iraq." *Journal of Historical Sociology* 31 (1): 25–38. 10.1111/johs.12189

Dodge, Toby. 2018b. "Iraq: A Year of Living Dangerously." Survival 60 (5): 41–48. 10.1080/00396338.2018.1518368

Dodge, Toby and Renad Mansour. 2020. "Sectarianization and Desectarianization in the Struggle for Iraq's Political Field." *The Review of Faith & International Affairs* 18 (1): 58–69. 10.1080/15570274.2020.1729513

Dreazen, Yochi. 2014. "Maliki Used to Have the Support of Both Iran and the U.S. Now He's Lost Them Both." *Foreign Policy*, August 2014. https://foreignpolicy.com/2014/08/13/maliki-used-to-have-the-support-of-both-iran-and-the-u-s-now-hes-lost-them-both/

Eisenstadt, Michael, Michael Knights, and Ahmed Ali. 2011. "Iran's Influence in Iraq - Countering Tehran's Whole-of-Government Approach." 111. *Policy Focus*. Washington D.C.: The Washington Institute for Near East Policy. https://www.washingtoninstitute.org/policy-analysis/irans-influence-iraq-countering-tehrans-whole-government-approach

Eisenstadt, Michael, and Michael Knights. 2017. "Mini-Hizballahs, Revolutionary Guard Knock-Offs, and the Future of Iran's Militant Proxies in Iraq." *War on the Rocks.* https://warontherocks.com/2017/05/mini-hizballahs-revolutionary-guard-knock-offs-and-the-future-of-irans-militant-proxies-in-iraq/

Fahim, Kareem, and Azam Ahmed. 2014. "Lawmakers Approve Cabinet in Iraq, but 2 Posts Are Empty." *New York Times*, 8 September 2014. https://www.nytimes.com/2014/09/09/world/middleeast/iraq.html

Gaston, Erica. 2017. *"Sunni Tribal Forces."* Berlin: Global Public Policy Institute. https://www.gppi.net/2017/08/30/sunni-tribal-forces

George, Susannah. 2014. "Breaking Badr." *Foreign Policy*, 11 June 2014. https://foreignpolicy.com/2014/11/06/breaking-badr/

Grinstead, Nick, Floor El Kamouni-Janssen, and Erwin van Veen. 2017. *A House Divided Political Relations and Coalition-Building between Iraq's Shi'a.* Den Haag: Clingendael. https://www.clingendael.org/pub/2017/a_house_divided/

Gulmohamad, Zana. 2020. "The Evolution of Iraq's Hashd al-Sha'abi (Popular Mobilization Forces)." In *The Regional Order in the Gulf* , edited by Philipp O. Amour, 259–301. Cham: Palgrave Macmillan. 10.1007/978-3-030-45465-4_9

Gulmohamad, Zana. 2021. "Munathamat Badr, from an Armed Wing to a Ruling Actor." Small Wars and Insurgencies online: 1–29. 10.1080/09592318.2021.1875310

Gunter, Michael M. 1993. "A de Facto Kurdish State in Northern Iraq." *Third World Quarterly* 14 (2): 295–319. 10.1080/01436599308420326

Gunter, Frank (2018). Immunizing Iraq Against al-Qaeda 3.0. *Orbis*, 62 (3), 389–408.

Haddad, Fanar. 2020. *Understanding 'Sectarianism': Sunni-Shi'a Relations in the Modern Arab World.* Oxford: Oxford University Press. 10.1093/oso/978019751062 9.001.0001

Hoekstra, Quint. 2020. "How Mosul fell: The Role of Coup-proofing in the 2014 Partial Collapse of the Iraqi Security Forces." *International Politics* 57 (4): 684–703. 10.1057/s41311-019-00199-3

126 *Iraq*

International Crisis Group. 2011. *"Failing Oversight: Iraq's Unchecked Government."* Brussels: International Crisis Group. https://www.crisisgroup.org/middle-east-north-africa/gulf-and-arabian-peninsula/iraq/failing-oversight-iraq-s-unchecked-government

International Monetary Fund. 2016. *"Economic Diversification in Oil-Exporting Arab Countries."* Washington D.C.: International Monetary Fund. https://www.imf.org/en/Publications/Policy-Papers/Issues/2016/12/31/Economic-Diversification-in-Oil-Exporting-Arab-Countries-PP5038

Isakhan, Benjamin, and Peter Mulherin. 2018. "Basra's Bid for Autonomy: Peaceful Progress toward a Decentralized Iraq". *The Middle East Journal* 72 (2): 267–285. 10.3751/72.2.15

Jabar, Faleh A. 2000. "Shaykhs and Ideologues: Detribalization and Retribalization in Iraq, 1968-1998." Middle East Report 215: 28–48. 10.2307/1520152

Jensen, Sterling. 2016. "The Fall of Iraq's Anbar Province." *Middle East Journal* 23 (1): 1–7. https://www.meforum.org/5687/fall-of-anbar-province

Kalin, Stephen and Maher Chmaytelli. 2016. "U.S., Iran keep Iraqi PM in place as he challenges ruling elite". Reuters 5 April. https://www.reuters.com/article/us-mideast-crisis-iraq-politics-insight-idUSKCN0X22NB

Kamaran Palani, Jaafar Khidir, Mark Dechesne, and Edwin Bakker. 2019. "Strategies to Gain International Recognition: Iraqi Kurdistan's September 2017 Referendum for Independence." *Ethnopolitics*. 10.1080/17449057.2019.1596467

Katzman, Kenneth. 2013. *"Iraq: Politics, Governance, and Human Rights."* Washington D.C.: Congressional Research Service. https://www.refworld.org/pdfid/52cff0d64.pdf

Katzman, Kenneth, and Carla E. Humud. 2016. *"Iraq: Politics, Governance, and Human Rights."* Washington D.C.: Congressional Research Service. https://fas.org/sgp/crs/mideast/RS21968.pdf

Knights, Michael. 2014. "ISIL's Political-Military Power in Iraq." *Combatting Terrorism Sentinel* 7 (8): 1–7. https://www.ctc.usma.edu/wp-content/uploads/2014/09/CTCSentinel-Vol7Iss85.pdf

Knights, Michael. 2016. *"The Future of Iraq's Armed Forces."* Baghdad: Al-Bayan Center for Planning and Studies. https://www.bayancenter.org/en/2016/03/650/

Lake, David A. 2016. *The Statebuilder's Dilemma: On the Limits of Foreign Intervention.* Itchica: Cornell University Press. 10.7591/9781501703836

Laub, Zachary. 2016. *"Does Iraq Have a Plan for After the Islamic State?"* Washington D.C.: Council of Foreign Affairs. https://www.cfr.org/interview/does-iraq-have-plan-after-islamic-state

Mansour, Renad. 2016. *"The Sunni Predicament in Iraq."* Washington D.C.: Carnegie Middle East Center. https://carnegieendowment.org/files/CMEC_59_Mansour_Sunni_Final.pdf

Mansour, Renad and Faleh A. Jabar. 2017. *"The Popular Mobilization Forces And Iraq's Future."* Washington D.C.: Carnegie Middle East Center. https://carnegieendow-ment.org/files/CMEC_63_Mansour_PMF_Final_Web.pdf

Mansour, Renad and van den Toorn, Christine. 2018. *The 2018 Iraqi Federal Elections: A Population in Transition.* LSE Middle East Centre Report. London: Middle East Centre and Institute of Regional and International Studies. http://eprints.lse.ac.uk/89698/

Marr, Phebe. 2017. *The Modern History of Iraq*. New York: Routledge. 10.4324/ 9780429494437

Michaels, Jim. 2015. "Iraq Political Disarray Slows Ramadi Campaign." *USA Today*, 21 September 2015. https://eu.usatoday.com/story/news/world/2015/09/21/ iraq-political-dissaray-slows-ramadi-campaign/72362740/

O'Connor, Tom and James Laporta. 2020. *Trump orders US drone strike, killing Iranian general who headed Quds* force. Newsweek, 2 January. https://www.newsweek.com/ iraq-militia-official-killed-us-iran-tensions-1480181

O'Driscoll, Dylan. 2014. "The Costs of Inadequacy: Violence and Elections in Iraq." *Ethnopolitics Papers, Exeter:* Exeter University. https://www.psa.ac.uk/sites/ default/files/page-files/EPP027_0.pdf

Ottaway, Marina. 2015. "Nation-Building in Iraq: Iran 1, the United States 0." *Insight Turkey* 17 (2): 9–19.

Paasche, Till F., and Michael M. Gunter. 2016. "Revisiting Western Strategies against the Islamic State in Iraq and Syria." *The Middle East Journal* 70 (1): 9–29. 10.3751/70.1.11

Pelham, Nicolas. 2015. "ISIS & the Shia Revival in Iraq." *The New York Review of Books*, 4 June 2015. https://www.nybooks.com/articles/2015/06/04/isis-shia-revival-iraq/

Pischedda, Costantino. 2020. *Conflict Among Rebels: Why Insurgent Groups Fight Each Other*. New York: Columbia University Press. 10.7312/pisc19866

Redaelli, Riccardo. (2018). *The Osmotic Path: The PMU and The Iraqi State*. Beirut: Carnegie Middle EastCenter. https://carnegie-mec.org/2018/10/30/osmotic-- path-pmu-and-iraqi-state-pub-77600

Risen, James, Tim Arango, Farnaz Fassihi, Mutaza Hussain, and Ronen Bergman. 2019. *The Iran Cables: A Spy Complex Revealed. The Intercept*. https://theintercept.com/ series/iran-cables/

Rizvi, Sajjad. 2010. "Political Mobilization and the Shi'i Religious Establishment (Marja'iyya)." *International Affairs* 86 (6): 1299–1313. 10.1111/j.1468-2346.2010 .00944.x

Rose Dury-Agri, Jessa, Omer Kassim, and Patrick Martin. 2017. "*Iraqi Security Forces and Popular Mobilization Forces: Orders of Battle.*" Washington D.C.: Institute for the Study of War. http://www.understandingwar.org/report/iraqi- security-forces-and-popular-mobilization-forces-orders-battle-0

Saleem, Zmkan Ali. 2021. *The King of Salah al-Din: The Power of Iraq's Sunni Elites*. London: London School of Economics. http://eprints.lse.ac.uk/108541/1/Ali_ Saleem_the_king_of_salah_al_din_published.pdf

Salehyan, Idean. 2020. "Militias and the Iraqi State". In *The Governor's Dilemma: Indirect Governance Beyond Principals and Agents*, edited by Kenneth W. Abbott, Bernhard Zangl, Duncan Snidal, and Philipp Genschel, 100–118. Oxford: Oxford University Press. 10.1093/oso/9780198855057.003.0005

Salmoni, Barak A. 2011. "Responsible Partnership." Washington D.C.: The Washington Institute for Near East Policy. https://www.washingtoninstitute.org/ policy-analysis/responsible-partnership-iraqi-national-security-sector-after-2011

Schmidt, Michael and Jack Healy. 2011. *Maliki's Broadened Powers Seen as a Threat in Iraq. New York Times* 4 March. http://www.nytimes.com/2011/03/05/world/ middleeast/05iraq.html

128 *Iraq*

Seliktar, Ofira and Farhad Rezaei. 2020. *Iran, Revolution, and Proxy Wars*. Cham: Palgrave Macmillan. 10.1007/978-3-030-29418-2

Stratfor. 2016. *"The Sacking of Iraq's Defense Minister."* Austin: Stratfor. https://www.stratfor.com/analysis/sacking-iraqs-defense-minister (Accessed 17 October 2017)

Thurber, Ches. 2014. "Militias as Sociopolitical Movements: Lessons from Iraq's Armed Shia Groups." *Small Wars & Insurgencies* 25 (5–6): 900–923. 10.1080/09592318.2014.945633

United States Government Accountability Office. 2017. *"Countering ISIS and Its Effects: Key Issues for Oversight."* Washinton D.C.: United States Government Accountability Office. https://www.gao.gov/products/gao-17-687sp

World Bank. 2014. *"The Unfulfilled Promise Of Oil and Growth: Poverty, Inclusion and Welfare in Iraq, 2007–2012"* 1. Poverty Global Practice. Washington, D.C. https://www.worldbank.org/en/country/iraq/publication/unfulfilled-promise-of-oil-and-growth

Yaphe, Judith. 2012. "Maliki's Manuevering in Iraq." *Foreign Policy*, 6 June 2012. https://foreignpolicy.com/2012/06/06/malikis-manuevering-in-iraq/

Zaid, Al-Ali. 2014. *The Struggle for Iraq's Future: How Corruption, Incompetence and Sectarianism Have Undermined Democracy*. New Haven: Yale University Press. 10.12987/9780300198539

6 Algeria: security institutions fighting for their survival

In the "dark decade" from 1992 to 2000, a violent insurgency war raged in Algeria, which killed at least 100,000 persons and nearly toppled the well-entrenched regime consisting of leaders from the intelligence service, security forces, and selected civilians. Economic stagnation and repression had led to massive popular discontent, which culminated when the Islamic opposition overwhelmingly won the first free election in 1991. Immediately, the military annulled the election and took power, but the attempts failed to crush the Islamic opposition, which turned into an insurgency movement. The threat from Islamist insurgents was so grave that Western intelligence services in 1992 predicted that the Algerian regime would collapse within 18 months (Sueur 2010, 61). Nonetheless, the secular, authoritarian regime survived and almost subdued the insurgency within 8 years. This chapter examines the interplay between the political settlement of Algeria and the strategic choices of the regime that made this turn in events possible.

The case adds to this study, because since the end of the Cold War Algeria is the only example of a regime mostly dominated by formal politics that faced an existential internal insurgency threat. The dominance of formal politics in Algeria's political settlement would be expected to correlate with different kinds of strategies from those of regimes in informal settings. Moreover, a local regime acting within formal politics would be expected to implement reforms to increase the effectiveness of the counterinsurgency campaign. The regime's resistance to demands for reforms would, from a theoretical perspective, only concern issues with which it disagrees due to ideological differences. What adds to the importance of the case is the in-direct, non-military Western intervention. On the one hand, the importance of formal politics would indicate a high level of Algerian acceptance of re-forms. On the other hand, the Western powers' distance to events in Algeria created ample room for simulated reforms.

The first section examines the importance of informal politics leading up to the annulled elections. The second section examines whether the prae-torian protection proposition can explain the choices of the Algerian regime with regard to security institutions and military strategy. The third section assesses the proposition of risk-averse alignment by studying the Algerian

DOI: 10.4324/9781003204978-6

130 *Algeria*

regime's use of alignment with militias and its reactions to international conditional economic aid. The fourth section evaluates the proposition of simulated statebuilding in regard to demands for economic, administrative, and democratic reforms.

The formal legacy of the Algerian war of independence

In 1991, three decades of Algerian independence had clearly not fulfilled the promises of development and prosperity made in the wake of the declaration of the new socialist, Arab, and Muslim republic. Nonetheless, the programmatic politics of that time still had some influence on the regime and its ruling coalition. When trying to determine the balance between formal and informal politics, there is a challenge of even identifying the regime and the factions influencing decisions. Several scholars refer to the Algerian regime's decision-making as "opaque" (Boserup and Martinez 2016, Werenfels 2007, Mortimer 2006). Still, the critical juncture of the military coup of December 1991 provides us with information on those who made the decisions and how they accommodated other elites and related to the Algerian society on the whole. This section argues that Algerian politics was predominantly formal, although clientelism was intertwined with programmatic decisions to reward factions within the ruling coalition. The first section examines the role of non-productive elites in the making of the political settlement. The second section examines the degree to which the regimes used clientelism to accommodate those non-productive elites. The third section examines the importance of programmatic politics.

The stalled revolution

From gaining independence until the end of the examined period, the fundamental political settlement of Algeria remained intact. Elites active in the resistance movement during the war of independence from 1954 to 1962 reaped the political, economic, and social benefits of independence. Around 1991, the post-war political settlement had become static and had great difficulties in accommodating the changing distribution of power in society due to high increase in population, an inefficient official economy, and the rise of radical Islamism (McDougall 2017, 280ff). One reason for the inability to adapt to the changing society was the mutual dependency of the factions of the ruling elite, whose power derived from their privileged status, not their ability to mobilize societal groups.

Eight years of embittered insurgency war led to the creation of the well-organized Algerian Liberation Army, founded by Algerians who had defected from the French army. Following independence, they outmanoeuvred other insurgent groups and translated their expertise in violence into control of the security forces, as they took up senior positions in the army and the intelligence institutions (Mortimer 2006, 156–157). In 1965, the army successfully launched

Algeria 131

a coup against President Ahmed Ben Bella and until 1999 all presidents were former high-ranking officers in the army. The security forces came to be the most powerful factions within the ruling coalition and perceived themselves as the guardians of the republic (Werenfels 2007, 44). Their outsize role was hardly the result of external threats or the size of the army, but a path-dependent result of the insertion of senior military commanders as regime leaders. When opposing societal actors became stronger, the security forces turned Algeria into what Clement Henry labels a "bunker state", where the regime fought popular unrest in order to promote its own vision of society (2004). The political role of the security forces enhanced the importance of so-called clans within and among the security institutions. Strong senior commanders developed factions within the officer corps, based on shared experiences, which they utilized in the behind-the-scene power struggles. However, the factions were formalized in organs like the *Haut Comité d'Etat*, where the dominant faction gained a seat alongside civilian politicians.

From the onset in 1954, the insurgents united politically in the *Front de Libération Nationale* (FLN). After independence, FLN was the regime's primary vehicle to mobilize political support, and the number of members of FLN reached 300,000 in the late 1970s (Ruedy 2005, 208). However, FLN did not accommodate traditional and non-productive elites, such as tribal leaders, but included individuals who supported the overall model of socialism and Algerian nationalism. In 1962, the sudden exodus of 800,000 French citizens left a void of educated and organized elites, which FLN tried to fill (Adamson 1998, 88). There is a parallel pattern in the economic sector, which did not so much accommodate non-productive factions, as create a non-productive faction of bureaucrats managing the economy. Similar to the socialist states in the Eastern Bloc, the trade unions, the administrators of the state-owned companies, and the state bureaucracy were closely connected to FLN and the regime. Together, the intertwined elites across the state constituted a "state class", which defined its interests in terms of the rents accumulated from the state (Ouaissa 2021, 53–54). Consequently, as far as the new factions were unproductive, they were formally accommodated through the state institutions and had an interest in upholding the formal institutions.

Conservative forces in the Algerian society were largely excluded from the political settlement. Islamists promoting the political role of religion had little access to the ruling coalition or state institutions. Instead, the regime promoted Islam as a defining characteristic of the Algerian society, but subjugated to the authority of the state (McDougall 2017, 261–262). Privileging the state amounted to a secularist vision of Algeria, although Islam featured prominently in official statements. However, in the 1980s the general rise of political Islamism in the Middle East and the failure of the oil-based centralized economy generated significant support for the excluded Islamist elites. The regime sought to accommodate the rising elites through acceptance of some elements of a scripture-based Salafi interpretation of Islam (Roberts 2003, 90–94).

132 *Algeria*

On the surface, the political settlement excluded the Berbers, who constituted 20–25 percent of the Algerian population, in an attempt to base Algerian nationalism on a common Arab culture and language. Moreover, in the 1980s, the regimes accommodated the demands of the Islamists to increase Arabization in education as well as in the juridical sector, which excluded the Berber community who mostly spoke Thamazighth and French. In 1989, when a multiparty system was adopted, Berbers organized themselves in two political parties, the *Rassemblement pour la Culture et la Démocratie* and *Movement Culturel Berbère*, which were more secular and leftist than the Arab population (Ruedy 2005, 240–241). In practice, most elements within the regime shared a secular political outlook with the Berber parties, whereas the Islamist parties saw Arabization as a way to gain influence (Benrabah 2004, 73–75). Therefore, the Berber parties were accommodated formally in the political settlement and the state industry absorbed many of the French-speaking Berbers.

In the first decades after independence, the political settlement in Algeria excluded relatively few, mainly Islamist elites. However, the economic downturn and the regional ideological changes increased the relative power of excluded Islamist elites, because they were able to mobilize among the disaffected young generations. The ruling coalition did not consist of elites who gained their strength from specific groups or classes in society, but was composed of elites who won their power through the institutions that were established in the aftermath of the Algerian war of independence.

Rewarding the ruling coalition formally and informally

Since Algeria gained independence, the country's economy had largely been based on income from oil and gas production, which in the 1990s constituted two-thirds of the total income and almost all of Algeria's export (International Monetary Fund 2000). Consequently, the question of the distribution of oil and gas funds was at the heart of many political decisions and provides an indicator of the importance of informal politics. In the first decades, the regime used oil and gas income to finance a grand-scale industrialization project. When forced industrialization failed to create a profitable industry, and agricultural production dropped, the regime increasingly used oil and gas income to finance the importation of food and consumer goods (Panta 2017, 1092–1093). The industrial policy accommodated the demands of the ruling coalition, because it created job opportunities for the party cadres. However, the regime failed to create enough jobs for the huge cohorts of young people, who had received a higher education thanks to the regime's investment in this sector. This inability created support for the Islamist elites as well as leading to large-scale riots in 1988, and not least an illegal economy fuelled by remittance and imported goods from Algerians in France (Ruf 1997, 7–8). The Islamists effectively mobilized among the individuals benefiting from the illegal economy.

Algeria 133

Until the late 1980s, the relative powerlessness of the excluded elites gave the ruling coalition little incentive to provide them informally with funds and privileges. However, within the ruling coalition privileges and funds were distributed both formally and informally. The International Crisis Group estimates that in the 1990s, the regime had 600,000–800,000 clients within the state and within newly privatized companies (2001, 10). Rather than direct payments, members of FLN or the organization for veterans from the war of independence received privileges in the form of contracts or licenses to benefit their businesses. Starting a new business was almost impossible for citizens outside the client network of the regime, at least in the formal economy. Moreover, the existence of wings within the security forces indicates that clientelism most likely served the purpose of securing the personal support of lower-level officials for senior officials with ambitions for power (Ouaissa 2021, 53). President Chadli Bendjedid took corruption to new levels to accommodate his client network when he was in power from 1978 to 1991 (Roberts 2003, 107). But even Bendjedid mobilized supporters within the ruling coalition who sympathized with the programmatic idea of a systematic liberal reform of the Algerian state.

In general, two aspects of the instrumentalization of the client networks differ from the informal use. First, the selection of officials was to some extent based on merit. French was a prerequisite for working in many parts of the state, and persons from families in the client network generally spoke French (Werenfels 2007, 87–88). Second, clients were selected for programmatic reasons, such as history (veterans from the war of independence) or their loyalty to the policy of the party and institutions that supported the regime. Although this went against the declared principles of serving the interest of the Algerian people, the selection of clients was based on their support of that vision.

Overall, clientelism was widespread, but was intertwined with and served the purpose of programmatic politics. Until the 1980s, the relatively secure position of the ruling coalition had allowed the regimes to distribute a great deal of funds and privileges to reward the supporters of the Algerian regime. Clients were selected along programmatic lines and they came to define their interests in line with those of the regime and the state. There is no doubt that non-programmatic exchanges were part of the factional battles for power. And from the point of view of the general Algerian population, the exchanges looked like corruption and nepotism. However, they served programmatic purposes and are therefore categorized as formal accommodation of factions within the ruling coalition.

A secular, nationalist vision of Algeria

In December 1991, the Islamic party *Front Islamique du Salut* won the first round of the first multiparty election in Algeria's history. They won 188 of 232 seats compared to FLN's 15 (Hill 2009, 43). FLN had been the single,

134   *Algeria*

legal party in the previous three decades, which meant that FLN had become the political manifestation of a nationalist, secular vision for Algeria. Losing power to a non-secular Islamist party would mean the end of three decades of nation and statebuilding, in which FLN leaders considered the interests of the people equal to the interests of the state and the party (Roberts 2003, 27). However, the principles of FLN were not directly connected to the policies implemented by the Algerian state.

The general staff and other senior commanders from the intelligence services, police, and gendarmerie held what Lahouri Addi called "supreme authority" of the state (1998, 46ff). Senior executives from primarily the security institutions had regular meetings in the so-called *le pouvoir* ("the power") – a consortium that met behind closed doors (Werenfels 2007). *Le pouvoir* had much more power than the parliament and more power than the president. Decisions made in *le pouvoir* ultimately sealed the fate of prime ministers and presidents (ibid). Political initiatives from FLN or the formal executive power of the president and his government had to be approved by the supreme authority of the factions specialized in violence, especially during the most intense part of the conflict. Thus, political principles of the civilian institutions did not necessarily translate into policy, if the influential commanders of the security forces were in opposition.

In January 1992, the most critical example of the limits to civilian control was the military coup and cancellation of the parliamentary elections. In the wake of the first round of parliamentary elections on 26 December 1991, the military removed President Bendjedid, banned the Islamist party *Front islamique du salut* (FIS), and cancelled the second round of the elections in a coup on 11 January 1992. An Islamist take-over of civilian power deviated so far from *le pouvoir*'s vision of the Algerian state and society that they were willing to throw away any pretensions of representing a popular will or democratic ideals. Obviously, *le pouvoir* was motivated by a strong self-interest in the coup to preserve its own power, but the subsequent events showed that the covert decision-makers in Algeria shared a secularist and nationalist vision of the state (Mortimer 1996, 22). The decision-making process in Algeria might have been opaque due to the power of the security institutions, and the factions within the ruling coalition might have disagreed on specific political issues, but the shared vision of Algerian politics provided a programmatic direction for political decisions.

To sum up, formal politics was able to accommodate most of the demands of the factions within the ruling coalition, who gained their power from the state institutions, not by mobilizing societal groups. Therefore, the regime could accommodate the factions by formal programmes to increase the capacity of the state institutions. For the most part, clientelism was intertwined with programmatic politics, which favoured persons loyal to the overall political vision of Algeria. The existence of factions and the decisive power of the security forces made the decision-making process opaque, but a

Algeria 135

public and formally formulated vision of Algeria tied the different decision-makers together. The political settlement of Algeria was primarily formal.

No praetorian protection: *le pouvoir* implements an elimination strategy

During the Cold War, the Algerian security institutions received weapons and training from the Soviet Union. Organizationally and doctrinally that meant that the army prepared for a conventional war, whereas the intelligence service and the gendarmerie were primarily used for internal repression. The regime had to choose a military organization and strategy best suited to addressing the new insurgency threat. This section argues that the regime acted as expected given that it mostly navigated formal politics. The regime changed its organization towards greater reliance on elite forces without building a praetorian force. Moreover, between 1992 and 1997, it used the elite forces and the regular forces in an uncompromising strategy of elimination that led to indiscriminate killings.

Changing the security institutions into a counterinsurgency force

The Algerian security institutions shared many weaknesses with other Arab armies, such as a centralized command and control structure, political appointments, and civil economic interests of senior commanders, which reduced the general level of professionalism (Pollack 2019). During the Cold War, the Algerian army was primarily organized for conventional warfare and had a high proportion of conscripts. The army only took up a small proportion of government expenditure compared to neighbouring states, which is surprising given the relative power of the army faction within the ruling coalition (Henry 2004, 71). Instead, the intelligence service and the gendarmerie were large organizations with a great deal of political power, as they were responsible for fighting internal threats to the political order in the mould of the KGB.

In 1992 the regime tasked Major General Lamari with establishing a dedicated anti-terrorism unit in order to increase the counterinsurgency capacity of the army. Until then, counter-terrorism was managed by two small elite units from the gendarmerie and the intelligence service. The new elite units were highly active from the onset and reached 60,000 service members in 1995 (Martinez 2000, 148). Moreover, Major General Lamari soon became a core member of the regime, when he became Chief of Staff in the army. Importantly, the army selectively used the newly added members of the elite units to conduct small-scale attacks to kill or arrest members of the Islamic insurgent groups, and to gather intelligence (ibid 2000, 149). The elite units were privileged with the highest increase in resources and men, most likely because of the operational need of having soldiers able to detect

136 *Algeria*

and attack insurgents living among civilians without warning them off, as the regular units did.

Additional regular units were established and the number of conscripts increased. On paper, the army grew from 126,000 men in 1992 to 270,000 men in 1997 (World Bank 2021). The increase was largely due to the inclusion of local vigilance militias in the formal structure (Benramdane 2004). More importantly, military expenditure rose from $601 million in 1991 to $1,909 million in 1997, measured in constant 2014 prices (SIPRI 2020). The increase in expenditure went hand in hand with an increase in professionalism. New materiel, such as computers, was implemented in most units within the security institutions (Benramdane 2004). This, together with a shared sense of purpose increased the cohesion of the army. As Zoubir notes: "Undoubtedly, the targeting of the military by the Islamists helped weld the military's cohesion and strengthen its esprit de corps, an event unforeseen by its armed opponents" (1998, 92). The number of men, available resources, and professionalism increased in the regular units, albeit at a lower rate than in the elite units.

The professionalism of the conscript-based regular units was not as high as that of the elite units. Even so, the regular units carried out two kinds of operations that supported the overall military strategy. First, they controlled access to insurgent-dominated areas in the suburbs of Algiers and Oran. From 1992 to 1994, when the crisis was most uncontrollable, the regime relied on containment of the strongest insurgency-held areas (Martinez 2000, 150). By limiting supplies and access to the outside world, the regime reduced popular support for the Emirs, the local insurgency leaders. Second, they conducted large-scale sweeping operations to remove insurgent bases and to signal determination to the public (Addi 2001). Overall, the regular army units had a place in the military strategy and received additional resources accordingly, although fewer than the elite units. Professionalizing and expanding the security forces when faced with an existential insurgent threat suggests that the security institutions were able to react to a new threat in a coordinated way. A certain level of control and hierarchy is necessary for the vast number of new units to adhere to the common strategy of the regime.

The internal debate about strategy

In the early phase of the insurgency, the regime reacted with a quick-paced repression of protestors and individuals suspected of insurgency activities. Since October 1988 violent protests alerted the internal security institutions to the risk of an insurgency. Following the military coup in January 1992, the regime banned the Islamic FIS party and arrested Abassi Madani and Ali Ben Hadj, the two leading members of the party. Moreover, to suppress protest the regime declared a state of emergency and began the hasty construction of concentration camps in the Sahara for FIS members arrested in

Algeria 137

the months following the coup. In 1992 and 1993, agents from the intelligence service and gendarmerie began killing and arresting militant or potentially militant Islamists (International Crisis Group 2004, 8).

However, the institutions dedicated to internal repression failed to deliver as the insurgency spread in 1992 and 1993, sparking an internal debate in the regime about the choice of counterinsurgency strategy. The most dominant wing of the regime was held by the so-called *éradicateurs*, who argued for a mobilization of all state resources to degrade the capacity of the insurgents to a negligible level – an elimination strategy. Some of the main proponents of the elimination strategy were General Mohamed Lamari, the Army Chief of Staff, General Tewfik Mediene, the Director of the Intelligence Service, General Smaïn Lamari, commander of the elite forces assigned to the Intelligence Service, and General Khaled Nezzar, the Minister of Defence (Addi 2001). The minor wing, known as the *conciliateurs,* argued for a two-pronged approach of applying violence to militant insurgents and compromising with non-violent Islamists (Roberts 1995, 251). The *conciliateurs* were headed by Liamine Zéroual, who was appointed President in 1994, General Muhammad Boughaba, the head of the Algiers military region and advisor to Zéroual during his presidency, and General Tayeb Derradji, the Commander of the Gendarmerie (Salies 1997).

Besides the elements of large-scale sweeping of insurgent-held areas and targeted elimination of insurgent cells, the security institutions used highly controversial methods. One way was to use the security institutions to "terrorize the terrorist" by applying excessive violence to sow fear among insurgents and sympathizers. Habib Souaïdia, a former officer in the elite forces, explains that the use of excessive violence was intended to force potential insurgents or persons marginally involved in the insurgency into passivity (Souaïdia 2002, 24). From this perspective the use of, e.g., extra-juridical killings, torture, and disappearances was part of an overall strategy, and not simply the result of an increased brutalization of the war (Pennell 2019).

One purpose, besides sowing fear among the insurgent groups, was to delegitimize the insurgents in the eyes of the population. The regime's military strategy could be considered population-centric, but instead of enhancing the popular view of the state, the strategy tried to scare the population away from the insurgents. The intelligence service strove to undermine the most militant insurgent group, the *Groupe Islamique Armé* (GIA), possibly by dubious methods. The mass killings of civilians in 1997 and 1998 remain the most controversial aspect of the Algerian war. GIA veterans themselves acknowledge that the group carried out many massacres against civilians in order to warn those that denounced the Jihadi project (Thurston 2017, 430). However, several sources claim that security forces pretending to be GIA carried out massacres to delegitimize the Islamist opposition (Benramdane 2004, Souaïdia 2002, Mortimer 2006). What is known for certain from the memories of Khaled Nezzar, former Chief of Staff and member of the *Haut Comité d'Etat,* is that the intelligence service

138 *Algeria*

infiltrated GIA to gain information and to cause an internal split (Nezzar and Maarfia 2003, 215). The infiltration of GIA also testifies to the regime's willingness to run risks in order to achieve its objectives. If the infiltrators knew about the massacres beforehand, yet did nothing, the regime must have calculated with the risk of a public backlash or international sanctions, if its actions came to light.

Until 1997, the only real attempt to break from the elimination strategy was initiated by then Minister of Defence Zéroual in October 1993, because in Zéroual's words "security policy alone is insufficient to rescue the country from its crisis [the solution lies in] dialogue and the participation of all national political forces, without exception" (Mortimer 1996, 33). This meant negotiating with arrested members of FIS. However in 1995, Zéroual was forced to abort negotiations publicly, due to pressure from the army (Roberts 1995, 259). This pattern repeated itself when the FLN faction, as well as several other parties, chose to negotiate with FIS on the principles of a political compromise. The negotiations were facilitated by the Sant'Egidio, a religious NGO in Rome, and Zéroual sent a secret negotiator to Rome, but rejected the outcome of the Sant'Egidio negotiations after pressure from hardliners in the regime (Ramonet 1999). In the period 1992–1997, the regime pursued an elimination strategy towards the insurgents, despite internal disagreements between the two wings of the regime.

The split of the insurgents gave rise to a third strategy

In 1997, the intelligence service secretly negotiated with the *Armée Islamique du Salut* (AIS) to end hostilities between AIS and the Algerian state, which culminated in AIS's unilateral ceasefire 1 October. The sudden negotiation came about as the uncompromising elimination strategy of the regime had decimated AIS. However, in practice the strategy from 1997 to 1999 continued the main elements of the elimination strategy, because it relied on delegitimizing the insurgents by pacifying the less extremist group. In 1997, the strategic situation of AIS was dim. AIS was close to the FIS party leaders and was mortified by GIA's tough approach, which included violence against civilians and thereby undermined national and international support for the Islamists (Mendelsohn 2019). GIA launched a *"takfir el moudhamah"* which meant a condemnation of large portions of society for having become apostate through their participation in the 1995 presidential elections. Operationally, the professionalization of the army and the numerous militia groups put relatively more pressure on AIS than on GIA, due to the operational focus of AIS on attacking the Algerian security institutions (ibid).

Within the regime, a third wing between the *éradicateurs* and *conciliateurs* was formed in 1996 and 1997. Tewfik Mediene, head of the Intelligence Service, and his right hand, General Smain Lamari, leader of the anti-terror unit of the Intelligence Service, saw negotiations with AIS as a way to split the insurgency and isolate GIA (Salies 1997). Secretly, they bypassed

Algeria 139

President Zéroual and negotiated directly with AIS, avoiding FIS. During the conflict, intelligence agents infiltrated AIS, which provided Mediene with intelligence on key leaders and their willingness to negotiate. It is worth noting that the intelligence service wing was able to reach an agreement with AIS, despite initial opposition from the *éradicateur* side led by Chief of Staff Mohammed Lamari (Sueur 2010, 66). Officially, the regime did not announce a reaction to the AIS's ceasefire until 1999, but the security institutions ceased operations against AIS, which at least suggests that the *éradicateurs* accepted the agreement.

By pacifying AIS, the regime was able to direct all its efforts against GIA. This group was founded on the principle of no negotiations (Thurston 2017, 423). Yet, the regime could force an internal split between less extreme factions and the most radical factions. In 1998, GIA was splintered by the founding of the *Groupe Salafiste pour la Prédication et le Combat* (GSPC), which left GIA almost powerless (Sueur 2010, 144). Whether due to infiltration or an increasingly unfavourable military situation, 800 insurgents from GIA accepted amnesty in 1999 together with 4,200 other insurgents. Subsequently, GSPC remained a nuisance, but not a threat, to the Algerian regime for the duration of the examined period. At that time, the level of violence fell dramatically, leading the army and intelligence service to accept the new President Bouteflika's "Law of Civil Concord", which restated the amnesty policy and called for an inclusive political process (Mecellem 2018, 243). However, the inclusive political process resembled a surrender by the insurgents.

In sum, the regime managed to increase the size and efficiency of both regular and elite forces in the examined period. The elite forces were not reserved for regime protection, but constituted the cornerstone of the military means. No Western training was allowed, nor necessary. The regime settled on an elimination strategy, which was supplemented by negotiations and infiltrations to cause splits within the insurgency groups. The organization and use of the security forces are therefore consistent with what would be expected of a regime in a formal setting, because the regime optimized the use of its military resources instead of fighting half-heartedly. The behaviour of the Algerian regime deviated from the proposition of praetorian protection, but was very close to the behaviour expected of regimes navigating formal politics. However, the regime could not rely entirely on the security forces to combat the insurgents and avoid an economic breakdown.

Risk-averse alignment: sovereignty first, alignment second

In 1993 and 1994, the regime was on the verge of defeat, due to the growing number of insurgents and their control of an increasing extent of territory. In addition, the cost of the war pushed the already fragile public finances close to bankruptcy. So how did the regime use alignment to balance the

140 *Algeria*

insurgents and move away from bankruptcy? This section argues that the regime acted differently from regimes in informal settings, because it fought to maintain the sovereignty of Algeria, and, thereby, its internal as well as external authority. First, the regime's approach to militias will be examined, and second, how the regime negotiated its debt obligations.

Arming the militias – mobilizing or balancing?

Militias can co-exist with regimes in states dominated by informal politics. By contrast, regimes in states dominated by formal politics would be expected to fight militias, or at least regulate their authority and subordinate them to the security institutions. In 1994 in Algeria, numerous self-protection militias formed to fight the Islamist insurgents. The question is to what extent the regime organized the militias or the militias were self-organized actors with whom the regime aligned reluctantly. In addition, it is necessary to consider if the militias were subjugated to the security institutions and to what extent the latter could control their actions. This part argues that the regime's relationship with the militias mostly adheres to the theoretical expectation, albeit with some exceptions. The regime was behind the establishment of many self-defence militias, but also aligned with self-organized militias. Moreover, the regime subjected the militias to the oversight of local police forces even though some militias conducted operations on their own.

Self-protection militias were formed in 1993 and 1994 against the Islamist insurgents, and most of them became organized in 1996 as part of the *groupes de légitimes défense* under the Ministry of the Interior. Militias were not a marginal part of the conflict, as they outsized the army and were often the first line of defence in the villages. Considerable disagreement persists on the origin of the militias. Bruno Salies argues that General Zéroual merely legalized existing militias in the fall of 1994, when Zéroual called for the formation of militias (1997). According to this view, the inability of the army to protect small villages or suburbs controlled by Islamists forced locals to organize militias spontaneously. By contrast, Jose Garçon argues that the idea of recruiting locals as militiamen to free army units from protection assignments was conceived by the regime (1997, 1998). Moreover, the creation of the militia units was originally described by Major General Mohamed Touati in the army journal El Djeich in March 1993 (Meddi 2005). In all probability the early militias reflected local security concerns, which the regime quickly took advantage of by arming the groups, many of which had a nucleus of former insurgents from the war of independence (Pennell 2019, 6).

However, although the army endorsed the formation or even set up part of the militias, two kinds of militias were beyond the control of the regime. First, in reaction to the general state of insecurity, tribes with little overt political presence organized self-defence militias to protect tribal members (Abdi 1997). Tribal influence was most pronounced in the rural parts of

Algeria 141

Algeria, where social or geographical mobility was less prevalent. In these areas, Arab tribal leaders might be said to accept the authority of the regime, in the sense that voter turnout was more favourable for pro-regime candidates. However, the nationalist project of Algeria since gaining independence was a modernist one, which tried to eliminate the political and social position of the tribes (Roberts 2003, 53–54). The decisions to set up self-defence militias are for that reason unlikely to have been attempts to protect the authority of the regime and state.

Second, the two main political parties of the Berbers founded and supported militias (Martinez 2000, 151). The Berber militias were active in Kabylia, and were effective enough to marginalize Islamist insurgents. Still, many of the local Berber militias were organized in the regime's Groupes de Légitimes Defense, and had a very local outlook (Aït Kaki 2003, 115). Moreover, the fact that many Berbers and the Berber political parties were part of the ruling coalition reduced the threat to the regime. The most obvious sign of the regime's accommodating view of the Berbers was the official recognition of the Berber language in 1995. However, in 2001, after the decline in violence civil Berber protests against the regime flared up, but the cause was primarily frustration over the lack of economic opportunities in Kabylia (International Crisis Group 2004, 11). However, the Berber militias did not use violence against the Algerian state, which probably reflects the Berber elites' wish to keep the political settlement together.

From 1996 onwards, insurgent groups and militias suffered from fragmentation, as commonly seen in prolonged insurgencies (Hafez 2020). In Algeria, many of the new militias took advantage of their power to get economic benefits. Many former FIS supporters found a livelihood serving in the militias, earning three times the minimum wage, and furthermore militias informally controlled illegal trade (Garçon 1997). Despite several attempts by the regime to discipline and direct the efforts of the militias, local grievances and economic disputes spurred extra-juridical killings and abuse of power (Benramdane 2004). Still, each militia remained small and dependent on receiving pay from the state. Once the security situation improved from 1999, the Algerian regime worked on and mostly succeeded in demobilizing and reintegrating the militias. The Ministry of the Interior used economic control of the *Groupes de Légitimes Defense* to demobilize the militias by cutting down the pay and materiel support (Meddi 2005).

The regime temporarily lost authority because of the formation and spread of militias. Yet, the overall assessment of the regime's strategy is that it had considerable control of the militias through the Ministry of the Interior. Even when the regime lost control of some militias in 1996 and 1997, it strived to regain it. The increased strength of the tribes and the Berbers was suppressed by the regime, once the security institutions became able to control the insurgents without the assistance of militias. The way the regime handled the militias is in line with the theoretical expectations that

142 *Algeria*

regimes navigating formal politics might have to rely on militias, but will subjugate them to the authority of the state and regime.

External alignments and economic assistance

In political settlements primarily dominated by informal politics, the regimes are expected to be relatively unconcerned with issues of sovereignty when aligning with external powers. By contrast, the expectation is that the Algerian regime would be very concerned with maintaining sovereignty, even during a crisis. If the crisis forces a regime in a formal setting to rely on external support, the regime will minimize the loss of sovereignty by keeping cooperation for less intrusive areas, such as the economy. In May 1994, with a stroke of the pen the economic foundation of the war effort changed. Although the deal between the EU, the World Bank, IMF, and the Algerian regime to restructure Algeria's public debt was inconspicuous compared to military interventions, it proved a turning point in the conflict. Despite its importance, the protection of sovereignty made the Algerian regime reluctant in its negotiations of the external alignments.

In 1993, the Algerian state was on the brink of bankruptcy after decades of economic decline and due to the sudden cost of expanding and professionalizing the security forces. The impact of the insurgency on the external debt of the Algerian state was huge: from 1993 to 1995 the external debt rose from 30 to 80 percent of GDP (International Monetary Fund 2000, 50). Due to Algeria's large oil and gas income, a restructuring of its debt could immediately provide the regime with $7 billion yearly to spend on the war effort, plus an additional $5 billion in yearly aid, which almost doubled the funds available to the regime. The dramatic change from 1995 to 1997 demonstrated the potential of the additional funds, which allowed the regime to maintain an elimination strategy through the continuous professionalization of the security forces as well as the financing of the numerous militias (Hill 2009, 50–52, Martinez 2000, 179). Yet, the regime hesitated to accept an international agreement.

Internally, the regime debated the terms of the EU and IMF from 1991 through 1993, but chose not to sign any agreements until May 1994, despite substantial EU payments being withheld until Algeria accepted IMF's structural adjustment programme (Roberts 2003, 324–27). The conditions of IMF called for massive cuts in public employment, privatization, and cuts in subsidies to consumer goods. In 1989 and 1991, the regime accepted minor IMF-imposed changes in the financial market in return for loans (Sueur 2010, 101). However, the major EU and IMF deal, negotiated from 1991 to 1994, had a more far-reaching impact on Algerian society. Most critically, some of the cuts played into the hands of the insurgents, because the public sector would be less able to absorb the large youth generations, and social welfare was decimated (International Crisis Group 2001, 11). Moreover, the

Algeria 143

deals made the regime dependent on the choices of external actors, who now had a say in its economic policy.

France was the driving force behind the EU and IMF's decision to assist Algeria financially. International donors were deeply sceptical of supporting the authoritarian Algerian regime in the midst of a major internal conflict. Japan, the biggest creditor, had no interest in renegotiating the debt payments and most member states within the EU opposed the idea of supporting a repressive regime that violated human rights and democratic principles (Roberts 2003, 326). However, behind the scenes Michel Camdessus, the French Executive Director of IMF, advocated most urgently that "countries which were allies of Algeria should immediately offer their help", and he finally succeeded (Ruf 1997, 12). Similarly, the French government implored EU member states to release the frozen payments and eventually persuaded them to prioritize stability and security concerns above democratization and human rights (Morisse-Schilbach 1999, 85).

Unilaterally, France decided to provide the Algerian regime with $6 billion of unconditional financial aid in 1994 (Martinez 2000, 228–229). Internally, the successive French governments in the early 1990s disagreed on the strategy vis-à-vis Algeria. Charles Pasqua, the French Minister of the Interior, strongly supported the *éradicateur* wing of the Algerian regime (Kapil 1995, 4). President François Mitterrand and later the Gaullist Prime Minister Edouard Balladur had reservations, but in the end reluctantly supported the Algerian regime (Darbouche and Zoubir 2013, 39). Additionally, the French and Algerian intelligence services cooperated from 1993, due to their shared focus on Islamist terrorism. After GIA terror attacks in France in 1995, the cooperation strengthened and the Algerian intelligence service provided most of the intelligence that influenced the French strategy towards GIA (Zoubir 1998, 85).

Several factors indicate that sovereignty was a major concern for the Algerian regime, and the external actors went to great lengths to provide support in a way that did not publicly encroach on Algerian sovereignty. The experience of the bloody and brutal Algerian war of independence made the Algerian population and elites reluctant to accept French involvement in the war in the 1990s. French politicians carefully sought to avoid the image of a former colonial power meddling in the internal affairs of Algeria. In 1998, when asked about what France could do in relation to the war in Algeria, Hubert Védrine, the French Minister of Foreign Affairs, declared "We cannot, we will not, assail Algerian sovereignty. Moreover, the Algerians, and not only the leaders, have rejected those who have maintained that they wanted to or proposed to interfere" (cited in Malmvig 2006, 140). The declaration might not hold up against the encompassing reforms the Algerian regime was subjugated to, but resonated well with the Algerian population's perception of what role France should play. The involvement of the international organizations of the EU, IMF, and the World Bank served two functions. In addition to increasing the available funds for assistance, France could turn external support and demands into a more

144   *Algeria*

anonymous and even technical assistance that would be less provocative to the Algerian public (Morisse-Schilbach 1999, 132). For the international organizations, the fact that the support was purely economic made it more acceptable.

In summary, the regime initially made use of internal alignment to turn militias into allies of the regime. However, the regime did so as a means to preserve its authority, by formally subjugating the militias to the Ministry of the Interior, and in practice forcing them to accept the dominance of the state, once the crisis waned. After avoiding external encroachment on Algerian sovereignty for years, the regime aligned externally to receive vital external economic support in order to continue and expand the war effort. Yet, the concerns for sovereignty meant that international support had to be framed in a less obtrusive, multinational, and technical way. In practice, international support had a potentially far-reaching impact on the Algerian society. The next section examines how the regime reacted to the demands for economic reforms as well as demands for democratization.

Simulated statebuilding to the satisfaction of le pouvoir and external donors

External actors went to great lengths to stress the importance of Algerian sovereignty when determining conditions for support. In practice, however, the demands of the external actors were equal to the administrative and political demands made in other Western interventions. The EU, France, and the United States insisted on the resumption of democracy in Algeria. The International Monetary Fund (IMF) and the World Bank demanded economic reforms. This section argues that Algeria in general adopted the reforms, but the regime made two key omissions that reflected the interests of the ruling coalition. The regime manipulated the elections to prevent Islamic parties from winning, and privatized public companies in a way that allowed the regime's powerbase to gain ownership. These practices were acceptable to the Western powers that shared the regime's fear of an Islamic take-over, despite Western critique of the human rights record of the Algerian regime. The first part examines the reintroduction of democracy, and the second part examines the implementation of economic reforms.

Good enough elections: the reintroduction of democracy

The abortion of the second round of the parliamentary election in December 1991 went against an international wave of democratization. In 1990, President Mitterrand introduced conditionality, declaring that "France will bind all its [aid] contributions to the efforts that will be made to move towards more freedom" (de Felice 2015, 26). Not surprisingly, the public stance of France, the United States, and later the EU was a call for a return to a democratic path in Algeria. In 1994, all three actors supported the Sant'Egidio negotiations between the banned FIS-party and other Algerian

Algeria 145

political parties (Pierre and Quandt 1995, 145). The regime's open exclusion of FIS was very difficult for the Western regimes to defend publicly, even though the Western powers shared some of the regime's concern about FIS's intentions.

Western demands avoided the thorny issue of limitations to what parties should be allowed to run when democracy was resumed in Algeria (Roberts 1995, 256). In August 1994, Allan Juppé, the French Minister of Foreign Affairs declared: "It is in France's interest to have a regime in Algeria which is not hostile to her. But an Islamic state would be anti-French, anti-European, anti-Western" (quoted in Malmvig 2006, 120). However, French politicians avoided the obvious issue that a reintroduction of democracy might have led to a repetition of the 1991 election. Until 1995 the EU was split between northern European states protesting against the Algerian state's human rights violations and French support for the regime. In the end, the EU's Foreign Ministers took a pragmatic course and expressed the hope that human rights and democracy would be respected by the Algerian regime (Morisse-Schilbach 1999, 71). Finally, the United States not only pushed for the resumption of democracy, but also engaged in a low-profile dialogue with the banned FIS party (Pierre and Quandt 1995, 145). The United States' position was most likely a pragmatic choice to lessen the consequences of a possible Islamic take-over.

After the cancelation of the elections in 1991, the Algerian regime strived for a formal political leadership with more legitimacy than a military regime. However, the military leaders intervened every time the formal political leadership overstepped its boundaries. The first example was the immediate return of Mohamed Boudiaf, who the military junta inserted as head of the provisional *Haut Comité d'Etat*. Boudiaf was a key figure from the war of independence and was untainted by the corruption associated with the political settlement after independence, mostly because he had been in exile in Morocco since 1964 (McDougall 2017, 303). However, conflicts broke out between Boudiaf and other members of the regime, because he promoted quick democratic and anti-corruption reforms. It does not seem likely that the senior army leadership was responsible for the assassination of Boudiaf in June 1992, yet it had stalled all his reform initiatives in the previous months (Sueur 2010, 59).

Instead, the regime slowly began preparing a return to elections by appointing Liamine Zéroual President in January 1994, before holding presidential elections in 1995. From 1995 to 1999, the regime held an additional presidential election in 1999, a referendum on a new constitution in 1996, and the parliamentary elections in 1997. The election processes were only partly free. Most prominently, FIS remained illegal and the two other Islamist parties, *Mouvement de la société en paix* and *Ennahda* were co-opted by the regime. Voters thus had few options outside the two parties most closely associated with the regime, the *Rassemblement National Démocratique* (RND) and FLN. In 1998, when Ennahda became too popular, the regime prevented its leader

146 *Algeria*

from running for president (Deeb and Yacoubian 1999). Moreover, the regime manipulated and rigged the elections in several ways to guarantee a majority for FLN and its offshoot RND (Roberts 2003, 192ff).

In contrast to the indirect and ad hoc control of the elections, the constitution of 1996 officially banned parties that "violate (...) [the] Republican nature of the State. (...) political parties cannot be founded on a religious, linguistic, racial, sexual, corporatist or regional basis" ("Algeria's Constitution of 1989, Reinstated in 1996, with Amendments through 2008" 2016, 9). In addition, the President could now overturn any new legislation and the parliament was divided into an upper and a lower house, with only the lower house being elected in a general election. The need to make a constitutional change in the rules of politics might reflect the formal elements of Algerian politics. The formal limitation of democracy was a clear signal of the boundaries of acceptable behaviour.

Having a civilian government elected by public votes had the advantage of creating a public centre of power, which the regime could point to when faced with international critique or demands. Moreover, as formulated by Gianni Del Panta, domestic critique became less dangerous to the regime: "(...) the dominant coalition has used the national assembly as a democratic façade and a tool to co-opt opposition forces, providing a safety valve for uncontrolled social unrest" (2017, 1096). Such a construction did not compromise the interests of the ruling coalition, as the factions could expect the regime to regulate any excesses of the civilian leaders.

The resumption of democratic elections in 1995 altered the public position of the Western powers. France and the United States underlined that the elected President Zéroual was now the legitimate head of state, and the electoral process was relatively fair, with a high voter turnout. In December 1996, EU Commissioner Marín visited Algiers, praised the elections, and announced a new aid package (Daguzan 2002, 143). The terror campaign of GIA in 1994 and 1995, including the hijacking of an Air France flight in December 1994 and the subsequent terror bombings in France in 1995, undoubtedly moved the French government towards uncompromising support for the regime. The EU and the United States decided that the limited democratization of Algeria was enough for them to support the regime publicly and provide the elections with international legitimacy.

In 1998, the wings within the regime settled on Boutiflika as a compromise candidate for the presidential election in 1999. In contrast to Zéroual, as a civilian Boutiflika was even easier for the Western powers to endorse. Moreover, Boutiflika appointed commissions to prepare juridical reforms and to limit the power of the security institutions, although none of the recommendations of the commissions were carried out (Holm 2003, 275). However, Boutiflika took small steps that increased his legitimacy and limited the power of the army. He launched the "Law of Civil Concord" and secured a parliamentary and popular vote in 1999. In 2004, Boutiflika declared that "gone is the time when the military institutions, for considerations of stability and national cohesion, intervened in the political game

Algeria 147

(...)" (Tlemcani 2008, 13). However, by that time the crisis was over, and the military leaders had accepted a more confined role, although they still protected the status quo towards the Islamists (Martinez 2016, 6).

The limited democratic reforms from 1995 onwards were enough to satisfy the public demands of the Western powers. Western backing came despite the constitutional limitations of the Algerian democracy and the continued dominance of the military, even after Boutiflika took office. Despite their knowledge of this, the Western powers accepted the democratic reforms as sufficient, given the alternative of an Islamic take-over. It is not possible to determine whether Algerian political reforms were a result of Western pressure, but the conclusion must be that the Algerian regime was able to satisfy the Western powers on the issue of political reforms.

Implementing macro reforms but simulating privatization

In 1994, the dire financial situation forced the Algerian regime to act. In the early 1990s, IMF and the World Bank imposed comprehensive economic reforms on states seeking financial aid. Western powers backed the approach of the two institutions, which presented Algeria with a range of demands for economic reforms. The regime's reaction to these demands took two different directions: on the one hand the regime diligently implemented macro reforms, such as inflation control, in a way that dramatically improved Algeria's economic outlook; on the other hand, the regime undermined the attempts to privatize state companies, or secretly handed the companies over to clients within the ruling coalition. This section argues that the duality of this behaviour reflects Algerian politics, which was mostly formal, but also exercised informal practices of distributing funds and privileges. Overall, the use of conditionality politics was mostly successful, as the regime adhered to the majority of the Western demands.

Western powers considered the economic crisis of Algeria as a root cause of the popular support for the Islamists. The perception in Paris and Washington was that the regime's inability to improve the economy was a key issue. A decade of economic decline caused widespread popular protest from 1988 and, along with the popular vote for FIS, all pointed towards improved economic conditions as being the key to improving popular support for the regime and marginalizing the insurgents (Malmvig 2006, 112–113, Morisse-Schilbach 1999, 66). The EU, France, and important creditors such as Japan delegated the design of economic reforms to IMF and the World Bank. In line with the general division of labour, IMF focused on Algeria's external debt at the fiscal level, whereas the World Bank concentrated on the structural adjustment at the macro and micro levels. At the macro level, the Algerian state had to lower inflation, reduce the public deficit, and create a floating exchange rate without forced devaluations. The micro level aimed to improve markets through the removal of state subsidies, privatization of public companies, and the removal of barriers to

148 *Algeria*

import and export (Hill 2009, 49). Collectively the reforms were a major neoliberal upheaval of the Algerian economy, which was state-driven with massive subsidies of consumer goods and unprofitable state industries financed by income from oil and gas production. More importantly, in the short term the reforms were likely to have negative effects on the livelihood of ordinary citizens.

Within two years, the macroeconomic indicators of Algeria had improved. At a macro level, the structural adjustment programmes drastically improved the economy, according to the IMF. Most importantly, debt services fell from around 80 to 40 percent of the total export, government finances had a positive balance in 1996 and 1997, before turning negative in 1998 due to the sharp fall in oil prices (International Monetary Fund 2000, 5). From that perspective, the regime had a self-interest in implementing the reforms. However, the cut in government spending increased unemployment, and the removal of state subsidies meant that the price of everyday consumer goods rose sharply (Hill 2009, 50–52). In fact, the regime had diligently implemented all macro-economic reforms and even micro-economic reforms that impoverished ordinary citizens, despite the potential for increased popular dissatisfaction with the regime.

However, the regime and actors within the ruling coalition manipulated and resisted privatization of public companies and the removal of restrictions on import and export. Formally, the Algerian state complied with the World Bank and passed the privatization law in 1995. In practice, trusted state officials made privatization a deliberately cumbersome process, which ensured that former generals, members of FLN, and increasingly younger clients gained ownership of the state-controlled companies (Werenfels 2002). The pressure to maintain control of state-owned companies in the hands of the ruling coalition came from the socialist wing of FLN and the UGTA, the dominant trade union. Moreover, junior officers became active in the hotel business, and acting and retired commanders outside the decision-making process took advantage of the large privatized companies (Martinez 2000, 124–125). They became the brokers between the regime and the lower-level factions within the ruling coalition without whom the regime would become isolated from its client network. This is not to suggest that the regime supported privatization. However, the regime was not the driving force in the informal undermining of privatization, which was dominated by other factions in the ruling coalition. When the ruling coalition needed informal accommodation, the outcome was simulated statebuilding.

From the 1980s, import became a lucrative business for most state-owned companies, often supplanting production as the main income. Restrictions on import and export of goods hampered the development of the private sector in Algeria, as the state did not allow companies to trade internationally outside the public monopolies. Algeria officially met the World Bank's demands for trade liberalization in 1995, but in practice the regime shut down competition by using bureaucratic delays or forcing state banks to deny credit to finance import (Aubenas 2004). Newly privatized companies thus upheld a

Algeria 149

favourable position, as an employee of Algiers's Chamber of Commerce noted, "The public monopolies have been replaced by private monopolies close to the people in power" (Karabadji 1998). Private monopolies of import were firmly situated within the ruling coalition, with little concern for the detrimental effects on economic growth and public prosperity.

Finally, the regime maintained tight control of Sonatrach, the state-owned oil and gas company, which provided almost 70 percent of the Algerian state's income and 97 percent of its export throughout the examined period (Werenfels 2002, International Crisis Group 2001). Rents from oil and gas production gave the regime a political instrument that was almost untouched by external demands for reforms. During the conflict, import remained low and internal industrial production actually dropped by 20 percent between 1993 and 1996. To maintain the intertwined relation between clientelism and the programmatic politics shared by the ruling coalition, the regime needed continued and unrestricted access to the distribution of oil and gas income. Regime insiders believed that as much as 25 percent of all oil and gas income went unaccounted for in the 1990s (Werenfels 2002). If the numbers are accurate, the formal and informal control of Sonatrach allowed the regime to keep the ruling coalition together, while at the same time complying with most external demands for reforms.

To sum up, the regime complied with demands for macroeconomic reforms, even those that increased unemployment and the cost of living. By contrast, the regime postponed, defused, or manipulated privatization and the removal of trade restrictions to maintain the privileges of clients within the ruling coalition. It is noteworthy that the reforms satisfied IMF, who declared the privatization reforms a relative success. The EU's and the United States' apprehension towards political Islam was reflected in the process of demanding the resumption of democracy. The vague Western position on the question of whether FIS should be allowed to run left room for the regime to partially comply with demands for democratization. The Algerian regime only needed to have the parliamentary and the presidential elections, while tightly controlling who was eligible. Without an Islamic opposition, democratic elections posed no threat to the regime. However, the regime still chose to manipulate elements of the elections, perhaps to increase the legitimacy of the regime, which is why the democratic reforms can only be considered partial implementation.

Conclusion

Algeria is a case of an existentially threatened regime in a formal political setting that received only economic and political, not military, Western assistance. The chapter found that the political settlement in Algeria was dominated by formal politics, despite the opaque decision-making process, because the small ruling coalition shared a broad political vision, and funds and privileges could be distributed according to formal rules, such as the

150　*Algeria*

membership of FLN. However, factional struggles fuelled the development of client networks based on personal loyalty, albeit not as the dominant feature of the political settlement. The regime used the strategies theoretically assigned to regimes in formal settings, with a few notable exceptions. Instead of coup-proofing and choosing ineffective strategies of punishment, the regime expanded and professionalized the security institutions, and pursued a strategy of elimination. Rather than relying on internal actors to balance the insurgents, the regime used militias as part of its strategy, but did so without losing authority. The bleak economic outlook forced the regime to rely on external actors, but the question of protecting Algerian sovereignty was at the heart of the interactions between Algeria and the EU, France, and the United States. Finally, the regime complied or partially complied with Western demands that did not hurt the interests of the ruling coalition. Macroeconomic reforms and elections changed Algeria's economic outlook and provided the Western powers with an argument for continued support of the regime.

The case of Algeria remains an outlier among the existentially threatened regimes. States with major elements of formal politics are generally less prone to be threatened existentially by insurgencies. Still, the next chapter draws on the contrasts provided by the Algerian case (together with the three other cases) to discuss how different levels and configurations of informal politics affect the regimes' strategy making and Western interventions.

References

Abdi, Nidam. 1997. "C'est Devenu Une Guerre de Tribus». De Retour d'Algérie, Samir Raconte Les Expéditions Punitives et La Peur Au Quotidien." *Libération*, 24 September 1997. https://www.liberation.fr/evenement/1997/09/24/c-est-devenu-une-guerre-de-tribus-de-retour-d-algerie-samir-raconte-les-expeditions-punitives-et-la-_214904/

Adamson, Kay. 1998. *Algeria*. London: Cassell.

Addi, Lahoua. 1998. "Algeria's Army, Algeria's Agony." *Foreign Affairs* 77 (4): 44–53.

Addi, Lahouari. 2001. "The Continuing War in Algeria." *Le Monde Diplomatique*, April 2001. https://mondediplo.com/2001/04/02algeria

Aït Kaki, Maxime. 2003. "Les Etats Du Maghreb Face Aux Revendications Berbères." *Politique Étrangère* 68 (1): 103–118. 10.3406/polit.2003.1185

2016 *"Algeria's Constitution of 1989, Reinstated in 1996, with Amendments through 2008."* 2016. Oxford: Oxford University Press. https://www.constituteproject.org/constitution/Algeria_2008.pdf

Aubenas, Florence. 2004. "Algérie: Les Friqués Du Chaos." *Libération*, 6 April 2004. https://www.liberation.fr/grand-angle/2004/04/06/algerie-les-friques-du-chaos_475087/

Benrabah, Mohamed. 2004. "Language and Politics in Algeria." *Nationalism and Ethnic Politics* 10 (1): 59–78. 10.1080/13537110490450773

Benramdane, Djamel. 2004. "Algeria: A Long and Dirty War." *Le Monde Diplomatique*, March 2004. https://mondediplo.com/2004/03/08algeriawar

Algeria 151

Boserup, Rasmus, and Luis Martinez, eds. 2016. *Algeria Modern: From Opacity to Complexity*. London: Hurst & Co.

Daguzan, Jean-François. 2002. "France, Democratization and North Africa." *Democratization* 9 (1): 135–148. 10.1080/714000234

Darbouche, Hakim, and Yahia H. Zoubir. 2013. "The Algerian Crisis in European and US Foreign Policies: A Hindsight Analysis." In *The Foreign Policies of the European Union and the United States in North Africa: Diverging or Converging Dynamics?*, edited by Francesco Cavatorta and Vincent Durac. London: Routledge.

Deeb, Jane M., and Yacoubian, M. (1999). *Algeria: Facing Presidential Elections*. 381. Policy. Washington D.C.

Felice, Damiano de. 2015. "Diverging Visions on Political Conditionality: The Role of Domestic Politics and International Socialization in French and British Aid." *World Development* 75: 26–45. 10.1016/j.worlddev.2015.01.010

Garçon, José. 1997. "Alger Remet de L'ordre Dans Les Milices. Le Contrôle Des Groupes Paramilitaires Est Devenu Un Enjeu de Pouvoir… et Un Argument Électoral." *Libération*, 14 March 1997. https://www.liberation.fr/planete/1997/03/14/alger-remet-de-l-ordre-dans-les-milices-le-controle-des-groupes-paramilitaires-est-devenu-un-enjeu-d_199931/

Garçon, José. 1998. "La Dérive Sanglante Des Milices En Algerie." *Libération*, 15 April 1998. https://www.liberation.fr/planete/1998/04/15/la-derive-sanglante-des-milices-en-algerie-une-douzaine-de-patriotes-suspectes-de-massacres-de-civil_235715/

Hafez, Mohammed M. 2020. "Fratricidal Rebels: Ideological Extremity and Warring Factionalism in Civil Wars." *Terrorism and Political Violence* 32 (3): 604–629. 10.1080/09546553.2017.1389726

Henry, Clement M. 2004. "Algeria's Agonies: Oil Rent Effects in a Bunker State." *The Journal of North African Studies* 9 (2): 68–81. 10.1080/1362938042000323347

Hill, J. N. C. 2009. "Challenging the Failed State Thesis: IMF and World Bank Intervention and the Algerian Civil War." *Civil Wars* 11 (1): 39–56. 10.1080/13698240802407033

Holm, Ulla. 2003. "Violence in Algeria: A Question of Securitization of State-Regime, Nation and Islam." *Alternatives: Turkish Journal of International Relations* 2 (2): 265–287. 10.21599/ATJIR.56120

International Crisis Group. 2001. *"Algeria's Economy: The Vicious Circle of Oil and Violence."* Brussels: International Crisis Group. https://www.crisisgroup.org/middle-east-north-africa/north-africa/algeria/algerias-economy-vicious-circle-oil-and-violence (4 August 2020)

International Crisis Group. 2004. "Islamism, Violence and Reform in Algeria: Turning the Page." Brussels: International Crisis Group. https://www.crisisgroup.org/middle-east-north-africa/north-africa/algeria/islamism-violence-and-reform-algeria-turning-page (4 August 2020)

International Monetary Fund. 2000. *"Algeria: Recent Economic Developments."* 00/105. Washington D.C.: International Monetary Fund. https://www.imf.org/external/pubs/ft/scr/2000/cr00105.pdf

Kapil, Arun. 1995. "Algeria's Crisis Intensifies: The Search for a 'Civic Pact.'" *Middle East Report*, 192: 2. 10.2307/3013347

Karabadji, Fayçal. 1998. "Mafia Threatens Algeria's Economy." *Le Monde Diplomatique*, September 1998. https://mondediplo.com/1998/09/05alger

152   *Algeria*

Malmvig, Helle. 2006. *State Sovereignty and Intervention, A Discourse Analysis of Interventionary and Non-Interventionary Practices in Kosovo and Algeria.* London: Routledge. 10.4324/9780203969458

Martinez, Luis. 2000. *The Algerian Civil War 1990-1998.* London: C. Hurst & Co.

Martinez, Luis. 2016. "Interest Groups in a Non-Democratic Regime." In *Algeria Modern*, edited by Luis Martineż and Rasmus Alenius Boserup. Oxford: Oxford University Press. 10.1093/acprof:oso/9780190491536.003.0002

McDougall, James. 2017. *A History of Algeria.* Cambridge: Cambridge University Press. 10.1017/9781139029230

Mecellem, Jessica G. 2018. "Misfortune or Injustice? The Political Work of Postconflict Narrative in Contemporary Algeria." *International Journal of Transitional Justice* 12 (2): 237–256. 10.1093/ijtj/ijy009

Meddi, Adléne. 2005. "Quel avenir pour les Patriotes?" *El Watan* 8 September 1997. https://algeria-watch.org/?p=48531

Mendelsohn, Barak. 2019. "The Battle for Algeria: Explaining Fratricide among Armed Nonstate Actors." *Studies in Conflict & Terrorism.* 10.1080/1057610X.2019.1580419

Morisse-Schilbach, Melanie. 1999. *L'Europe et La Question Algérienne: Vers Une Européanisation de La Politique Algérienne de La France.* Paris: Presses universitaires de France.

Mortimer, Robert. 1996. "Islamists, Soldiers, and Democrats: The Second Algerian War." *Middle East Journal* 50 (1): 18–39. 10.1163/2468-1733_shafr_SIM220070004

Mortimer, Robert. 2006. "State and Army in Algeria: The 'Bouteflika Effect *The Journal of North African Studies* 11 (2): 155–171. 10.1080/13629380600704837

Nezzar, Khaled, and Mohamed Maarfia. 2003. *Le Procès de Paris: L'armée Algérienne Face À La Disinformation.* Paris: Edition Médiane.

Ouaissa, Rachid. 2021. "Algeria: Between Transformation and Re-Configuration." In *Re-configurations: Contextualising transformation processes and lasting crises in the Middle East and North Africa"*, edited by Ouaissa Pannewick, and Strohmaier. Cham: Springer International Publishing. 10.1007/978-3-658-31160-5_4

Panta, Gianni Del. 2017. "Weathering the Storm: Why Was There No Arab Uprising in Algeria?" *Democratization* 24 (6): 1085–1102. 10.1080/13510347.2016.1275575

Pennell, C. R. 2019. "The Algerian State, Islamist Insurgents, and Civilians Caught in Double Jeopardy by the Violence of the Civil War of the 1990s." *Terrorism and Political Violence.* 10.1080/09546553.2019.1629910

Pierre, Andrew J., and William B. Quandt. 1995. "Algeria's War on Itself." *Foreign Policy* (99) July, pp. 131–148. 10.2307/1149010

Pollack, Kenneth M. 2019. *Armies of Sand: The Past, Present, and Future of Arab Military Effectiveness.* New York: Oxford University Press.

Ramonet, Ignacio. 1999. "Peace for Algeria." *Le Monde Diplomatique*, July 1999. https://mondediplo.com/1999/07/01leader

Roberts, Hugh. 1995. "Algeria's Ruinous Impasse and the Honourable Way out." *International Affairs* (Royal Institute of International Affairs 1944-) 71 (2): 247–267. 10.2307/2623433

Roberts, Hugh. 2003. *The Battlefield Algeria 1988-2002.* London: Verso.

Ruedy, John Douglas. 2005. *Modern Algeria: The Origins and Development of a Nation.* Bloomington: Indiana University Press.

Ruf, Werner. 1997. "The Flight of Rent: The Rise and Fall of a National Economy." *The Journal of North African Studies* 2 (1): 1–15. 10.1080/13629389708718285

Algeria 153

Salies, Bruno Callies de. 1997. "Algeria in the Grip of Terror." *Le Monde Diplomatique*, September 1997. https://mondediplo.com/1997/10/alger1

SIPRI. 2020. *Stockholm International Peace Research Institute Yearbook: Armaments, Disarmament and International Security*. Stockholm: SIPRI. https://www.sipri.org/yearbook/2020

Souaïdia, Habib. 2002. *La Sale Guerre: Le Témoignage D'un Ancien Officier Des Forces Spéciales de L'armée Algérienne*. Paris: Editions La Découverte.

Sueur, James D. Le. 2010. *Between Terror and Democracy: Algeria since 1989*. London: Zed Books. 10.5040/9781350218390

Thurston, Alexander. 2017. "Algeria's GIA: The First Major Armed Group to Fully Subordinate Jihadism to Salafism." *Islamic Law and Society* 24: 412–436. ep.f-jernadgang.kb.dk/10.1163/15685195-00244P05

Tlemcani, Rachid. 2008. *"Algeria Under Bouteflika: Civil Strife and National Reconciliation."* 7. *Carnegie Papers*. Carnegie Papers. Washington D.C.: Carnegie Endowment for International Peace. https://carnegieendowment.org/files/cmec7_tlemcani_algeria_final.pdf

Werenfels, Isabelle. 2002. "Obstacles to Privatisation of State Owned Industries in Algeria: The Political Economy of a Distributive Conflict." *The Journal of North African Studies* 7 (1): 1–28. 10.1080/13629380208718455

Werenfels, Isabelle. 2007. *Managing Instability in Algeria: Elites and Political Change Since 1995*. Abingdon: Routledge.

World Bank. 2021. *"Armed Forces Personel, Algeria."* Armed Forces Personnel, Total. Washington D.C. 2017. http://data.worldbank.org/indicator/MS.MIL.TOTL.P1?locations=DZ (Accessed 21 April 2021)

Zoubir, Yahia H. 1998. "The Algerian Political Crisis: Origins and Prospects for the Future of Democracy." *The Journal of North African Studies* 3 (1): 74–100. 10.1080/13629389808718310.

7 Do politics, organizations, or persons derail reforms?

Derailing reforms is a common, but not universal regime reaction to Western demands for reforms during an existential crisis. The four case studies found a range of regime reactions that affected the security institutions, military strategy, alignment, sovereignty, and, ultimately, the implementation of administrative and political reforms. Even within the single-case studies, the regimes' reactions varied across time and issues. To make sense of the variation, this chapter conducts a cross-case comparison focusing on the co-variation between the importance of informal politics and regime strategy, as well as the form of Western intervention. Yet, the chapter also pays attention to the diversity of regime strategies and how they reflect the different ways that informal politics unfolded in four unique political settlements, each containing a certain power constellation and distribution of formal and informal politics. Moreover, the diverse forms of Western interventions in the four cases interplayed with the political settlement, which created specific political dynamics. Taking one further step back, the chapter discusses two alternative explanations at the organizational and individual levels to evaluate the likelihood that informal politics is the primary cause of regimes' derailing Western-initiated reforms.

In the first part of the chapter, three sections examine the co-variation between the importance of informal politics and the strategy of praetorian protection, risk-averse alignment, and simulated statebuilding, respectively. The second part first discusses the explanatory power of regarding dysfunctional security institutions as the intentional actions of the regime leaders. Last, the explanatory power of a political psychology explanation of foreign policy blindness is evaluated.

Informal politics and the security forces

When regimes are existentially threatened by violence, organizing and applying force would presumably be a key concern to any regime. Looking at the organization and application of security forces across the four cases, it becomes clear that states react in different ways to a common challenge. However, table 7.1 exposes a pattern in the choice of strategies that suggests

DOI: 10.4324/9781003204978-7

Derailment of reforms 155

Table 7.1 Variance in importance of informal politics and the organization, training, and application of force

	Importance of informal politics	Privileged elite force reserved for regime protection?	Coup-proofing affecting Western training	Regular forces deprived of resources and used for co-optation	Choice of strategy
Chad	High	Yes[†]	Yes	Yes[†]	Punishment[†]
Mali (ATT)	High	Yes	Yes	Yes[†]	Punishment
Mali (IBK)	High	Yes	Yes	Yes[†]	Punishment[†]
Iraq (al-Maliki)	Medium	No	–	Yes	Punishment
Iraq (al-Abadi)	Medium	No	No[*]	No[**]	Elimination-[**]
Algeria	Low	No	–	No	Elimination

Notes
* Training supplied by the West had little effect on the efficiency of the security forces, but the analysis did show that coup-proofing caused this.
** Intelligence, artillery, and air power provided by the West, as well as the impact of militias, make an accurate assessment of the capabilities and strategy of the Iraqi forces difficult.
† Empirical observations of how the need for accommodating the ruling coalition influenced the strategic behaviour of the regime.

that the level of informal politics shapes the regimes' choices in a way similar to the theoretical expectations. This section discusses this co-variation, but also the specific ways that the political settlements affected the regime choices. For example, the seemingly matching choices of the Chadian and the Malian regimes hide important differences in the composition of the elite forces, and the choice of militias to be co-opted into the regular forces.

Western intervention practices in relation to capacity-building in the four cases varied from no training or advisory in Algeria, over a limited training mission focusing on counter-terrorism in Chad, to extensive training, advisory, and assist programmes in response to existential threats in Iraq and Mali. The impact of such programmes across four cases tells a story about how some of the preferred practices of contemporary Western interventions clash with or corroborate regime strategies. The ability of Algeria to improve the performance of its security forces without external training calls into question the importance of such practices, although the abysmal human rights record of the Algerian security forces also shows the dark side of its effective elimination strategy. To organize the section, the discussion proceeds in two parts. First comes an examination of the variation in the organization of the security forces, the purpose of the elite forces, and the impact of Western training. Second, a discussion of the military strategy, with a special attention to the conspicuous ineffectiveness of the punishment strategy, which seemed even less effective than theoretically assumed.

156　*Derailment of reforms*

How existential crises affect the organization of the security forces

Whether an insurgency constituted the only, or even the primary, threat to the regime had profound effects on the organization of the security forces. In cases where a coup threatened the regimes, they refrained from organizing the security forces to function effectively against an insurgency. Instead elite forces were diverged from the counterinsurgency effort to counter the threat of a coup. The case studies showed a variation between, on the one hand, Chad and both Malian regimes, and, on the other hand, Algeria and both Iraqi regimes. In Chad and Mali the regimes mostly held back the elite forces for regime protection. Geographically, SATG and DSGGIE units in Chad were stationed around N'djamena, and in Mali the ATT regime kept most of the 33rd Para in Bamako far from the front. This prioritization seems sensible in the light of the coups in Chad in 2004 and in Mali in 2012 and 2020. In Iraq, CTS had a dual role of regime protection and offensive operations. The al-Maliki premiership used CTS for regime protection, and al-Abadi retained personal control of CTS. Nevertheless, it also constituted the cornerstone of the Iraqi state's military engagement and was promoted as a symbol of an effective state. Elite forces in Algeria continuously engaged the insurgents and even infiltrated GIA to create internal divisions. Most likely, the Algerian regime did not coup-proof despite the 1991 coup, because the security forces held much of the power before the coup.

In three of the cases, the regimes' prioritization of elite forces coincided with the Western post 9/11 security agenda. The dedicated Western counter-terrorism programmes in Chad, Iraq, and Mali created or expanded elite units that came to be closely associated with regime survival. Although the units' missions differed from small-scale counter-terrorist operations, the units proved valuable to the intervening powers in especially Iraq, but also Chadian elite forces became a bargaining chip for the regime that deployed them to Western supported operations in the Central African Republic, Mali, and Nigeria after the threat subsided in Chad. From the onset, the expectation was that the regimes' attempts to coup-proof would hamper the effectiveness of the training given by the intervening powers, so that only trusted elite units would be allowed to benefit from training. The theoretical expectations match the empirical observations rather accurately. Trusted units, such as the 33rd Para in Mali or the DSGGIE in Chad, were allowed to stay together and sustain their acquired tactical and logistical proficiency.

The lingering question is why certain regimes have to fear coups, whereas others are free to concentrate on threats outside the state. Based on the patterns of the organization and training of the regular forces, an important part of the answer is the degree to which the military functions as an alliance of militarized elites with power bases outside the state. In Chad and Mali, the armies lacked tactical and operational proficiency due to insufficient training, logistics, and materiel. The inattention paid to the efficiency of the

Derailment of reforms 157

regular forces was almost certainly due to their purpose. The case studies of Chad and Mali showed that an important function of the regular forces was the co-optation of militias and insurgents. For example, the inflated number of soldiers in Chad shows that their pay was, in fact, the price for co-optation, and, therefore, related to a logic of informal politics rather than a military logic. It is hardly surprising that the regimes built parallel elite security forces to offer protection against regular units with diverse loyalties. However, the cases showed more nuances. In Mali, MINUSMA promoted the co-optation of northern militarized elites into the regular forces as a way to foster inclusion and the legitimacy of the security forces. Moreover, even though the IBK regime might not have shared the lofty ambitions of MINUSMA, the newly integrated units only operated in the peripheral northern regions, thereby posing less of a political risk. In contrast, the Déby regime allowed co-opted elites access to government offices and senior military positions. In practice, the co-opted elites held little power except for the access to state resources, but the wide-ranging actions of the Déby regime illustrate the political importance of co-optation into regular forces in Chad.

In Algeria conscripts in the regular units were the backbone of the army, and as the conflict grew so did the number of conscripts. The regular forces were assigned many trivial tasks, but nothing resembling the passivity of the regular forces in Chad and Mali. Clearly, regular forces held an important place in the security forces. More puzzling are the Iraqi regimes' approaches to the regular forces. Militarized elites with powerbases outside the state populated the regular forces, especially in the paramilitary Federal Police. Al-Abadi would have been justified in considering these elites a coup threat, but the regimes used the CTS and to a lesser extent the presidential brigades for offensive operations, not merely regime protection. One reason might be that the militarized elite wielded influence through the formal politics in the parliament, which reduced their motivation for violently overthrowing the regime. Another element might be the role of Iran behind the scene that increased trust and cooperation between the regime and the diverse Shia Islamists groups. The result was that the al-Abadi regime oversaw the rebuilding of regular units, even though their loyalty to the government varied widely.

The current discourse on Western interventions favours a narrow focus on security force assistance at the expense of wide-ranging liberal reforms to increase the legitimacy of the state, as discussed in the introduction. The choice to accept the political status quo has consequences for the prospect of Western training efforts. While the narrow counter-terrorism training wields tactical results, it mainly enhances the prospect of regime survival and coup-protection rather than the counter-terror effort. Moreover, the effectiveness of training regular units depends on the political dynamics among elites inside and outside the ruling coalition and inside and outside the state. In the four cases, those dynamics were only marginally influenced by Western

158   *Derailment of reforms*

intervention practices. By prioritizing tactical improvements among local elite units, Western powers avoided the thorny and intricate questions of elite politics and institutionalization of security forces.

The passivity of the regular forces and punishment strategy

Fighting an insurgency with security forces suited for coup-proofing and the co-optation of militias and insurgents puts a limit to the number of feasible military strategies to use against the insurgents. Nonetheless, the negligible role of the regular forces in the military strategies in Chad, Mali, and their limited role in Iraq deviated from a praetorian protection proposition. The theoretical expectation was that the regimes would rely on regular forces to carry out an inefficient strategy of punishment to raise the cost of the insurgency. But the passive and sporadic application of violence by the regular forces hardly constituted a punishment strategy. Instead, militias and even private military companies applied most of the indiscriminate force. By comparison the Algerian regime developed a strategy of elimination, which relied on the combined efforts of the regular and the elite units as well as the intelligence service and the gendarmerie. What separated Algeria from the three other cases was the willingness of the regime to use military engagements to change the balance of force before initiating a political process, which then resembled a fait accompli, due to the desperate situation of the insurgents from 1997 and onwards.

The tactical use of the regular forces in Chad, Mali, and partially in Iraq was inefficient. In Chad and Mali, the regular forces rarely engaged with the enemies – even the instances of indiscriminate use of violence against civilians were infrequent. In Iraq, the regular forces were sporadically used for applying indiscriminate violence. During the Sunni protests in 2012 and 2013, the regular units took part in the crackdowns. Moreover, the regular units' importance grew from the nadir in 2014, not least due to the United States' insistence on rebuilding and finding a role for ISF after 2014. Nonetheless, the three regimes were not entirely passive, but relied on militias or private military companies to apply indiscriminate violence. In Chad, the private companies operating the aircraft of the Chadian Air Force carried out bombings of columns and even rear bases in Darfur in 2008 and 2009. In Mali, the regime used the Imghad ETIA unit in the autumn of 2011, and IBK utilized the Platform Group and self-protection militias to inflict punishment on the Coordination Group and Fulani militants after 2014. Still, the punishment strategies employed different means to those predicted by the theoretical expectations, as the regular army only played a marginal role.

Overall, the importance of informal politics co-varied with the choice of strategy. External efforts to (re)train regular units did not necessarily translate into changes in the military strategy. In the case of Iraq, the al-Abadi regime chose to make limited use of the regrouped regular army divisions, but the training efforts of EUTM in Mali hardly marked the military strategy of the IBK regime. The inefficiency of the regular forces must in part have been

Derailment of reforms 159

caused by the regimes' need to disregard them as a relevant tactical instrument. Politically, the regular forces had an important function of co-optation as well as providing a formal institution for informal accommodation to take place and funds to be transferred. Later, the question of why organizational dysfunction happens will be discussed.

Alignment and the role of programmatic politics

In the face of an existential threat, all the examined regimes needed to make internal and external alignments to stave off the insurgents. Chapter two laid out the risk-averse alignment proposition, suggesting that regimes in informal settings align with the actors with the lowest associated risk, with little concern for maintaining state authority. For pragmatic reasons they align with diverse cultural or ideological groups and provide them with access to patronage from the state. By contrast, regimes in states dominated by formal politics are expected to assert authority internally and protect their sovereignty when aligning with external actors. Table 7.2 shows a clear difference in the alignment strategies of the regimes that co-vary with the importance of informal politics in the political settlement. Yet, the applied alignment strategies also reflected specific power distributions that were unique to each case, and provided the regimes with different possibilities and impossibilities. Especially the pragmatism of militant elites who initially opposed the regimes influenced the specific alignment strategies of the regimes. Moreover, the Western military interventions had different forms that influenced the ways the regimes could cooperate with other alignments.

Three comparisons structure this section. First, a comparison of the preferences for domestic alignment in order to discuss the differences in the regimes' behaviour. Second, a comparison of the use of co-optation and a discussion of the importance of the programmatic foundation of the insurgents. Third, a comparison of the regimes' external alignments as to the question of sovereignty and risk aversion.

Domestic alignment and the political settlement

All regimes favoured alignments with internal rather than external actors. In Chad and Mali, the Déby and ATT regimes sought internal alignments at the onset of the crisis, especially among ethnic groups in the most contested regions, eastern Chad and northern Mali, respectively. In Algeria, the regime chose to make use of local vigilance groups from 1993, before turning to Western powers and international organizations in 1994. The case of the IBK regime is less apparent, because external actors were already present once IBK was elected President. Still, his strong relationships with the Platform Group and, e.g., Dogon self-defence militias seem to suggest that the regime favoured internal rather than external alignment. Similarly, in the hectic summer of 2014, the al-Maliki regime most likely sought to align with

160 *Derailment of reforms*

Table 7.2 Variance in the importance of informal politics and the choices of alignment

	Importance of informal politics	Favouring domestic alignments over external alignments?	Co-optation of rivals and insurgents through the use of patronage?	External alignment with the least risk to regime survival?
Chad	High	Yes	Yes[†]	Yes
Mali (ATT)	High	Yes	Yes[†]	Yes
Mali (IBK)	High	Yes	Yes[†]	–
Iraq (Maliki)	Medium	Yes[*]	No	Yes
Iraq (Abadi)	Medium	Yes	No	Yes
Algeria	Low	Yes	No	No

Notes
[†] Empirical observations of how the need for accommodating the ruling coalition influenced the strategic behaviour of the regime
[*] Very short period between the outbreak of fighting, the organization of the militias, and the alignment with the United States.

pro-Iranian militias and to seize on al-Sistani's call for the formation of nationalist militias, but the pace of IS's offensive made it analytically difficult to separate attempts of internal and external alignments. Finally, the al-Abadi regime catered to the demands of the Shia militias, despite its dependence on the United States to fight IS.

Domestic alignments fall into three different types: alignment with militias within the ruling coalition, alignment with militias of excluded elites (apart from the insurgent groups), and alignment with insurgents. Mobilizing militias within the ruling coalition affects the position of the regime. Although the factions of the ruling coalition support the regime, they are also rivals aiming to maximize their influence and economic benefits. A mobilized militia changes the distribution of power within the ruling coalition and increases the standing of the militarized faction, which puts pressure on the regime for increased accommodation. In parallel, alignment with militarized elites outside the ruling coalition, but not part of the insurgency alliances, means the regime must find ways to accommodate a broader group of elites, at least temporarily.

The way the regimes in the four cases dealt with this challenge reflects the importance of informal politics. No attempts were made by the Déby regime to enforce authority on mobilized militias, instead the regime accepted the ever-changing composition of the security forces and the alliance of militias. Less extremely, but notably pragmatically, the regimes of ATT and IBK accepted that the Imghad Tuareg group under El Haj Gamou shifted in and out of the army and pursued its own ends in northern Mali. Importantly, accommodating those militias was not a zero-sum game. In Chad, the spike in oil prices allowed for the accommodation of more militias inside and outside the security forces, without subtracting from the accommodation of the ruling coalition. In Mali, the market for smuggling allowed the regimes

Derailment of reforms 161

to accommodate more northern elites, without hurting the interests of the Bamako-based elites, because privileges took the form of acceptance of informal rules. Nevertheless, the regimes had to accept the erosion of the power of formal state institutions and an even wider distribution of power.

By contrast, in the formal setting of Algeria the regime imposed the state's authority on the self-defence groups by subjugating them to the command of the gendarmerie. In addition, the Algerian state kept the militias as lower-level clients that operated as local, community-based groups rather than allowing them to spread or join larger militias. In Iraq, the regimes enforced state authority to a limited extent, e.g., through the legal regulation of the Peshmergas and the regulation of PMFs. However, in reality the militias had more power than legally outlined, and at times their actions went against the regime. In a political settlement dominated by formal politics, the concern for state authority reflects the need to uphold the formal institutions that accommodate the ruling coalition's need for protection, funds, and privileges. Without strong control of the militias, the ruling coalition in Algeria would have run the risk of other societal actors gaining military power and the ability to destabilize the political settlement. In Iraq, the militarized factions controlled militias, but the regimes' power lay primarily within the state, which explains the regimes' attempt to take control of the security forces and lessen the autonomy of the PMF militias.

Co-optation and the character of the insurgency

Co-optation of members of the insurgency alliance varied greatly across the four cases in terms of the regimes' flexibility and pragmatism when choosing internal allies. The regimes in Algeria and Iraq were the least pragmatic. The al-Maliki regime ended the alignments with Sunni tribes, which the United States established during the surge in 2006 and 2007. In parallel, the Algerian regime only approached AIS once the military campaign had brought the group to its knees in 1997. On the other hand, the Déby regime in Chad and, to a less extent, the ATT regime in Mali showed extreme pragmatism and negotiated with insurgent groups across societal cleavages. Déby's alignment with all tribes involved in the conflict stands out as a pure example of pragmatism. This finding does not imply that the Déby had no sectarian or cultural affinities; merely that they were subdued to short-sighted considerations to ensure regime survival. The regimes had no reservations in aligning with insurgents across sectarian or tribal divides once regime survival depended on such pragmatic choices. Power-sharing has been highly prioritized in international state-building efforts, but no examples in this study indicated that co-opted insurgent groups translated co-optation into influence on regime decisions.

In parallel, insurgent elites embraced or tolerated routine co-optation in informal settings. When President IBK provided former Arab insurgents with a *carte blanche* to expand drug smuggling in northern Mali, the Arab

162 Derailment of reforms

elites accepted the co-optation, and the Bamako-based elites raised few protests. By contrast, in the formal setting of Algeria, AIS only gave in to laying down arms at the point when they were militarily defeated. The pattern of co-optation suggests that informal politics affects the way co-optation is carried out in terms of pragmatism as to who is co-opted, how they react, and whether or not the ruling coalition accepts the co-optation. A wide distribution of power is one of the defining characteristics of political settlements dominated by informal politics. Moreover, protracted or recurrent conflicts often increase the power of lower-level militarized factions, who are difficult to control for the factions of the ruling coalition (Kalyvas 2003, DeVore and Stähli 2020). Yet, the logic of fragmentation also works the other way round, since insurgent alliances find it difficult to keep together when faced with persistent attempts by the regimes to co-opt a part of the alliances (Bakke et al. 2012). The success of the Déby and IBK regimes in splitting the insurgency alliances reflects the many insurgency factions' ability to make independent decisions.

It is also possible that the different patterns in co-optation are due to variation in the internal cohesion of the insurgent groups. Insurgent groups with a strong, ideological motivation are generally in a good position to avoid fragmentation (Weinstein 2006, 260–265). IS in Iraq and GIA in Algeria were highly cohesive groups due to ideological indoctrination and brutality towards defectors. Moreover, they offered an alternative political vision that was the opposite of informal politics – e.g., a strong focus on banning informal accommodation such as corruption or favouritism within the juridical system. Militant Islamist groups including IS, al-Shabaab in Somalia, or AQIM, the successor of GIA, in Mali, all succeeded in controlling territory until their success provoked an external intervention.

However, the kinds of challenges faced by cohesive groups depend on the importance of informal politics. In an informal setting with a wide distribution of power, the coherent group competes with militarized domestic elites for resources and recruitment. In Mali, in order to control territory AQIM had to align with other, less coherent groups, who fragmented the insurgent alliance within a few years as they shifted sides to maximize their influence. In more formal settings, a cohesive group might find societal elites more responsive to its programmatic ideas, but face regimes that have a greater reliance on state institutions than on domestic alignment. Co-optation is a key strategy of the regimes and one that shapes the strategic environment in informal settings.

External alignment and sovereignty

The case studies showed that external alignments mostly took place once internal alignment proved insufficient to stem the insurgency threat. Nevertheless, a variation is detectable in what the regimes cherished and defended when aligning externally. When informal politics was most

Derailment of reforms 163

important to the political settlement, the regimes routinely traded sovereignty and authority in return for external intervention during a crisis, but were highly risk-averse when a potential external alignment might have posed a threat to the regime's hold on power. In formal settings, the regimes and the ruling coalitions were far more concerned about the violation of the principles of sovereignty, even when the regimes were existentially threatened. The difference was probably due to the extent to which programmatic politics held the ruling coalition together.

On the one hand, the regimes in Chad and Mali showed no secondary concerns besides regime survival. Both regimes allowed French forces to carry out military operations whose underlying tactics and strategy only partly fitted the interests of the states. Operation Barkhane was an anti-terror mission to increase the safety of France, despite the fact that the French strikes might have been unpopular among Arabs and Tuaregs in Mali. In Chad, the problem of the French military presence was not so much the infringement on Chadian sovereignty as it was the opposite. The French military presence was mainly a mission to protect Chad (and French interests) from outside aggression, originally from Libya but now from violence in Darfur and Sudan. In 2008, the French hesitance to support the regime during the insurgent attack drove Déby towards earnest negotiations with Sudan. The military junta in Mali preferred an intervention by ECOWAS rather than a French one. Given their military inferiority, an ECOWAS intervention would have reduced the risk of forcing the military junta from power, but would have increased the risk of a prolonged conflict. Concerns for sovereignty or military effectiveness were less important than avoiding the risk of losing power.

On the other hand, sovereignty, understood in the sense of non-interference in domestic affairs by outside powers, was the dominant principle according to which the Algerian regime engaged with external powers. Sovereignty took on such a level of significance that Western military support beyond the sale of weapons was unacceptable to the regime. As a result, Western powers framed their support as unobtrusive, technical aid provided by international organizations, such as the EU and IMF. In Iraq, the alliance of nationalists and pro-Iranian Shia parties, many of which had violently opposed the American military, had a strong ideological preference for ending the external alignment with the United States, and the nationalist Shia-party remained wary of Iranian interference. However, the split within the Shia bloc meant that sovereignty was most important to the nationalist bloc of al-Sadr and other elites associated with the cleric al-Sistani. The willingness to trade sovereignty for external alignment was limited by the importance of nationalist principles in Algeria, and was somewhat limited in Iraq.

This variance raises the question of whether concern for sovereignty only thrives in states where the political settlement allows programmatic politics to matter. Resistance to foreign intruders is also manifest in states dominated by informal politics, but based on the Malian case resistance and

164   *Derailment of reforms*

protests are most common among the public, not the regime (Guichaoua 2020, 900–901). From the perspective of the regime, the main concern of survival is not attached to the principle of sovereignty. Rather, political settlements highly dominated by informal politics deliberately circumvent the authority of the state to accommodate strong non-productive elites. Under such circumstances, the coherence of the ruling coalition is unlikely to hinge on a principled concern for sovereignty. This would explain why the Chadian regime accepted French, EU, and UN operations on Chadian ground. A different picture is seen in political settlements dominated by formal politics that provide room for programmatic politics. Programmatic politics is more than a luxury concern, because upholding the current formal institutions, such as the security institutions in Algeria, is important to keeping together the ruling coalition, in which factions are accommodated through the current formal setup.

Across the four cases, the regimes preferred domestic to external alignment. Nevertheless, regimes in informal settings pragmatically aligned across societal cleavages, and liberally co-opted former insurgent groups. When aligning externally their primary concern was the risk to regime survival, not infringement of sovereignty as such. In more formal settings, principally Algeria and to a lesser extent Iraq, the regimes subdued or tried to subdue militias to the authority of the security forces and focused on reducing infringements of the state's sovereignty, when they needed to align externally.

Simulated statebuilding and Western demands

External alignments may come with demands for reforms to address what the intervener perceives as the root causes of the conflict. The proposition of simulated statebuilding expects the local regimes to simulate implementation to preserve the vital ruling coalitions without antagonizing the Western powers, at least in political settlements dominated by informal politics. A comparison of the four cases and their instances of simulated statebuilding suggests a slightly more nuanced story. This section analyses the relationship between informal politics, Western pressure, and the use of simulated statebuilding. Moreover, it discusses the empirical observations of the impact of the veto power of the ruling coalition and the impact of a regional power as a hedge against Western demands. A subsequent section will discuss why Western interveners in most cases condoned simulated statebuilding.

In the four case studies there were 16 instances of Western powers and international organizations making demands for administrative and political reforms. Table 7.3 summarizes the Western demands and codes them according to the importance of informal politics, the Western use of either conditionality or inducement, the reaction of the regimes, and the West's response to the regimes' reaction. Inducement strategies combine a demand for an administrative or political reform with a reward, while conditionality

Derailment of reforms 165

strategies add a threat of punishment in case of non-compliance. The principal-agent approach expects conditionality strategies to manipulate the regimes' cost-benefit calculation most effectively and, thus, have a higher rate of success. Moreover, the choice of a conditionality strategy might indicate that the Western powers put greater emphasis on a particular reform.

Overall, there is co-variation between the importance of informal politics and the use of simulated statebuilding. In six out of eight instances, regimes in informal settings chose to simulate implementation. Only in one instance did a regime in an informal setting choose to implement a Western-imposed reform. In comparison, the regimes in mixed or formal settings chose to comply fully, partially, or with a delay, in four out of eight instances, but still used simulated statebuilding in three out of eight instances. However, aid-giving strategies and implementation also co-varied, which indicates that the regimes could actually implement reforms, when they really mattered to the Western powers. External interveners used inducement in six instances and conditionality in ten. Inducement strategies produced one case of compliance, whereas the regimes complied in five out of ten cases when Western powers added a threat of punishment.

Nevertheless, compliance must be considered in conjunction with the importance of informal politics. Four out of the five instances of compliance were in a mixed or formal setting, in which a higher degree of compliance was indeed expected, since the regime and the ruling coalition for the most part had little to lose by complying. By contrast, in an informal setting the only case of compliance was the resumption of elections in Mali. Otherwise, Chad and Mali's regimes chose to simulate implementation or not to comply at all. The instances of non-compliance were concurrent with the World Bank's attempt to establish an elaborate control mechanism to control oil distribution in Chad, which forced the regime to declare its non-compliance officially. Nevertheless, an effective conditionality strategy depends on the willingness of the Western power to punish non-compliance and, more significantly, simulated implementation. Western powers conspicuously failed to use punishment as part of the declared conditionality strategy. Later in the chapter, the question of Western acceptance of failed reforms is discussed as part of the alternative explanations of foreign policy blindness.

The influence of the ruling coalition and regional powers

No state is without informal politics, which was evident in the informal accommodation of factions in the ruling coalition in the otherwise formal or mixed politics of Algeria and Iraq. Moreover, Iran and Sudan played significant roles as the regimes' hedges against Western interference and as independent actors in Iraq's and Chad's domestic politics, respectively. Based on empirical observations of the interactions between the factions of the ruling coalition and the regime, it is likely that the factions – especially

166   *Derailment of reforms*

Table 7.3 Overview of Western demands for political and administrative reforms

Interaction (Regime; Western power; demand)	Importance of informal politics	Inducement or conditionality?	Reaction of the regime (compliance, partial compliance, non-compliance, simulated implementation)	Western reaction to regime (acceptance, protest, consequence)
Chad; World Bank; distribution of oil income	High	Conditionality	Non-compliance	Consequence
Mali; France; restoring democracy	High	Conditionality	Compliance	Acceptance
Mali; France/UN; peace agreement with Arabs and Tuaregs	High	Conditionality	Simulated implementation	Protest and acceptance
Mali; international donors; comprehensive development plan for northern Mali	High	Conditionality	Simulated implementation	Acceptance
Chad; EU; democratization in 2007	High	Inducement	Simulated implementation	Acceptance
Chad; EU; anti-corruption and good governance	High	Inducement	Simulated implementation	Acceptance
Chad; EU; resumption of elections in 2011	High	Inducement	Simulated implementation	Acceptance
Mali; international donors; anti-corruption and administrative reforms in northern Mali	High	Conditionality	Simulated implementation	Protest and acceptance
Iraq; USA; inclusion of Sunnis in the national guard	Medium	Conditionality	Delay and partial compliance	Acceptance
Iraq; USA; inclusive government	Medium	Conditionality	Partial compliance	Acceptance
Iraq; USA; keeping al-Obedi	Medium	Conditionality	Non-compliance	Acceptance
Iraq; USA; anti-corruption	Medium	Inducement	Simulated implementation	Acceptance
Iraq; USA; Political control of Shia militias	Medium	Inducement	Simulated implementation	Acceptance

(Continued)

Derailment of reforms 167

Table 7.3 (Continued)

Interaction (Regime; Western power; demand)	Importance of informal politics	Inducement or conditionality?	Reaction of the regime (compliance, partial compliance, non-compliance, simulated implementation)	Western reaction to regime (acceptance, protest, consequence)
Algeria; World Bank; macro-economic reforms	Low	Conditionality	Compliance	Acceptance
Algeria; World Bank; privatization of public companies	Low	Conditionality	Simulated implementation	Acceptance
Algeria; France/ USA; resumption of elections	Low	Inducement	Partial compliance	Acceptance

militarized factions – drove the regimes toward simulating reforms. Still, external actors were not without influence on the interplay between factions of the ruling coalitions and the regimes. The long-standing relations of Iran and Sudan with factions in Iraq and Chad, respectively, gave them indirect influence on the implementation of Western-imposed reforms.

One of the most valuable insights was the attempt by IMF to privatize state-owned companies in Algeria. The observations of the behaviour of the factions within the ruling coalition demonstrated not only the strength and importance of the ruling coalition, but also the fact that informal accommodation played an important, though minor, role in political settlements otherwise dominated by formal politics. More specifically, the unanimous resistance to privatization within the ruling coalition in Algeria gave key actors concerned with the management of the state-owned companies a free hand to stop any real privatization. Another observation that stresses the importance of the ruling coalition was the veto power of the pro-Iranian elites in the parliament and on the battlefield, which forced the al-Abadi regime to simulate the implementation of reforms imposed by the United States. The empirical examples of the veto power included the mostly symbolic inclusion of Sunni and Kurdish ministers in the government, the obstruction of the formal inclusion of Sunni militias in a national guard, the blocked attempt to create a non-partisan government, and the Shia militias vetting of Sunni militias in liberated areas. In all cases, reforms threatened

168 *Derailment of reforms*

the informal rules that benefited the pro-Iranian factions beyond the stipulations of the formal rules.

The influence of the ruling coalition might also result in the support for reforms of an institution for its own benefit, against the interest of the regime. This is obviously a rare observation in states with political settlements dominated by informal politics, but nonetheless one made in Mali in relation to the resumption of democracy. In the single instance when a regime in informal politics chose to carry out a reform demanded by the West, the factions of the former ruling coalition supported the reintroduction of democracy in Mali. The Bamako-based factions of the ruling coalition had refused to cooperate with the military junta. Instead of seeking informal accommodation from the military junta, the Bamako factions realized that they would benefit from a resumption of elections, as they would gain renewed access to patronage and control of the political development. Reintroducing democracy in Mali was, on paper, a clear-cut successful application of a conditionality strategy, but the interest of the ruling coalition made the circumstances highly favourable.

Well-positioned regional powers with a history of interacting with societal elites in the examined states had the ability to influence the interplay between factions of the ruling coalitions and the regimes, which in turn affected the implementation of Western-imposed reforms. Sudan and Iran wielded more economic and military power than Chad and Iraq, and had strong interests in the domestic situations in the two states. Although the Iraqi and Chadian regimes manipulated the regional powers to their own ends, the regional powers used their superior power to influence the militarized factions. In Iraq, Iran had developed close ties with the Shia parties since the 1980s and supported the Shia militias and parties after the American invasion. Iran did not alter its course once a Shia sectarian regime came to power in 2006, but kept supporting specific Shia factions, and included new ones, such as Hezbollah and AAH. After 2014, Iran harnessed specific factions to manipulate the pace and scale of political reforms in Iraq in ways that suited Iranian interests. To al-Abadi, Iran's involvement was not so much a way of mitigating the risk of relying on the United States, as Iran was a veto power that strengthened the factions that kept the informal elements of Iraqi politics in place.

Sudan took a more confrontational approach to the Chadian regime. Not only did the al-Bashir regime offer the insurgents staging areas in western Sudan, but it also influenced the choice of leaders of the insurgency alliance. The EU's attempt to establish a political dialogue in 2007 might have convinced two insurgency leaders to accept co-optation, but the remaining part of the insurgency groups kept up arms and stayed safe in their Sudanese rear bases. The importance of the Sudanese sanctuaries forced Déby to realign with Sudan to lower the risk of insurgency razzias against

Derailment of reforms 169

N'Djamena. When the realignment was in place, the regime could use Sudan as a hedge against Western pressure and abandonment. However, the two examples also demonstrate that regional powers had shifting roles during the examined period of being threats, allies of the regime, or factions within the ruling coalition.

There is a stark contrast between the approach of the Western powers and that of the regional powers. Whereas Western powers mainly dealt with regimes or promoted marginalized groups in society, Iran and Sudan chose to influence factions within the ruling coalition as a way to maximize their influence in the neighbouring states. The approach of the regional powers demanded a long-term commitment and knowledge of the interactions between the ruling coalition and the regime, but at a low economic and human cost. The benefit was that when the regime acted independently of the regional powers, these could increase the power of the factions they supported to keep the regime in check. In the end, military vulnerability forced Déby to reconcile with Sudan, and al-Abadi had to make a compromise or abandon any reform initiative that went against the interests of pro-Iranian elites. A well-connected regional power with strong connections among the ruling coalition is likely to lessen the chance of reforms.

Western demands for administrative and political reforms have a moderate prospect of success even when the local regime is situated in a formal or mixed setting. Nevertheless, there is a lower rate of success in informal settings, even when the Western powers use a strategy of conditionality. Empirical observations support the proposition that the regime is forced to use simulated statebuilding because of the veto power of the factions of the ruling coalition, especially when they are supported by regional powers.

Alternative explanations

In the four cases, the regimes acted in ways that co-varied with the importance of informal politics. Still, to move the comparison of the cases closer to a discussion of possible causality, the explanatory power of informal politics must be evaluated against other potential explanations. Besides the distribution of power in the political settlement, domestic explanations at the organizational and the individual analytical levels deserve consideration. The organizational dysfunction explanation considers organizational shortcomings in authoritarian states as the regimes' deliberate design to foster loyalty and prevent coups. From this perspective, derailment of reforms is a calculated choice made by the local regimes. The political-psychology explanation focuses on the effects of selecting loyalists in the inner decision-making circle. Factionalism and the risk of coups incite the regime leader to select like-minded, personally loyal individuals as ministers, advisors, or, e.g., ambassadors. The effect might be foreign policy blindness and the miscalculation of Western signals. Non-cooperation in

170 *Derailment of reforms*

this explanation is not the result of inability or unwillingness of the regime, but the result of a lack of understanding of the international context. After introducing the dysfunctional organization explanation, a discussion of its explanatory power of the four cases follows, with a specific focus on the causal relation between non-cooperation, dysfunctional organizations, and informal politics. Afterwards, the political-psychological explanation of non-cooperation is introduced and discussed based on the cases, with a special focus on whether the use of simulated statebuilding expresses the regimes' foreign policy blindness towards Western signals.

Organizational dysfunction

An important puzzle in strategic studies is the difference in military efficiency even when states invest the same in terms of personnel, money, and materiel. A group of scholars point to the organizational structure and culture: choices as to professionalization, training, and unity of command are more important than the input of resources (Stanley and Brooks 2007; Talmadge 2015). In the same vein, civilian state organizations produce very different output, even though measurable input is the same. Especially, the research has focused on the glaring inefficiencies of many authoritarian states. Due to a low level of legitimacy, authoritarian states might respond by creating dysfunctional organizations to protect the regime from threats arising from power concentration in state institutions, particularly security institutions. So far, the assumption has been that the praetorian protection was the regime's response to societal elites' *intrusion* into the security institutions, not the security institutions in themselves. However, state institutions might be more autonomous, and their weakness and incompetence might be by *design* of the regime leader, not the result of power struggles among societal elites.

An explanation that considers organizational dysfunction as a deliberate design would answer the question of why existentially threatened regimes derail western reforms in two ways. First, when a regime leader has spent years creating delicately balanced state institutions, the first reaction will be resistance to changes. Only severe external threats will convince the regime of the need to reform dysfunctional organizations if they deem dysfunction a necessary condition to remain in power. Caitlin Talmadge's study of Saddam Hussein shows that it took years of military backlashes in the war against Iran to convince Hussein to roll back coup-proofing measures in the security institutions (2015, 226ff). Second, dysfunctional intelligence and security institutions might underestimate the actual extent of an internal threat and they might misunderstand Western signals and conditions for support.

Methodologically, it can be difficult to separate the explanation of organizational dysfunction by design and this study's explanation that organizational dysfunction is the outcome of state organizations being intruded

Derailment of reforms 171

by non-state elites. In terms of expected behaviour, both explanations hold that regimes counterbalance the regular army with units directly controlled by the political leadership. The strategy of establishing counterbalancing forces mirrors the coup-proofing aspect of the praetorian protection strategy. However, the two explanations differ when it comes to direct regime intervention in the regular forces. The explanation of organizational dysfunction by design argues that the regime gains political control by creating a highly centralized and rigid command structure in order to avoid independent initiatives within the armed forces (Brown et al. 2016). Barriers to information sharing across services or units further debilitate the security institutions' ability to react to a threat, but achieve the goal of hindering coordination among potential coup-plotters. The establishment of several intelligence and security services with overlapping areas of responsibility creates competition and mutual distrust, which prevents one particular organization from gaining superior power.

The alternative explanation of organizational dysfunction by design makes sense of much of the empirical findings of the four case studies. Above all, three of the regimes used elite forces as counterbalancing against regular forces. In the case of Chad, the reform of the elite units came about as a consequence of the failed coup in 2004. Equally, the same three regimes navigating informal or mixed politics inserted political clients as senior commanders. The regimes of Déby, al-Maliki, ATT, and IBK all selected senior commanders among their political clients. Especially the actions of Prime Minister al-Maliki seem in line with the dysfunction-by-design proposition. Maliki circumvented the command structure by ordering certain units to report directly to the prime minister's office, replaced many senior commanders, and expelled a significant number of Sunnis from the security forces. Each of the documented steps was a deliberate action taken by Maliki to de-professionalize and coup-proof the security institutions.

Moreover, the alternative explanation adds explanatory power to the lacking coup-proofing measures in Algeria, the quintessentially authoritarian state. Dysfunction by design might be rectified once a sufficiently severe threat arises. Arguably, the improvement in military efficiency during the 1990s supports this proposition. The new elite forces were not meant to be counter-forces to the regular units. And despite the power struggles between the intelligence services and the military, civil-military unity prevailed, partly due to the heavy dominance of the leaders of the security forces. Arguably, the well-developed formalization of the Algerian state apparatus and FLN meant that personal control and coup proofing became less important than fighting the common threat from Islamist societal elites.

The difference between the two explanations becomes important when looking at the role of the regular forces and the effect of Western training. Regime leaders do not have the freedom to design organizational

172 *Derailment of reforms*

dysfunction if informal rules are prevalent inside and outside state institutions in order to satisfy the demands of militarized elites in the ruling coalition. Instead, dysfunction is the outcome of competing bids for control of the security institutions made by the different militarized elites. If the regime leader had designed the security institutions, their activities would have been highly controlled. However, the cross-case comparison showed that the tactical non-use of the regular forces was due to the peculiarities of informal politics. Informal accommodation meant that the co-opted militias of the militarized factions in the ruling coalition and co-opted insurgents were in practice outside the chain of command or even the regimes' direct control.

As in an alliance, the regime had to convince the militarized elites to partake in tactical engagements. For example, in Chad co-opted militias might have fought their own clan members engaged in the insurgency, but chose passivity. Also, the problem of free-riding meant that, e.g., the otherwise effective ETIA unit commanded by Colonel Gamou Imghad chose to flee once it became clear that northern Mali would fall. From the perspective of the militarized factions, risking their own client network in pursuit of regime survival is less appealing than forcing the regime to find other ways to balance the threat. Even in the case of Iraq, the Badr-militia controlled large units within the paramilitary and military forces. In many cases, those units followed their own bidding and selected a course of action different from that of other parts of the security institutions. The examples from the three cases support the proposition that organizational dysfunction arises from the intrusion of non-state actors.

The comparison of the two explanations suggests that organizational dysfunction by design is most commonly found in states where formal politics dominates the political settlement. Once formal rules organize the work within a security institution, the senior commanders gain power, influence, and connections by holding the position within the institution. Thereby, the senior commanders control power independent of non-state elites and, possibly, independent of the regime leader. The dilemma of choosing between efficient, independent security institutions and inefficient, dependent institutions is a choice which only certain regimes face. Historically, several dictatorships and autocracies, such as Syria, have chosen inefficient, but dependent institutions as the research on military efficiency has shown (de Bruin 2018). Nevertheless, they are merely particular instances of organizational dysfunction, in which the regime had the possibility of creating efficient security institutions. More generally, a political settlement dominated by formal rules is a necessary, but not sufficient condition for military efficiency. The literature on organizational dysfunction by design lays forth why regimes navigating formal politics differ in their ability to create efficient institutions. However, this study's explanation of dysfunction by intrusion explains why the large group of regimes navigating informal politics cannot rectify organizational dysfunction, even in the face of a major threat.

Foreign policy blindness, and the inability to read Western signals

In 1956, Friedrich and Brzezinski described what they labelled a vacuum effect surrounding a dictator (1956). The more an authoritarian regime represses dissent and criticism, the less the regime leader knows about the true state of the regime's popularity. Describing African authoritarian leaders, Judith Barker and Richard Sandbrook notice the leaders' need for veneration and obedience among his personally loyal followers, who also serve as advisors. To avoid rivals, an authoritarian leader will swiftly fire or reshuffle any minister, general, or governor, who develops an independent power base (1985, 90). Today, the political psychology literature describes the vacuum as an extreme example of groupthink, which is often the sub-optimal outcome of a decision-making process that takes place only among like-minded individuals. The inability to discuss and challenge the regime leader's perception of external actors might lead to foreign policy blindness, as described by Or Honig and Zimkind 2017. Research on the initiation of conflicts shows that in autocratic regimes, the strength of the domestic audience correlates with the regime leader's decision to initiate conflicts (Weeks 2012; Colgan and Weeks 2015, Li and Chen 2021). Sycophants, who hold their position at the discretion of the regime leader, are less likely to challenge the same leader's ill-fated decision to enter an armed conflict. In contrast, a strong domestic audience of party organizations or military organizations provides the inner circle of the regime with a shield against the whims of the regime leader.

Foreign policy blindness provides a third answer to the research question. In this perspective, the derailing of Western imposed reforms happens because the existentially threatened local regime underestimates the severity of the internal threat and disregards Western threats and demands. The puzzling behaviour of the al-Maliki regime that ignored signals from the United States might be an example of foreign policy blindness. Years of American disinterest and withdrawal might have convinced al-Maliki of the unlikeliness that the United States would seek to replace him in the middle of an existential crisis. The placement of 'Malikiyouns' in the inner-circle screened al-Maliki from dissenting views that might have indicated that Iran and the United States were about to abandon his regime.

According to this explanation, regimes with a strong domestic audience would react more appropriately to Western signals and demands. There is considerable room for the analyst to determine what constitutes an appropriate reaction. In the context of this study at least, it means recognizing military backlashes that the security institutions cannot overcome. In terms of reading western signals, an appropriate reaction depends on the regime's ability to decipher the importance a Western power attaches to a specific demand for reforms. While the regime can safely ignore general demands

174   *Derailment of reforms*

for, e.g., inclusion with vague threats and rewards, the regime must be able to pick up specific demands that they are obliged to follow if they do not want to lose rewards or face punishment.

In accordance with the explanation of foreign policy blindness and the strength of domestic audiences, the cases of Algeria and Iraq during the al-Abadi regime recorded most instances of compliance. In Algeria, the regime clearly understood the severity of the threat from the militant Islamists, and expanded and professionalized the security institutions accordingly. Moreover, the military junta recognized that access to loans was necessary, and that macro-economic action and inaction would be observable for external powers. For a decade, the World Bank and the IMF had monitored the implementation of macro-economic reforms in many states, and had the expertise to assess the honesty of Algerian macro-economic reforms. With strong intelligence and military institutions, the regime leaders in Algeria, in all likelihood, had to include opposing views in their decision-making process. This might have reduced their foreign policy blindness.

In parallel, until 2003 Prime Minister al-Abadi had spent his adult life in the United Kingdom providing him with an intricate understanding of Western culture and ways of communicating. During his premiership, Western-imposed reforms ultimately failed, but al-Abadi clearly understood Western intentions. Al-Abadi initiated technocratic reforms, sought to include Sunni elites in the security institutions and so forth but partly failed due to the resistance among pro-Iranian Shia parties. In the cases of Chad and Mali, it is more difficult to see to what extent the regime leaders understood Western intentions. If non-implementation is any indication, the regimes in both states seem to have suffered from blindness to Western intentions.

Rather than being cases of foreign policy blindness, the reactions of the regimes must also be interpreted together with the Western reactions. In the 10 instances of non-compliance or simulated compliance, only the World Bank made threats to leave the oil project in Chad, which hardly placed the Chadian regime in an unfavourable position, since the oil lines were finished at that point. In the other instances, Western powers in all likelihood understood the lack of compliance, yet they mostly chose to accept or protest against non-compliance and simulated implementation without punishing the regimes. In Mali, the EU even chose to increase aid for good governance reforms, regardless of the Malian regime's failure to live up to the demands made in 2013. Contrary to the idea of foreign policy blindness, the use of simulated statebuilding might demonstrate a very accurate reading of Western signals.

The introduction discussed the broad shift in Western intervention practices from liberal peacebuilding to regime stability. Nevertheless, the introduction argues that Western military interventions in each case reflect specific political interests, and prioritize between short-term stability and long-term reforms. When the Western powers and international organizations in the four cases chose to accept non-compliance and simulated

Derailment of reforms 175

implementation in response to demands for administrative and political reforms, one explanation is that they preferred short-term stability in order to maintain a friendly relationship with the local regimes. In all four cases, the regimes were existentially threatened by the insurgencies, which pushed Western preferences further towards short-term stability. In the case of Iraq, the offensive of IS also threatened Syria and potentially Jordan, which would endanger the perceived regional interest of the United States. In Chad, France and the United States considered hostilities in conjunction with the Darfur conflict, and the intervention in Mali was part of the general concern about instability in North Africa and the Sahel region after the Western intervention in Libya. Even in the cases where the interventions aim to establish long-term stability brought about by administrative and political reforms, as in Mali, the interventionist parties are often willing to settle for much less.

Regime leaders, who accurately understand the interventionists' dilemmas, are able to play on Western powers' need to demonstrate tangible signs of progress. An image of voters with ink on their thumbs is a strong indication of change and inclusion. Even if Western intelligence services have sufficient information on, e.g., informal undermining of an election, there are still no easy choices for Western decision-makers. Pressing concerns for stability are likely to lead Western powers to accept the practice of simulated statebuilding, such as rigging elections. Moreover, Western political elites often need to convince their domestic audiences to support Western interventions. Andrew Mack identified public opinion in the metropolitan (Western) states as the centre of gravity for Western powers in counterinsurgency wars, because such wars seldom involve vital national interests, and a counterinsurgency strategy is difficult to explain to the public (1975). To maintain public and elite support, Western powers can utilize demands for reforms as a way to appeal to domestically held liberal norms of democracy and human rights (Gelpi et al. 2009, 193ff; Patterson 2016, 155). Furthermore, in an international context there is a common need to establish consensus on terminating aid in, e.g., the EU or the World Bank, where considerable diplomatic work lies behind the aid and reform programmes in the first place. Knowing this political logic of Western powers, simulated statebuilding might be a necessary strategy for local regimes, but also a much less risky strategy than it appears. To cut off aid, despite reforms being formally implemented, would require Western powers to publicly display detailed evidence of the regime's shortcomings, and acknowledge years of misguided trust in a local ally.

Regimes playing skilfully on Western dilemmas and indecisiveness suggest that the mechanisms behind foreign policy blindness might be more intricate than previously shown. According to Honig and Zimskind, in many cases authoritarian regime leaders have ways to overcome foreign policy blindness (2017). Well-known and trusted advisors might dare to hold dissident views, and the inner-circle might include Western-educated advisors. Likewise,

176   *Derailment of reforms*

backstage diplomacy provides access to more honest assessment of Western intentions, e.g., through meetings set up by the intelligence services. Finally, hiring Western consultancy groups, engaging in public diplomacy, or remedial image management are all ways to understand Western signals, and possibly modify Western perception of the regime.

These alternative ways to transmit Western signals into the decision-making process seem to portray the case studies very well. For years, the regimes had repeatedly negotiated with Western NGO's, diplomats, and military attachés. Unlike the most isolated dictatorships, regimes in states dominated by informal politics interact routinely with external actors. Even when Idriss Déby, an autocratic leader, chose relatives for his inner-circle of decision-makers, they often met with representatives of Western powers and international organizations. The examined regimes' understanding of Western powers suggests that the explanation of foreign policy blindness has a narrow scope condition. First, many regimes today straddle the line between democracies and autocracies, as was apparent in Chad. Moreover, autocracies have very different levels of control. Finally, as discussed earlier, autocratic regimes with strong domestic audiences are less prone to foreign policy blindness. In fact, states with the combination of strong and autonomous state institutions and a regime leader with a weak domestic audience might be rare instances, at least when considering states battling an existential internal threat. The cases of Chad, Mali, and Iraq demonstrate that the domestic audience might be competing parties, militias, religious leaders, and even regional powers. Regime leaders in informal settings navigate a political world that is mostly not of their own making. Foreign policy blindness would be challenged by dissident views from competing elites, who may not even be part of the state or ruling party. Overall, foreign policy blindness has relatively little explanatory power in the four cases, compared to the organizational dysfunction explanation.

Conclusion

By making a cross-case comparison of the four case studies, this chapter identified a clear co-variation between informal politics and the strategies of the regimes facing an existential threat. The need to cater to the demands of militarized elites in Chad and Mali affected the regimes' strategies towards praetorian protection, risk-averse alignment, and simulated statebuilding. In the case of Algeria, and to some extent Iraq, the regime survival strategies made use of the state institutions as agents, rather than vessels for co-optation and clientelism. Yet, the unique history, power constellation, and agency of the regime in each case gave rise to differences in the strategies. For example, the culture of co-optation meant that several militias and insurgent groups were highly attuned to the possibility of co-optation, which

Derailment of reforms 177

undermined insurgent cohesion and led to an even greater mistrust of the regular forces, especially in Chad. Another example is the way that simulated statebuilding followed an intricate pattern of formal and informal politics in especially Algeria and Iraq.

The chapter also discussed alternative explanations of derailment of reforms during existential crises. The explanation of foreign policy blindness had little explanatory power in the four case studies. To the contrary, the regimes were able to use the language of reforms, and had a very good grasp of Western unwillingness to punish simulated statebuilding. The second competing explanation, the organizational dysfunction explanation, aptly accounted for the sharp distinction between elite and regular forces. Moreover, organizational dysfunction offers a convincing explanation of the deliberate actions of al-Maliki to undermine the professionalization of the security forces. Yet, it could not explain the lack of control of the regular forces in Chad and Mali, the systematic practice of co-optation of non-state militias or insurgents, nor the empirical observations of systematic pressure from the ruling coalitions. The next chapter concludes and discusses the wider ramifications of this study.

References

Bakke, K. M., Cunningham, K. G., and Seymour, L. J. M. 2012. "A Plague of Initials: Fragmentation, Cohesion, and Infighting in Civil Wars." *Perspectives on Politics* 10 (2): 265–283. 10.1017/S1537592712000667

Bruin, Erica De. 2018. "Preventing coups d'état: How counterbalancing works." *Journal of Conflict Resolution* 62 (7): 1433–1458. 10.1177/0022002717692652

Brown, Cameron S., Christopher J. Fariss, and R. Blake McMahon. 2016. "Recouping after Coup-Proofing: Compromised Military Effectiveness and Strategic Substitution." *International Interactions* 42 (1): 1–30. 10.1080/03050629. 2015.1046598

Colgan, Jeff D., and Jessica L. P. Weeks. 2015. "Revolution, Personalist Dictatorships, and International Conflict." *International Organization* 69 (1): 163–194. 10.1017/ S0020818314000307

DeVore, Marc R., and Armin Stähli. 2020. "Anarchy's Anatomy: Two-tiered Security Systems and Libya's Civil Wars." *Journal of Strategic Studies* 43 (3): 392–420. 10.1080/01402390.2018.1479256

Friedrich, Karl, and Zbigniew Brzezinski. 1956. *Totalitarian Dictatorship and Autocracy*. Cambridge: Harvard University Press.

Gelpi, Christopher, Peter D. Feaver, and Jason Reifler. 2009. *Paying the Human Costs of War: American Public Opinion and Casualties in Military Conflicts.* Princeton: Princeton University Press. 10.1515/9781400830091

Guichaoua, Yvan. 2020. "The Bitter Harvest of French Interventionism in the Sahel." *International Affairs* 96 (4): 895–911. 10.1093/ia/iiaa094

Honig, Or A., and Sarah Zimskind. 2017. "Not Completely Blind: What Dictators Do To Improve Their Reading of the World." *Comparative Strategy* 36 (3): 241–256. 10.1080/01495933.2017.1338481

178 *Derailment of reforms*

Kalyvas, N. 2003. "The Ontology of 'Political Violence': Action and Identity in Civil Wars." *Perspectives on Politics* 1 (3): 475–494.

Li, Xiaojun and Dingding Chen. 2021. "Public Opinion, International Reputation, and Audience Costs in an Authoritarian Regime." *Conflict Management and Peace Science* 38 (5) 543–560. 10.1177/0738894220906374

Mack, Andrew. 1975. "Why Big Nations Lose Small Wars: The Politics of Asymmetric Conflict." *World Politics* 27 (2): 175–200. 10.2307/2009880

Patterson, William. 2016. *Democratic Counterinsurgents: How Democracies Can Prevail in Irregular Warfare*. London: Palgrave Macmillan. 10.1057/978-1-137-60060-8

Sandbrook, Richard, and Judith Barker. 1985. *The Politics of Africa's Economic Stagnation*. Cambridge: Cambridge University Press. 10.1017/CBO9780511558931

Stanley, Elizabeth. A., and Rita. A. Brooks, eds. 2007. *Creating Military Power: The Sources of Military Effectiveness*. Stanford: Stanford University Press. 10.11126/stanford/9780804753999.001.0001

Talmadge, Caitlin. 2015. *The Dictator's Army: Battlefield Effectiveness in Authoritarian Regimes*. Ithaca: Cornell University Press. 10.7591/9781501701764

Weeks, Jessica L. 2012. "Strongmen and Straw Men: Authoritarian Regimes and the Initiation of International Conflict." *American Political Science Review* 106 (2): 326–348. 10.1017/S0003055412000111

Weinstein, Jeremy M. 2006. *Inside Rebellion: The Politics of Insurgent Violence*. Cambridge: Cambridge University Press. 10.1017/CBO9780511808654

8 Betting on institutions or persons?

Why did the al-Maliki regime not undertake administrative and political reforms when the reward would be Western military support that would tip the military balance in the regime's favour? The previous examinations sought to cast light on the intricate informal and formal interplay among ruling elites, regimes, and Western intervening powers that shaped the actions of regimes in existential crises, such as the al-Maliki regime. This chapter brings together the theoretical framework and the empirical studies to answer the overarching research question of this book. Afterwards, the chapter discusses the wider ramifications of the increasing acceptance of the role of informal politics in the evolving Western intervention practices discussed in the introduction. It discusses the advantages and drawbacks of accepting and utilizing informal politics, by comparing the French and the US approaches to interventions.

Informal politics is at the heart of elite relations

This book set out to answer the research question, *why do existentially threatened regimes derail Western demands for administrative and political reforms when they depend on Western assistance for survival?* Taking its departure from the observation that upholding the domestic status quo seems essential to regimes, the first working question was *what domestic factors prevent the regimes from meeting Western demands?* Based on a state-in-society approach and political settlement theory, the key theoretical argument was that in order to stay in power the regimes depend on non-productive elites, specialized in violence, whom the regimes must accommodate by using informal politics. In those instances, external pressure for reforms is tantamount to demanding a change in the political settlement at the expense of the factions in the ruling coalition. As difficult as such a change would be during more peaceful periods, it would be impossible during a crisis, because the factions specialized in violence have the power to prevent them. Although the study relied on a co-variational logic between the importance of informal politics and regime strategies, the four case studies found important examples of non-productive elites that defended or fought their way to informal

DOI: 10.4324/9781003204978-8

180   *Betting on institutions or persons?*

arrangements. However, the case studies of political settlements with a higher element of formal politics also observed instances of elites within the ruling coalition undermining reforms informally. In general, a detailed examination of particular political settlements is necessary in order to understand fully the composition of formal and informal accommodation of elites within the ruling coalition.

The second working question was *how do these internal factors shape the strategic choices of the regimes?* From a theoretical point of view, this study argued that during an existential crisis the regime's freedom of action is limited to three complementary kinds of strategies, namely praetorian protection, risk-averse alignment, and simulated statebuilding. In various ways, all three types of strategies employ and reinforce informal politics and derail administrative and political reforms. The praetorian preference means that regimes undermine efforts to build capable security institutions, the risk-averse alignment strategy implies that regimes are willing to undermine the authority and sovereignty of the state to counter an insurgency threat, and simulated statebuilding evades other reforms without confronting the Western powers.

The convoluted praetorian protection strategy was the default choice for the two regimes in informal settings. As the cross-case comparison in chapter seven showed, the regimes in informal settings were unwilling to expose their elite forces and mainly reserved them for regime protection. Furthermore, chapter seven discussed the rival explanation that the dysfunction was by design of the regime leader to prevent the rise of alternative centres of power. However, this explanation cannot account for the fact that regular forces served little purpose beyond being the vessel for co-opting militias and insurgents, and were hardly ever used for punishment. The findings might partly be due to peculiarities of the cases, and an examination of the cases of Somalia and Sierra Leone might point to a more active role of the regular forces, but this is doubtful[1]. Therefore, the regimes undermined the professionalization of the regular forces, despite the Western provision of training opportunities. Praetorian protection stood out as a strategy of necessity brought about by the uncertain position of the regimes and their limited ability to transform co-opted units into professional military units, along with the inherent danger this poses.

All examined regimes applied alignment-based strategies, which might be unsurprising in the light of their dire circumstances. As summarized in Chapter 7, all the four regimes were reluctant to put their faith in other actors in order to survive, and they all preferred internal to external alignment. In this regard, the level of informal politics made little difference. However, the regimes in informal settings were pragmatic and chose to align across ethnic and sectarian divides to stay in power. Most notably, the wide distribution of power among domestic elites made fragmentation and realignment a common occurrence, which the regimes benefited from. This logic differed from the concern for state authority found in the two cases

Betting on institutions or persons? 181

where formal politics was more important. In Algeria and partly in Iraq, the regimes concerned themselves with programmatic principles and sovereignty besides regime survival when aligning externally, because these were important to a more formal political settlement. By contrast, regimes in informal settings appeared unconcerned with principles other than regime survival in their external alignments.

The analysis found that the pressure of informal politics did indeed require regimes to simulate statebuilding when they aligned with Western powers. However, the cases of Algeria and Iraq showed the need for a subtler understanding of instances when regimes simulate statebuilding. When reforms threatened the interests of factions of the ruling coalitions or their clients, the regimes chose to simulate statebuilding, which highlights the relative strength of factions to keep informal politics in place. Moreover, in Chad and Iraq regional powers strengthened militant elites inside and outside the ruling coalition that hindered statebuilding initiatives. A systematic observation was that Western powers accepted the use of simulated statebuilding. This observation is detrimental to the alternative explanation that local regimes suffer from foreign policy blindness. Instead, the local regimes most likely had a keen awareness of the importance of short-term crisis management to the intervening Western powers rather than a commitment to administrative and political reforms. During long-term Western interventions, the need to evoke liberal progress is a way to gain public support for the engagement, but a need that is accommodated by the regimes' nominal implementation of reforms. Local regimes seem to have ways to pick up the dual concerns of the Western powers. This might reflect that regimes navigating informal politics are far from being isolated dictatorships. On the contrary, they face a very active domestic audience within the ruling coalition, which subjugates the regime to constant criticism and forces it to understand political allies and opponents.

The importance of informal politics to a political settlement is most likely a key factor to explain why existentially threatened regimes derail Western reforms, even when they depend on assistance from the West. Consequently, the dynamic of informal politics most likely influences the strategies of other existentially threatened regimes, even though in ways particular to the specificities of these political settlements and the regional power distribution. The universalistic strands of literature within security study would benefit from an engagement with theories within the peacebuilding literature that unfolds local conflict dynamics. Had the theoretical framework black-boxed domestic politics and simply assumed that the interests of the regimes differed from those of the West, it would not have been able to explain why existentially threatened regimes ran the risk of Western powers abandoning them. By modestly expanding on the demands for contextual knowledge, the reward is an analytical tool that moves beyond distinctions such as strong/weak states or resilient/fragile states. As we saw in Algeria and in Iraq, informal politics can be part of otherwise formalized politics. By asking to

182 *Betting on institutions or persons?*

what extent and in what areas informal politics dominates in an existentially threatened state, a political settlement framework can make sense of why some demands for reforms fail and others succeed.

Implications for Western interventions

Since the withdrawal of combat troops from Afghanistan and Iraq, Western powers have acted in a paradoxical way. Western policy debates about the feasibility of interventions have turned more sceptical, yet Western powers have directly, or indirectly, been involved in a number of new interventions in, e.g., the Central African Republic, Iraq, Libya, Mali, and Syria in addition to ongoing interventions in, e.g., Bosnia, Kosovo, the Democratic Republic of Congo, and Somalia. On the ground, the paradox has been dealt with by adopting a reticent posture and utilizing existing power structures, regional powers, or private military companies as discussed in the introduction. The attention of this study to the utility and importance of informal politics raises the question of the feasibility, legitimacy, and consequences of reinforcing existing power structures. To discuss the policy implications of this study, this section expands on the shift towards indirect and small footprint operations. Afterwards, it compares in the person-centric approach of France with the approach of the United States a historical light, and discusses the ramifications of leveraging informal, personal connections.

Small footprint interventions and the acceptance of status quo

In 2011, Robert Gates, US Secretary of Defense, summed up the prevailing view on Western interventions by saying that "any future defense secretary who advises the president to again send a big American land army into Asia or into the Middle East or Africa should 'have his head examined,' as General MacArthur so delicately put it" (quoted in Shanker 2011). In 2014 the Parliament of the United Kingdom rejected the Government's proposed air campaign in Syria, thereby breaking with the custom of foreign policy being the prerogative of the Government. The rejection was also the culmination of the United Kingdom's growing scepticism towards large-scale interventions. Among decision-makers in France, the view on interventions was more favourable, as shown in the case study of Mali. Nevertheless, in operations Serval and Barkhane France followed the general trend of deploying relatively few land troops (Tenenbaum 2017, 570–571). In the introduction, the abandonment of large-scale interventions was associated with a shift away from statebuilding. Removing Western combat troops has obfuscated violence for the Western public, and the alternative modes of intervention have created a practice of permanent stabilization operations (Gelot and Sandor 2019).

Not surprisingly, Somalia has been a showcase, or even a laboratory, for new small footprint interventions (Moe et al., 2017, Demmers and Gould 2018). Since

Betting on institutions or persons? 183

the infamous "Black Hawk Down" incident in Mogadishu in 1993, Somalia has epitomized Western casualty aversion and unwillingness to deploy combat troops. To handle the perceived threat from the Islamic Courts, and later on al-Shabaab, Western powers have built a security assemblage consisting of all but Western conventional forces. Special forces have trained local security forces or have conducted direct action against high-level al-Shabaab members, US drones have conducted reconnaissance and have carried out strikes against militant leaders, and a host of private military companies have provided, e.g., logistics and close protection units. To compensate for the light footprint, Western powers have used diplomacy and aid to bring together an alliance of East African states in the African Union Mission in Somalia (AMISOM). Western powers have been funding, training, and assisting AMISOM. Manipulating clan politics has been the way to link these means with the goal of removing or marginalizing first the Islamic Courts and afterwards al-Shabaab. After the Ethiopian army, and later AMISOM, had driven back the al-Shabaab militia, the major clans in the Mogadishu area set up the Transitional Federal Government under the auspices of the Western powers. The political crisis of Somalia in the spring of 2021 demonstrates the illusiveness of a strong central Somalian state, but so far AMISOM has proven sufficiently resilient despite the high number of casualties (Kirechu 2021). It has lasted over a decade with little public debate about its termination, even though the intervention has achieved little stability, not to speak of peace. Key elements of the "Somalia experiment" can be found in other current Western interventions. The case study of Iraq showed how the Western powers relied on special forces, air power, and local forces. In Mali, only weeks before the French intervention, a regional intervention force was supposed to lead the military campaign with assistance from France. Moreover, many of the elements have been applied by Western powers in Afghanistan after 2014, the other Sahel states, and in Yemen.

The open-ended (or unending) character of contemporary military interventions has been picked up in both the security studies and peacebuilding literature. Within security studies, the debate is about the strategic potential and consequences of the current intervention practices, such as drone warfare and military assistance to local forces (Krieg and Rickli 2019). The cynical political side to the operational shift is an increased willingness to leave root causes mostly unattended and willingness to accept high levels of violence in the local societies (Biddle et al. 2018, 44). Small footprint operations require so few resources and result in so few – Western – casualties that they can be sustained over an extended period, and perhaps indefinitely. Within the peacebuilding literature, the focus is less centred on military or elite issues. Yet, the ambition to build resilient societies after conflicts has led to calls for ever more long-term and open-ended engagements among practitioners and observers (Bargués-Pedreny 2020, 274ff, Paffenholz 2021). The need to adapt constantly to a dynamic environment makes the creation of resilience a potentially never-ending quest.

184 *Betting on institutions or persons?*

However, taking a quick historical perspective of Western intervention practices after decolonialization shows that Western powers often have engaged in semi-permanent small footprint interventions. Moreover, it shows that even among small footprint interventions with few ambitions of statebuilding markedly different political dynamics are at play. The former colonial powers of Britain and France had a deep knowledge of local elite politics and personal connections to the new post-colonial regimes. In contrast, acute global security concerns, such as the Cold War, have often forced the United States to intervene in local conflicts with little prior knowledge. To focus the discussion, the following section compares the approaches of France and the United States to indirect, small footprint interventions. More specifically, the purpose is to tease out the difference between the French approach of nurturing close, personal relations to its former African colonies and the approach of the United States of leveraging local proxies for global purposes.

French post-colonial ties and the United States' use of proxies for global purposes

Every year since 1973 African leaders from the former French colonies gather to engage in confidential discussions with the French President in the Franco-African summit. President Emmanuel Macron has continued the personal involvement in the former French colonies and often travelled there to meet state leaders, despite his public denouncement of the colonial past (Bryant 2021). The longevity and depth of the personal relations only tell part of the story of the close relationship between France and its former African colonies. In these specific parts of Africa, France has developed an advanced understanding of the power dynamics and influence of societal elites. During the Cold War, when the two superpowers saw regional and local dynamics through the lens of the global ideological struggle, France identified a niche role of being the great power that preserved close ties to its former colonies and kept them non-communist, without conflating local power dynamics with a global black-and-white ideological clash. In contrast, the United States took little notice of domestic issues of its allies in, e.g., Africa, as long as the allies maintained a nominal anti-communist stand.

In most cases after the end of the Cold War the United States has appraised generalized concepts above local power dynamic when deciding on a course of action in an intervention. From Iraq being a democratic beacon for the Middle East to the overarching concept of war on terror, a universal concept came before the understanding of the power distribution among societal elites. In certain regions, such as Latin America, the US approach resembled the French approach with personal contacts and an understanding of the ruling coalition and marginalized elites. Nevertheless, there is a general historical difference between the French use of personal relations to existing power holders and the US approach of considering local politics

Betting on institutions or persons? 185

from a universal perspective. This historical difference provides us with important insights into the potential and limitation of interventions that are not based on administrative and political reforms.

During the dramatic days in N'djamena in Chad in 2008, the French assessment and actions epitomized the French approach of making use of personal relations. No principles guided French diplomats in their choice between supporting President Déby or the alliance of insurgent groups. Just as France was willing to abandon the Habré regime in 1990, so was France willing to abandon the Déby regime in order to maintain good relations with the insurgent leaders. Once they chose to support the president, French diplomats and officers had few quarrels about being intimately involved in the tactical decisions of the regime, because they had been personally involved with the President even before Déby took office. French officials knew that the insurgents did not represent a break with informal politics in Chad, but were merely aiming at modifying the existing clientelistic configuration. In April 2021, President Macron swiftly took advantage of the French state's deep personal knowledge of Chadian elites to provide political support for Mahamat Déby, the son of the deceased President. Put more generally, the French approach in Francophone Africa rests on the assumptions that any intervention requires close relationships to the key power holders, and political solutions must be based on the existing power structure either among the ruling coalition or among powerful elites outside.

French understanding of and participation in the elite power plays in Francophone Africa have deep roots in the transition from the colonial to the post-colonial period. In Tony Chafer's formulation, decolonization did not mark an end, but rather a restructuring of the imperial relationship (2016, 137). Besides the high-profile summits and state visits, French foreign aid was mainly directed to its former African colonies, and the common currency, CFA Franc, was used in Francophone Africa and administered from Paris. Cultural, educational, and administrative programmes as well as defence agreements, in some cases, meant that more French citizens worked in the former colonies than during the colonial period (ibid, 144). After the independence of the colonies, France permanently stationed 10,000–15,000 troops in Africa.

In addition, bureaucratically and politically, French relations to Francophone Africa were different from traditional foreign policy. Until 1994, an "African cell" was responsible for African policy and placed directly under the President. In parallel, the Ministry of Co-Operation, the former Ministry for the Colonies, administered foreign aid related to the former colonies, which were therefore outside the domain of the Ministry of Foreign Affairs. Francophone Africa was not treated as part of the realm of French foreign policy, but as a distinct policy area (Châtaigner 2006). Arguably, the activities and organization of the French policy created a common culture among African and French elites, which came to share the idea that France had a special understanding of Francophone Africa (Gouttebrune 2002, 1038–1039).

186   *Betting on institutions or persons?*

French participation in the power plays of the elites in Francophone Africa also had a somewhat murkier side, which gave rise to the pejorative term *Francafrique*. In François-Xavier Verschaves' critique, the personalized and clientelistic intermingling of interests meant that French policy was guided by the interests of a small group of businesses and political elites (1998). Even worse, corruption and kickback were ubiquitous practices, and French parties were susceptible to corruption, because they received large amounts of money from African leaders (Alleno 2020). Another outcome of the intermingling of French and Africa interests was the routine military interventions, in some cases in support of coups d'etat. In the period from 1960 to 1995, on average France intervened militarily in its former colonies every year (Chafer 2016, 137). The permanent and personal relations created a deep understanding among French decision-makers, civil administration, intelligence and military services of formal and, especially, informal elements of politics in Francophone Africa.

In comparison, the global projection of diplomatic and military power of the United States led to very diverse alignments with local regimes. By engaging in a global power struggle with the Soviet Union, the United States suddenly needed to ally with regimes in many newly independent states in Africa, the Middle East, and Asia. American decision-makers saw local conflicts in a global perspective, which regimes deftly took advantage of by framing themselves as staunch anti-communists (David 1991). After 2001, the global character of the al-Qaeda network similarly prompted the United States to engage with states previously neglected by decision-makers in Washington. When the United States rushed to build alliances with, e.g., Uzbekistan or Yemen, diplomats, intelligence and military officers had to deal with actors, of whom they had little prior knowledge (Byman 2008, 203ff). Or, as in the Sahel states, the United States launched a one-size-fits-all regional counter-terrorism programme, creating new elite counter-terrorism units in heavily coup-proofed militaries.

Since the beginning of the Cold War, the United States has built up massive diplomatic, intelligence, and military services to oversee the vast number of allies and proxies. However, understanding the intricacies of informal politics requires a substantial amount of time and effort. In 2014, behind the scene the United States was deftly involved in the negotiation of the ouster of al-Maliki, due to the many contacts to Iraqi elites established by US officials in the decade since the invasion. Still, the range and depth of the US personal relations hardly matched those of Iran, who had nurtured their connection through the years of US disengagement from Iraq. The many diverse alliances of the United States have led to debates about the viability of sustaining a global network of alliances. For decades, the dominant position has been to continue most alliances, even though this does not always extend to perceived peripheral states. Many perceived peripheral states and elites have been abandoned by the United States, because of the tendency of US senior leaders to see the local conflicts through a

Betting on institutions or persons? 187

global lens. The abandonment of the Mujahedeen elites in Afghanistan at the end of the Cold War meant that the United States had few contacts in those theatres immediately after the 9/11 attacks. Without trust, personal contacts, or knowledge, the United States needed years of involvement to compensate. Still, the current debate about US grand strategy centres on whether to continue the "forever wars". Former President Donald Trump and President Joe Biden share a resentment against long-term military commitments, as noticeable in the Trump administration's decision to abandon the Syrian Defence Forces, and the Biden administration's continuation of the withdrawal of US forces from Afghanistan. For all the US critics of the decisions, the debate reflects that once the narrative of the "War on Terror" gave way to the narrative of great power rivalry, decision-makers questioned alignments with peripheral states en bloc, not based on individual merits or a common history.

The United States differs from France at the senior administrative and political levels, where the organizational capacity to cope with peripheral states is severely limited. Since 9/11, most of the military outposts and training missions of the United States have a permanent status, and junior diplomatic, intelligence, and military representatives show a keen understanding of local politics. However, it is difficult to convey knowledge to the senior levels for various reasons. First, within the last two decades, the State Department has lost influence and means compared to the military commands, which reduces the importance of the political and diplomatic aspects of alignments (Ucko 2019). Second, the senior level cannot automatically take over personal contacts established by junior representatives, because political attention is a scarce resource. On a daily basis, the White House and State Department might deal with issues in Eastern Europe, the South China Sea, or South America that draw away attention from perceived peripheral states. The symbolism of head-to-head meetings between senior leaders is difficult to replicate at the junior level, yet global concerns truncate the available time of the President and senior leaders. To meet regularly with regime leaders from states, which might one day become important to US security, is beyond the capacity of the Secretary of State or the President. The continuity of the French approach at the senior level cannot easily be duplicated by the United States.

Still, since the 1990s, French policy towards its former colonies has in some respects moved closer to the policy of the United States. Three highly publicized changes have aimed to de-personalize the French approach towards its former colonies. First, in 1990 President Mitterrand initiated a conditionality-based approach to its former colonies to promote democracy and economic reforms, which was to replace trust and longevity with inducement and potential punishment. The genocide in Rwanda amplified the move towards detachment and conditionality, because France received criticism for its close connection to the Hutu-dominated government (Kroslak 2007). Second, multilateralism and Europeanization became the main vehicles for French

188 *Betting on institutions or persons?*

engagement. The cases of Algeria, Chad, and Mali showed how international organizations, such as the EU, IMF and the UN, were supposed to be the vehicles for implementation of reforms. In principle, a multilateral approach removed the privileged position of the former French colonies and subjugated them to universal criteria to determine international aid. Third, France began promoting "African solutions to African problems", a catch phrase for advancing regional cooperation and national capacity building. Capacity building was now supposed to promote rule-of-law, protection of civilians, and the ability to conduct regional peacekeeping. France, for instance, supported the development of ECOWAS into a regional peacebuilding actor (Wyss 2017). On paper, the post-Cold War approach cut historical and personal ties and promoted universal solutions to security challenges.

In reality, the French and US approaches to local regimes still differ, because the French approach maintains many of the practices from the Cold War. French demands for democracy, human rights, or market reforms were never rigorous, as the case studies of Chad and Mali demonstrated. Other case studies find the same pattern in French behaviour in, e.g., the Ivory Coast and Niger (Bovcon 2013). In parallel, France has maintained bilateral personal contacts and aid to its former colonies, despite its professed adherence to multilateral institutions. By supporting multilateral institution building in Francophone Africa, France also deflected criticism of its unilateral politics (Erforth 2020, 576–577). Moreover, France has managed to influence EU's prioritization in Africa, effectively turning French priorities in especially the Sahel region into EU projects. Finally, the launch of operation Barkhane put an end to the strong emphasis on African solutions. Notwithstanding decades of avowed change, France still bases its policy on a deep bilateral involvement in its former colonies. However, with strapped resources, France complements its unilateral efforts by cooperating closely with local security forces and by making multilateral arrangements.

The difference in the approaches of France and the United States is on display in their self-declared partnership in Africa (Obama and Hollande 2014). Division of labour is at the heart of the partnership and reflects the difference in personal ties. French resources shortage makes US capacities such as airlift, intelligence, reconnaissance, surveillance, and special forces capacity-building valuable to the French efforts (Rye Olsen 2018). In return, the United States takes advantage of long-established French contacts and its deep understanding of the elite interplay. Such a division of labour lessens the need of the United States for political engagement in Francophone Africa.

The achievability and desirability of leveraging personal ties

The French approach of nurturing personal, political connections generates a more inclusive understanding of informal politics. Still, the approach begs the question of what problems arise from close alliances with local regimes and political elites. Close alliances allow for an intimate involvement in conflicts

Betting on institutions or persons? 189

pertaining small adjustment to the rules of the political settlement, which in some cases makes quick crisis management possible. On the other hand, close alliances also weaken the bargaining position of the Western power, and arrangements with autocratic leaders may have limited public legitimacy. Yet, taking a transactional approach to local regimes makes it difficult to build knowledge of informal politics in order to monitor compliance with Western demands. More to the point, handling long-term threats, such as the growth of militant Jihadism through short-term corrections of local regime behaviour is unlikely to yield significant results. In that light, building long-term personal relations with selected regimes might be the least bad option, if military interventions are relevant in the first place.

Understanding informal politics is different from influencing it and very different from changing it. If other external interveners choose to duplicate the French approach, they might, in time, gain knowledge about the ruling coalition, informal and formal rules, and possibly knowledge about marginalized elites. The benefit of the approach is primarily the longevity of the relations. France maintains relations with a number of states and regimes that understand their security as tied to maintaining a workable relation with Paris. External military interventions are most likely to take place in conflict-ridden states with political settlements favouring militant elites or other non-productive elites, who increase the risk of long-term violence and recurrent crises. Choosing when to end military engagements in such states is often an arbitrary decision, in the sense that external decision-makers know that new crises are likely to follow afterwards. To pull out of, e.g., Afghanistan was a hard decision fraught with risk. Once the decision was taken the Afghan regime quickly unravelled, and international terrorism may once again emanate from the country. In that light, maintaining long-term political relations is a way to reconcile the need for permanent political monitoring and access to decision-makers with the need to reduce military engagements for as long periods as possible.

Permanent political relations also make an external power the hub of external interventions. In the Sahel region, France's possession of valuable insight and connections makes France the natural organizer and co-ordinator of external activities in the region. The military engagements of, e.g., Germany and the EU in Mali and Niger heavily rely on French infrastructure and political negotiations with the regimes. The case studies also show how France translated knowledge and connections with local regimes into influence on, e.g., the World Bank, which enabled them to make use of much larger economic resources. Close, personal connections are difficult to establish quickly once a crisis breaks out. Having them in advance provides an external power with political influence, because other external actors come to rely on these connections.

From the perspective of the intervener, the downside is that local regimes can also take advantage of durable relations. Local regime leaders might utilize external powers in their internal attempts to sideline rivals or get

190 *Betting on institutions or persons?*

away with repression of the opposition or the civil society (Hagmann and Reynthens 2016). By accepting a current political settlement as the lesser evil, the external power risks underwriting a political stasis that democratic actors in the civil societies might have been able to challenge. Moreover, the critique of corrupt practices and personal gains in French Africa politics might not be a particular French experience, but rather the logical result of long-term cooperation in informal contexts. Finally, an assured commitment to local regimes creates moral hazards, as pointed out by the principal-agent theory. Regimes might act recklessly in the face of threats from excluded elites if they come to expect Western powers to intervene. This might create a vicious circle of more unconcerned regime behaviour and more frequent Western interventions.

A tit-for-tat, transactional approach seeks to evade the moral hazard of enduring, personal relations. The reviewed principal-agent literature recommends that Western powers do not become entangled with persons and keep a distance to local regimes. A transactional approach might be better suited for a global power. The difficulty of providing a large number of developmental states across continents with senior political attention, suggest that the United States would only be engaged periodically with developmental states, and only in ways that maximized US influence. Moreover, in the view of a group of scholars that have recently applied the principal-agent approach to proxy warfare, aid programmes should be "(...)designed from the beginning to provide divisible, reversible, contingent assistance with intrusive monitoring will offer more potential to create leverage for maintaining proxy incentives (...)" (Biddle 2019, 273). The need for a tit-for-tat approach arises from misaligned interests. Intrusive monitoring of the regime's activities becomes necessary when the external power mistrusts the local regime, and conditionality compensates for misaligned interests by temporarily manipulating the interests of the local regime.

For several reasons, these policy prescriptions are deceptively easy. First of all, this study has shown that Western powers accept simulated state-building in most cases. Western governments walk a tightrope when they have to convince their domestic audiences of the need to intervene and simultaneously convince a local regime that aid is conditional only. But for the sake of the argument an assumption may be that Western powers will be able to conduct strict conditionality-based strategies with intrusive monitoring and still maintain domestic support for the intervention. Then the second problem is that military or civilian reforms mostly succeed in states dominated by formal politics. Although there were examples of a successful conditionality policy in Algeria, it only carries little importance because Western powers mostly intervene in states dominated by informal politics. Informal politics offers too many ways to deflate, circumvent, or manipulate a strict conditionality strategy. Divisible aid and divisible punishment may succeed in their own right. Still, considering them a series of interactions, regimes are able to negate most concessions at a later stage, offset them by

Betting on institutions or persons? 191

doing the opposite in other policy areas or institutions, or are able to simulate their implementation.

The third problem is closely related and stems from the argument made earlier, namely that most often internal threats are long-lasting in states dominated by informal politics. Violence is a common part of the repertoire of excluded elites, who may wield it with devastating effects. Thus, a strategy of manipulating incentives potentially faces decades of intrusive monitoring and difficult decisions whether to cut or continue aid. In the meantime, new issues, new political leadership, and new priorities will gradually undermine the strategy by taking away senior political attention. The final problem is that a transactional approach shapes the expectations and behaviour of the local regime. In the short run, this might be a negligible concern, as the local regime most likely has nowhere else to turn. Nevertheless, Western aloofness and willingness to punish or even abandon the regime induce the local regime to look for alternatives. Allowing regional powers greater influence or accommodating more militarized elites are ways for the regime to guard itself against a tit-for-tat Western approach. The principal-agent perspective offers important explanations of the lacking influence of external powers. Still, the plasticity of informal politics and the longevity of threats make a principal-agent theory a porous foundation for policy prescriptions.

When weighting the achievability and desirability of personal and informal ties at the elite level, the argument easily becomes detached from the practice of interventions and post-conflict reconstruction. The comparison of the French and US approaches focused on the level of state-to-state interactions, which even leaves out the interplay between the regime and domestic elites. Moreover, it leaves out the level of societal dynamics among civil societies and local elites that garner much attention within the peacebuilding literature and practices. A narrow elite focus might be politically suspect, as it evokes colonial practices and puts Western security interests before the interests of the population in the targeted states. In that light, the interplay between regime and intervener must be considered in relation to the complex dynamics of violent conflicts. On the other hand, the regime and the ruling coalition cannot simply be bypassed, whether as an analytical level or in policy implementation. An exclusive focus on local communities, NGOs, or other parts of the civil society runs the risk of drawing resistance from the national elites. To avoid that, initiatives to create "peace from below" would probably benefit from a long-term, personal engagement with the regime and its ruling coalition. At least as long as it is not equated with unconditional support of the incumbent regime, fixed power-sharing agreements, or neglect of societal need.

The possibility of peace is intimately connected to the dynamics of power politics among elites. Jan Pospisil explores ways to move the current peacebuilding debate beyond a "state of affirmation" (2019 18ff, see also Moe and Stepputat 2018). That is, a deep skepticism among practitioners and theorists of the conceptual and contextual authority of current peacebuilding approaches to

192 *Betting on institutions or persons?*

create solutions to violent conflicts. To break the "state of affirmation", while retaining a pragmatic approach, Pospisil imagines a "formalised political un-settlement" that "focuses on continuation in stagnancy, on the fluid elements that enable this continuation and on the hidden practices at work in these fluid elements" (2019, 200). A pragmatic approach to creative solutions to the complex problems of peacebuilding requires a continuous political dialogue and understanding of the personal and non-codified politics, rather than the imposition of pre-conceived reforms.

The conception of political settlement-as-conflict implies that a political settlement remains a dynamic interplay between power and institutions, which a (potential) intervener needs to study continuously. An intervener with the ambition to transcend stability and aim at peacebuilding would have to acknowledge the complexity of the conflict dynamic (ibid, 41ff). On the other hand, the intervener already disturbs the distribution of power by intervening. In this lies opportunity. Although the outcome of a certain action to transform the political settlement cannot be determined in advance in a complex system of an internationalized conflict, the intervener can probe different initiatives and analyse the effects. Especially the informal accommodation of militant elites appears to be a key element to either facilitate or undermine the economic foundation of the elites' power. In such cases, a deep understanding of the political settlement underlying the power of the regime is essential before engaging militant elites.

This study and the "affirmative state" of peacebuilding suggest that interveners can only hope for small changes in the political settlement. However, even minor changes in the configurations of power and institutions may lay the seed for a long-term change, once violence declines. Certain configurations allow the slow establishment of productive economic activities and new forms of collective actions, such as labour unions or programmatic political parties without provoking a backlash from the militant elites. The explorations of "constructive" configurations of power and institutions and the circumstances under which they come about are promising avenues of research. After all, during the Cold War, the region suffering the most from extreme poverty and internal violence was not Africa, the Middle East, South Asia, but East Asia. There is no external cookie-cutter method for transforming societies, but even poor and conflict-ridden societies may change.

Note

1 In Somalia, Robinson and Matisek found that the armed forces remain highly fragmented and are mainly vessels for armed elites to profit from foreign military assistance (2021, 192). In Sierra Leone, William Reno strongly argues that factionalism and rivalry dominated the armed forces in the 1990s (2007, 327ff).

References

Alleno, Kevin. 2020. "La «Françafrique», Instrument d'un Soft Power Associatif et «sTigmate» Pour la Politique Africaine de la France." *Dans Relations internationals* 2 (182): 99–113. 10.3917/ri.182.0099

Bargués-Pedreny, Pol. 2020. "Resilience Is 'always More' Than Our Practices: Limits, Critiques, and Skepticism About International Intervention." *Contemporary Security Policy* 41 (2): 263–286. 10.1080/13523260.2019.1678856

Biddle, Stephen. 2019. "Policy Implications for the United States." In *Proxy Wars: Suppressing Violence through Local Agents*, edited by D. A. Lake, and E. Berman. Itchaca: Cornell University Press. 10.7591/9781501733093-013

Biddle, Stephen, Julia Macdonald, and Ryan Baker. 2018. "Small Footprint, Small Payoff: The Military Effectiveness of Security Force Assistance." *Journal of Strategic Studies* 41 (1–2): 89–142. 10.1080/01402390.2017.1307745

Bovcon, Maja. 2013. "Françafrique and Regime Theory." *European Journal of International Relations* 19 (1): 5–26. 10.1177/1354066111413309

Bryant, Lisa. 2021. *Amid France's Africa Reset, Old Ties Underscore Challenge of Breaking With Past*. Voice of America May 31. 31 May. https://www.voanews.com/europe/amid-frances-africa-reset-old-ties-underscore-challenge-breaking-past (15 June 2021)

Byman, Daniel. 2008. *The Five Front War: The Better Way to Fight Global Jihad*. Hoboken: John Wiley & Sons.

Chafer, Tony. 2016. "French African Policy in Historical Perspective." In *Readings in the International Relations of Africa*, edited by T. Young, 165–182. Indiana: Indiana University Press.

Châtaigner, Jean M. 2006. "Principes et Réalités De La Politique Africaine de la France." *Afrique contemporaine* 4: 247–261. 10.3917/afco.220.0247

David, Stephen R. 1991. *Choosing Sides: Alignment and Realignment in the Third World*. Baltimore: Johns Hopkins University Press.

Demmers, Jolle, and Lauren Gould. 2018. "An Assemblage Approach to Liquid Warfare: AFRICOM and the 'Hunt' for Joseph Kony." *Security Dialogue* 49 (5): 364–381. 10.1177/0967010618777890

Erforth, Benedikt. 2020. "Multilateralism as a Tool: Exploring French Military Cooperation in the Sahel." *Journal of Strategic Studies* 43 (4): 560–582. 10.1080/01402390.2020.1733986

Gelot, Linnéa, and Adam Sandor. 2019. "African Security and Global Militarism." *Conflict, Security and Development* 19 (6): 521–542. 10.1080/14678802.2019.1688959

Gouttebrune, François. 2002. "La France et l'Afrique: le crépuscule d' une ambition stratégique?" *Politique estrangère* 67 (4): 1033–1047.

Hagmann, Tobias, and Filip Reynthens. 2016. *Aid and Authoritarianism in Africa: Development without Democracy*. London: Zed Books.

Kirechu, Peter. 2021. "Somalia's Electoral Crisis in Extremis." War on the Rocks, 2 April. https://warontherocks.com/2021/04/somalias-electoral-crisis-in-extremis/ (14 June 2021).

Krieg, Andreas, and Jean-Marc Rickli. 2019. *Surrogate Warfare: The Transformation of War in the Twenty-First Century*. Washington D.C.: Georgetown University Press. 10.2307/j.ctvf34hnd

Kroslak, Daniella. 2007. *The Role of France in the Rwandan Genocide*. London: Hurst & Co.

194 *Betting on institutions or persons?*

Moe, Louise Wiuff, and Stepputat, Finn (2018). Introduction: Peacebuilding in an Era of Pragmatism. *International Affairs* 94 (2), 293–299. 10.1093/ia/iiy035.

Moe, Louise Wiuff, and Markus-Michael Müller. 2017. "Introduction: Complexity, Resilience and the 'Local Turn' in Counterinsurgency." In *Reconfiguring Intervention: Complexity, Resilience and the "Local Turn" in Counterinsurgent Warfare*, edited by Louise Wiuff Moe and Markus-Michael Müller, 1–27. London: Palgrave Macmillan UK. 10.1057/978-1-137-58877-7_1

Obama, Barack, and Hollande, François. 2014. "France and the U.S. Enjoy a Renewed Alliance." *Washington Post*, 10 February. https://www.washingtonpost.com/opinions/obama-and-hollande-france-and-the-us-enjoy-a-renewed-alliance/2014/02/09/039ffd34 –91af-11e3-b46a-5a3d0d2130da_story.html (20 December 2020).

Pospisil, Jan. 2019. *Peace in Political Unsettlement: Beyond Solving Conflict*. Cham: Palgrave Macmillan. 10.1007/978-3-030-04318-6

Reno, William. 2007. "Patronage Politics and the Behavior of Armed Groups." *Civil Wars* 9 (4): 324–342. 10.1080/13698240701699409

Robinson, Colin D., and Matisek, Jahara. 2021. "Military Advising and Assistance in Somalia: Fragmented Interveners, Fragmented Somali Military Forces." *Defence Studies* 21 (2): 181–203. 10.1080/14702436.2021.1885976

Olsen, Gorm Rye. 2018. "Transatlantic Cooperation on Terrorism and Islamist Radicalisation in Africa: The Franco-American Axis." *European Security* 27 (1): 41–57. 10.1080/09662839.2017.1420059

Paffenholz, Thania. 2021. "Perpetual Peacebuilding: A New Paradigm to Move Beyond the Linearity of Liberal Peacebuilding." *Journal of Intervention and Statebuilding* 15 (3): 367–385. 10.1080/17502977.2021.1925423

Shanker, Thom. 2011. "Warning Against Wars Like Iraq and Afghanistan." *New York Times*, 25 February 2011. https://www.nytimes.com/2011/02/26/world/26gates.html (14 November 2019)

Tenenbaum, Élie. 2017. "French Exception or Western Variation? A Historical Look at the French Irregular Way of War." *Journal of Strategic Studies* 40 (4): 554–576. 10.1080/01402390.2016.1220368

Ucko, David H. 2019. "Systems Failure: The US Way of Irregular Warfare." *Small Wars & Insurgencies* 30 (1): 223–254. 10.1080/09592318.2018.1552426

Verschave, François-Xavier. 1998. *La Françafrique: Le Plus Long Scandale de la République*. Paris: Les Arènes.

Wyss, Marco. 2017. "France and the Economic Community of West African States: Peacekeeping Partnership in Theory and Practice." *Journal of Contemporary African Studies* 35 (4): 487–505. 10.1080/02589001.2017.1348600

Index

administrative reforms 5, 34–36; in
    Algeria 147–149; in Chad 62–65; in
    Iraq 118–123; in Mali 91–94
advice and assist missions *see* small
    footprint operations
African Union 183
Acyl, A. 58
Acyl, H. 58
aid 36–37, 75–6, 93, 142–7, 185;
    conditionality 35–36, 144, 147, 165–9;
    cut–off 35–6, 175–6; inducement 35,
    66, 165–167; strategies 165, 190–1;
    see also military assistance
air power 54, 110, 183
al-Qaeda 74, 84, 89–94, 104, 186;
    see also GSPC; JNIM
Abadi, H. 101–2, 110–12, 115–17,
    119–23
Ahrar party 103, 118
Algeria 129ff, 155–6, 161–5, 171–2;
    administrative reforms 144–7;
    alignment 139–43; military strategy
    136–9; political reforms 147–9;
    political settlement 130–5
Algerian Liberation Army 130
Algiers Accord 90
alignment 8, 31–4, 38; in Algeria
    139–44; in Chad 57–62; in Iraq 112–7;
    in Mali 83–9
alliance 26–7, 32, 156–7, 160, 172, 186–9;
    against IS 111, 115–7; insurgency 34,
    48, 57–60, 84, 87, 161–2; literature on
    14, 32; *see also* alignment
Ameri, H. 104–5, 116
Anbar Province 109–11
Anser Dine 84, 90
Armée Nationale Tchadienne 53–7, 59

anti–corruption *see* administrative
    reforms
arab tribes *see* tribes
arabization 132
armed forces *see* security forces
Armée Islamique du Salut 138–9
Asa'ib Ahl al–Haq 106, 113, 115, 117,
    121–2, 168

Ba'ath party 102, 104, 109
Badr militia 103–6, 108, 111–12, 115–18,
    121–2, 172
Baghdad 1, 106, 113, 116, 119
balancing *see* alignment
Bamako 73–5, 77–87, 89–91
Barkhane 80, 88, 90, 163, 182
Barzani, M. 113, 116
Bashir, U. 48, 61, 169
Bendjedid, C. 133–4
berber 132, 141
Biden, J. 119, 187
Boudiaf, M. 145
Bouteflika, A. 139

case selection 39–41
case study method 37–8
Chad 47ff, 155–61, 163–169, 174–6, 185,
    188; administrative reforms 62–5;
    alignment 57–62; military strategy
    55–7; oil export 49–50, 62–3; political
    reforms 64–6; political
    settlement 48–52
civil war 7, 12–3, 20, 48, 78, 104
clan: Arab 74; in the Algerian army 131;
    in Somalia 183; Tuareg 74, 79;
    Zaghawa 49, 52, 57, 59, 172
client network 2, 7, 23–4, 26, 29, 170; in

196 *Index*

Algeria 133–4, 148–9; in Chad 49–50; in Iraq 104–105, 107–9, 112, 120–1; in Mali 74–6, 77–8, 81, 87, 92–3
clientelism 24–25, 42n; *see also* client network
Cold War 39, 135, 184, 186–8, 192
command structure 26–7, 29–31, 170–3; in Algeria 130–1, 134–5, 137, 161; in Chad 48–49, 54–55; in Iraq 108, 110–11, 118, 121–2; in Mali 77–8; *see also* security forces
conciliateurs 137–8
constitution: Algerian 145–7; Chadian 50–1, 65; Malian 73; Iraqi 102–5, 120, 123n
Coordination Group 85, 87–8, 90, 158
corruption 7, 23, 162, 186; off–budget funds 23–24, 41; in Algeria 133, 145; in Chad 50, 63; in Iraq 105, 108, 119–21; in Mali 73–5, 91–4
Cotontchad 49–50
counterinsurgency 3–4, 29–32, 175; in Algeria 129, 135, 137; in Chad 58, 63; in Iraq 111–2; in Mali 82, 85
counterterrorism 3, 29, 35, 40, 155–7, 186; in Algeria 135; in Chad 52, 55; in Iraq 108; in Mali 78, 80, 83
coup 2–3, 10, 27–9, 31, 42n; in Algeria 1965 130–1; in Algeria 1992 134, 136–7; in Chad in 1989 48, 57; attempt in Chad 2004 51–2; in Mali 1991 73, 77; in Mali 2012 72, 74, 77–8, 84; in Mali 2020 72, 76–7, 79–81, 91
coup–proofing 7, 10, 29–31, 38, 155–8, 170–2; in Algeria 150; in Chad 51, 54, 57; in Iraq 107–9, 112, 121, 123; in Mali 77–8, 80–1; *see also* praetorian protection
criminality *see* illegal economy
crisis management 181, 189
cross case comparison 39–41, 154ff

Daesh see Islamic State
Dan Na Ambassagou 88
Darfur 47–9, 52–4, 56–9, 61–4, 158, 175
Dawa party 102–6, 108, 114, 119
debt 142–3, 147–8
Deby, I. 47–55, 57ff, 157, 160–2, 169, 185
decentralization *see* administrative reforms
decolonialization 184

democratization 1–4, 10, 35–6; in Chad 51, 66; in Mali 76, 87; in Algeria 143–6, 149; *see also* political reforms
developmental state 20, 22, 190
Direction générale des services de sécurité des institutions de l'État 52–4, 56, 66
Dicko; Mahmoud 76, 91
Dogon tribe 88, 160; *see also Dan Na Ambassagou*
domestic audience 173–6
ECOWAS 85–6, 163

elections 2, 11–2, 34, 165, 175; Algeria parliamentary 1991/1992 129, 133–4, 144–5; Algerian presidential 1995 139, 145–6; Chad presidential 2006 50–1, 65; Chad parliamentary and presidential 2011 66; Iraq parliamentary 2010 103; Iraq parliamentary 2014 113; Iraq parliamentary 2018 101, 117, 120–1; Mali 2013 89–90; *see also* political reforms
Elias, B. 14
elite forces 7, 31, 155–6, 171–2, 180; in Algeria 135, 137, 139; Chad 57; in Mali 81, 83; in Iraq 107, 109; *see also* presidential guards
elite 6–7, 9–12, 21–6, 28–35, 160–9, 176, 179–81; in Algeria 130–4, 143, 147–150; in Chad 47–9, 51–2, 57–9, 62, 66–7; in Iraqi 101–7, 113–16, 121–3; in Mali 73–7, 82–5, 88–9, 91–4; *see also* ruling coalition
Ennahda 145–6
Épervier 60, 66
Éradicateurs 137–9
Erdemi, T. 59
ethnic groups 10, 22, 33, 53, 91, 159
ethnic stacking 29
EU Training Mission Mali 80–1, 86, 159
EUFOR Chad/CAR 56, 64–5
European Union 163–4, 169, 174–5, 188–9; in Chad 56, 64–7; in Mali 80–2, 91–5; in Algeria 142–6, 149–50
EUCAP Sahel Mali 80
extra–juridical killings 56, 88, 137–8, 141

factions *see* elite
foreign policy blindness 173–6
formal politics 23–5, 31–6, 159–61, 172–3, 180–1, 190; in Algeria 129,

Index 197

133–5, 140, 142, 149ff, 164; in Chad
51–2; in Iraq 106–7, 116–17, 123; in
Mali 76–7
francafrique 40, 186
France 40, 163, 175, 182–9; and Algeria
131, 143–7, 150; and Chad 47–8, 51,
54–5, 60–67; and Mali 82–7, 89–92
francophone Africa 185–8
Front de Libération Nationale 131,
133–4, 138, 145–6, 148, 150
Front Islamique du Salut 133–4, 136–9,
141, 145–9

Gamou, E. 79, 81, 84, 160, 172
Gao 81–2
GATIA 87–8
Ghali, I. 84
ghost soldiers 54, 109; *see also* security
forces
Goïta, A. 81
good governance *see* administrative
reforms
government 2–3; in Algeria; in Chad 60,
65; in Iraq 103–7, 111, 115, 118–19,
122–3; in Mali 79, 84, 87–91, 93;
see also regime
Groupe Islamique Armé 137–9, 143, 146
*Groupe Salafiste pour la Prédication et le
Combat* 139; *see also* al Qaeda
Groupes de Légitimes Défense 140–1
Guterres, A. 90

Habré, H. 48–9, 51, 185
Haut Comité d'Etat 131, 137, 145
Hezbollah in Iraq 106, 113, 115, 118,
122, 168
High Islamic Council 76, 91
Hilal, A. 62
Hollande, F. 85, 188
human rights 5, 36, 56, 143–5, 155, 175
Hussein, S. 102–4, 107–8, 171

Ibrahim, K. 58, 62
ideology 11, 24–5, 107, 129, 159;
conservative 107; Islamism 132, 162;
shia activism 106, 163; socialist 106;
see also pragmatism;
see also programmatic politics
illegal economy 6–7, 23, 132, 141; narco
73–7, 87, 161–2
image management 2, 32, 176
import 132–3, 148–9; *see also* illegal
economy

indirect approach 110, 129, 182, 184
industry 75, 132
informal politics 6–9, 23–5, 33–34,
154–5, 161ff, 180–2; in Algeria
130–135, 148–9; in Chad 48–52, 66; in
Iraq 102–7, 123; in Mali 73–7, 94–5;
policy implications of 188–92;
see also formal politics
Inherent Resolve 110–11
institutionalization 158;
see also administrative reforms;
political reforms
institution 5–9, 21–3, 25–7, 33–7, 170–3,
192; in Algeria 130–4; in Chad 49, 52,
64–5; in Iraq 102, 105–7, 111–12,
120–2; in Mali 75–6, 91–4;
see also security institutions
insurgency 7, 25–7, 33–5, 161–2, 180; in
Algeria 129–31, 136–9; in Chad 47–49,
57–61; in Iraq 104, 112–13; in Mali 73,
78–9, 87
intelligence 8, 16, 158, 186–8; assistance
40, 55, 86, 110–11; estimate 54;
officers 80, 139; agencies 30–1, 88,
129–30, 134–9, 171–2, 175–6
International Monetary Fund 63, 93,
142–4, 147–9, 163, 188
intervention 2–6, 12–4, 20, 27, 39–41;
current 182–4; dilemma of 175; in
Mali 85–87, 94, 163; without reforms
157–158, 185–6, 189–91
Iran 112–13, 117, 157, 163, 165–9; war
with Iraq 103, 171; pro–Iranian
militias 104, 111, 113, 115, 121–2;
pro–Iranian parties 103–4, 106–7,
116–17, 119–21; revolutionary
Guard 115
Iraq 101ff; administrative reforms
119–123; alignment 112–17; military
strategy 109–12; political reforms
118–19; political settlement 102–7
Islamic State 1, 88, 101, 107–8, 122
Islamist 4, 35, 51, 104, 140, 162;
militants in Mali 87, 90, 92;
movements 62; opposition 131–2, 137;
parties 12, 106, 134, 145–7; *see also* al
Qaeda; Islamic State; pro–Iranian
Shia militias

Jama'at Nasr al–Islam wal Muslimin 88;
see also al Qaeda
Janjaweed 48, 56–8, 61–2

198 Index

Justice and Equality Movement 54,
57–9, 61–2; *see also* Darfur

Keita, I.K. 77, 79–83, 87ff
Khan, M. 6–7, 22
Khartoum 59, 61
Kidal 81–2, 84, 91
Kirkuk 116
Kurdish autonomous region 103,
113, 116
Kurdistan Democratic Party 103, 106–7,
113, 115–16

Ladwig, W. 13
Lamari, S. 135, 137–9
Law of Civil Concord 139, 146
liberal peacebuilding 3–5, 8, 10, 12, 175
liberal reform *see* administrative
reforms; political reforms
Libya: and Chad 49, 60–1, 163; civil war
2011- 42n, 78, 84; Western
intervention 175, 182
Liptako 88, 91

M5–RFP 91
Macron, E. 184–5
Mahdi army 103, 113; *see also* the Peace
Companies
Mahdi, A. A. 117, 121
Mali 72ff; administrative reforms 91–4;
alignment 83–9; military strategy
78–83; political reforms 89–91;
political settlement 73–77
Maliki, N. 1, 103–5, 107–10, 112–15,
119–22
Malikiyouns 105, 173
Mara, M. 82, 91
Migdal, J. 21
military strategy 8, 28–31, 38, 82–3,
109–12, 135–9, 158–9;
see also praetorian protection;
strategy
military *see* security forces
military assistance 8, 13, 183; in Chad
54; in Mali 78, 85; in Iraq 103,
114, 116
militia 7–8, 21, 23–26, 31–4, 158, 160–1,
172; in Algeria 136, 138, 140–2, 144; in
Chad 56–9; in Iraq 103–5, 107,
110–18, 121–2; in Mali 81, 83–5, 88–91
MINURCAT 66
MINUSMA 80, 82–3, 88, 90
Mitterrand, F. 143–4, 187

mixed politics 25, 165, 171;
see also politics
money 23, 38, 41, 49–50, 75, 105;
see also corruption
Mopti 74, 81–4, 86, 88, 91, 94
moral hazard 190
Mosul 1, 101, 109, 111, 115–16, 118
Mouvement de la société en paix 145
*Mouvement National pour la Libération
de l'Azawad* 79, 84, 87
Mouvement Patriotique du Salut
51–2, 65–66
multilateralism 187
MUJAO 87, 91

N'Djamena 49, 53–7, 59–61, 63–5, 156,
169, 185
narcotics *see* illegal economy
nationalism 131–2
natural resources 41; oil and gas 49–53,
57–8, 62–4, 132, 148–9; gold 75; oil
curse 41
neoliberal reforms *see* structural
adjustment programmes
Nezzar, K. 137–8
Nineveh province 109
non-cooperation 14, 170
non-programmatic politics 24, 29, 170,
184–9; *see also* informal politics
Nour, M. 59–60
Nouri, M. 51

Obama, B. 1, 4, 101, 115, 117–18, 122
Obeidi, A. 108, 111, 118–19
oil *see* natural resources
organizational dysfunction 170–3, 176–7

party 24–5, 34, 38, 173, 186, 192; in
Algeria 132–4, 136, 138, 141, 144–6; in
Chad 48, 51–2, 65–6; in Iraq 102–7,
113–14, 116, 118–21, 163; in Mali
75–6, 87, 91
Patriotic Union of Kurdistan 103, 106,
113, 116
patronage 27, 29, 32, 42n, 159–60; in
Algeria; in Chad 49–52, 54, 57, 59; in
Iraq 106–7, 122; in Mali 74–5, 89;
see also client networks
patron-client 22, 24, 29; *see also* client
networks
peace agreement 13, 22, 33; in Chad 59,
61–2; in Mali 72, 78–9, 86–7, 89–91, 94

Index 199

peace companies 113–14, 122;
  see also Mahdi army
peacebuilding 39–40, 67, 72, 188; in
  Mali; *see also* liberal peacebuilding
peacebuilding literature 1, 13, 22, 181,
  183, 191
peacekeeping 3–4, 188
personal politics *see* non–programmatic
  politics
Peshmerga 103, 107, 115–16, 121, 161
Platform group 85, 87–8, 90, 94–95, 158
political reforms 5, 34–5;
  democratization 65–66, 89–90, 144–7;
  ethnic inclusion 118–19; , peace
  process 90–1
political settlement 6ff, 20ff, 154ff, 168,
  172–3, 179–82, 189–92; in Algeria
  130–5; in Chad 48–52; in Iraq 102–7;
  in Mali 73–7
political settlement theory 6–7, 13, 22
Popular Mobilization Forces 112, 114,
  116, 118, 121–2, 161
Pospisil, J. 191–2
power distribution 22, 24, 77, 159,
  181, 184
power-sharing 102–4, 107, 119, 191
praetorian protection 7–8, 28–31, 38,
  154–9, 170–1, 180; in Algeria 135–9; in
  Chad 52–57; in Iraq 107–12; in Mali
  77–83; *see also* punishment strategy;
  see also coup proofing
presidential guard 30; 33rd Parachute
  Regiment 77–9, 80, 84, 156; DGSSIE
  52–4, 56, 66; Counter Terrorism
  Service 108–12
principal-agent theory 13–14, 165, 190–1
private military companies 3, 53,
  158, 182–3
privatization 142, 147–9
programmatic politics *see* formal politics

*Rassemblement National
  Démocratique* 145–6
*Rassemblement pour la Démocratie et la
  Liberté* 59
regime survival 2ff, 13–14, 20–2, 33–4,
  156–7, 161–4, 177–181; in Algeria; in
  Chad 60, 62, 65–7; in Iraq 114; in
  Mali 89
regime 2–4, 20ff, 154ff, 179–81;
  authoritarian 36, 41, 129, 173, 176;
  existentially threatened 4–5, 14–15;
  le pouvoir 134–5, 144; *see also* Abadi;

  see also Déby; Habré; Keita; Maliki;
  Touré
regional powers 8, 35, 38, 165–9, 181–2,
  191; *see also* Iran; Sudan
rent 7, 41, 105, 131, 149
repression 1, 48–9, 109, 120, 135–7, 190
resilience 3–4, 183
risk-averse alignment *see* alignment
ruling coalition 31–9, 184–5, 191; in
  Algeria 130–2; in Chad 48–9; in Iraq
  102–4; in Mali 73–4 *see* elites

Sadr, M. 103–6, 113–15, 117–22, 163
Sahel 9, 40, 55, 94, 175, 183, 186–9
Saleh; I. 65
Sanogo, A. 78, 85–7
Sant'Egidio 138, 145
Sistani, A. 106, 113–15, 120–2, 160, 163
Special Anti–Terrorist Group 52–6, 156
secular 11, 129, 131–4
security forces 7, 26, 28–31, 33–4, 183,
  188; in Algeria 135–6; in Chad 52–5;
  in Iraq 107–11; in Mali 77–82;
  see also presidential guards; special
  forces
security sector reform 10, 64, 79–82
security studies 1, 12–3, 183
Serval 72, 80, 82, 89, 182
Shia: clerics 106, 161; elites 101–7,
  113–16, 121–3; militias 103–5, 107,
  110–18, 121–2; shrines 113;
  see also Popular Mobilization Forces;
  see also Sistani
Sierra Leone 39–40, 180
simulated statebuilding 8–9, 34–7,
  164–9, 175–77, 180–1, 190; in Algeria
  144–9; in Chad 62–6; in Iraq 117–23;
  in Mali 89–94
small footprint operations 182–4;
  see also indirect approach
smuggling *see* illegal economy
Soleimani, Q. x; *see also* Iran 115, 122
Somalia 40, 162, 180, 182–3
Sonatrach 149
Songhay 84
sovereignty 33–4, 60, 139–144, 163–4,
  180, 183
special forces 40, 53, 79, 110, 183, 188;
  see also elite forces
stability 27, 35, 82, 143, 175; regime
  stability 8, 34, 63–5, 93; stability
  operations 3; political stability 22,
  76, 192

200　Index

state: authority 90, 92, 159, 161, 180; legitimacy 3, 5, 10, 21, 157, 170; state–in–society 15, 21–22, 179; weak 21, 36, 181; *see also* institutions; developmental states
State and Law Coalition 113, 118–19
state company 49–50, 149
State Department 52, 56, 187
statebuilding 1, 3, 67, 101, 134, 182; liberal 12, 47; *see also* administrative reforms; liberal peacebuilding; simulated statebuilding
strategy 15, 27–8, 175, 187, 190–1; *see also* military strategy; praetorian protection; risk–averse alignment; simulated statebuilding
structural adjustment programmes 35, 142, 148
Sudan 48, 51, 163, 166–9; proxy war with Chad 52, 57–9; rapprochement with 60–2, 64, 66; *see also* Darfur
Sunni Arab 1, 101–4, 108–9, 112–14, 116–19
Supreme Council of the Islamic Revolution 103
Syria 104, 111, 117, 122, 175
Saairun coalition 120

terrorism 32, 35, 94
threat: existential 1–6, 24–5, 27–8, 39, 47, 154–5, 163; from coup 29, 31–2, 78, 108, 156–7, 170–1; from insurgency in Algeria 129, 135–6, 139; from insurgency in Chad 31, 52, 54, 60; from insurgency in Mali 78, 82–4, 87–8; from insurgency in Iraq 112–13, 118; from Western powers 34, 173–4, 181; shared perception 14, 114, 116

Timbuktu 74, 82
Toubou 48, 57, 59, 62
Touré, A. T. 72–81, 83–5, 89, 92–3
training missions 80, 155, 187; *see also* EU Training Mission Mali; EUCAP Sahel Mali
Trans–Saharan Counter–Terrorism Initiative 52
Traoré, D. 79, 84–6, 89
Tribal Mobilization Forces 118
tribe 21, 48–9, 56–9, 73–4, 102, 140–1; *see also* Berber; Sunni Arab; Toubou; Tuareg; Zaghawa
Trump, D. 117, 122, 187
Tuareg 73–4, 78–9, 82–5, 87, 89, 92

United Kingdom 64, 86, 182
United Nations 3–4, 40, 82, 85, 164, 188; Security Council 64, 88, 90, 92
United States 3, 158–61, 173–5, 184, 186–8, 190; and Algeria 144–6, 149; and Chad 52–3, 54, 60, 63–66; and Iraq 1, 101–4, 108, 110, 112–21, 123; and Mali 78, 80, 86–8, 93–4

war on terror 184
warlords *see* militarized elites
Western military intervention *see* interventions
White House 114, 187
World Bank 62–4, 66, 142–4, 147–8, 165–6, 174

Zaghawa 48–9, 51–3, 57–60, 62
Zéroual; Liamine 137–40, 145–6

Printed in the United States
by Baker & Taylor Publisher Services